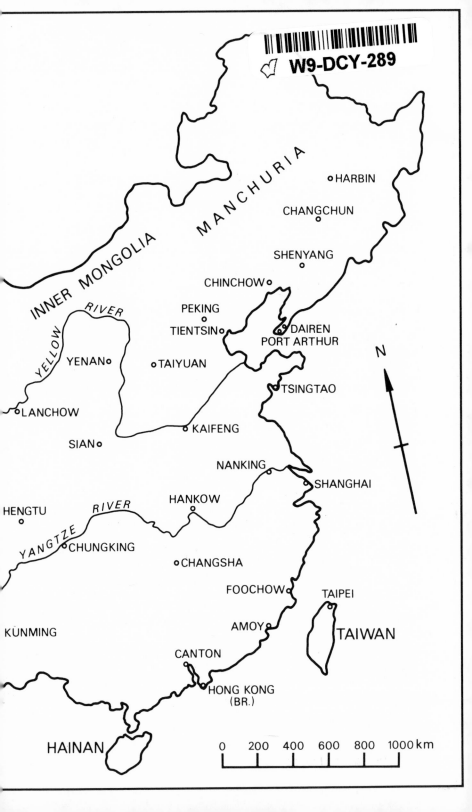

W9-DCY-289

HARBIN

CHANGCHUN

SHENYANG

CHINCHOW

MANCHURIA

INNER MONGOLIA

YELLOW RIVER

PEKING
TIENTSIN

DAIREN
PORT ARTHUR

YENAN

TAIYUAN

TSINGTAO

LANCHOW

KAIFENG

SIAN

NANKING

SHANGHAI

HENGTU

HANKOW

YANGTZE RIVER

CHUNGKING

CHANGSHA

FOOCHOW

TAIPEI

KUNMING

AMOY

TAIWAN

CANTON

HONG KONG
(BR.)

HAINAN

N

0   200   400   600   800   1000 km

Dilemma in China:

America's Policy Debate, 1945

by

Kenneth S. Chern

1980

Archon Books

Hamden, Connecticut

Library of Congress Cataloging in Publication Data
Chern, Kenneth S 1946–
  Dilemma in China

  Bibliography: p. 251
  Includes index.
  1. United States—Foreign relations—China.
2. China—Foreign relations—United States. 3. United
States—Foreign relations—1945–1953. I. Title.
E183.8.C5C434   327.73′051   79–21200
ISBN 0-208-01829-8

© Kenneth S. Chern 1980

First published 1980 as an Archon Book

an imprint of The Shoe String Press, Inc.

Hamden, Connecticut 06514

Printed in the United States of America

for Ronni

CONTENTS

Dilemma in China

"We bet on the wrong horse in Russia in the last war. I certainly hope we are not going to repeat that mistake in China."

— Baptist minister to
Secretary of State Byrnes,
November 1945

Preface

In January 1945, Mao Tse-tung and Chou En-lai, leaders of the waxing Chinese Communist Party, transmitted to American Army officers a most unusual request: they asked to come to Washington to talk with President Franklin D. Roosevelt about establishing "a working relationship" with the United States. The offer met no response.[1] Thirty-four years later, in January 1979, America and the People's Republic of China established full diplomatic relations. President Jimmy Carter invited Deputy Vice-Premier Teng Hsiao-p'ing, Chou En-lai's protégé, on a triumphal journey to Washington—a journey that Chou and Mao did not live to make. The thirty-four intervening years saw the climax of the Chinese revolution, a Sino-American bloodbath in Korea, two crises in the Taiwan Strait, a war in Vietnam, and finally, a Sino-American reconciliation. With normalization of relations, the Cold War in Asia has come to an end, technically as well as in practice.

This book seeks to explain why the Sino-American confrontation occurred at all. Analyzing the Cold War in Asia, historians mistakenly have dated widespread American concern about postwar China to the failure of the Marshall mission in 1946 and the convening of a Republican Congress in 1947. Earlier, East Asia was reputedly at the edge of the public's consciousness, while Europe and the Middle East occasioned more visible Soviet-American disputes. General indifference to China immediately after World War II and the Truman Administration's failure to inform the nation about critical Chinese issues allegedly contributed to the shock and partisanship which gripped Washington following the communization of China in 1949.[2] In contrast, I will argue that the vigorous China debate which actually occured in 1945 was a critical turning point in United States China policy, and a determinant of the Sino-American animosity which erupted later.

We currently live in a fluid period of great power readjustment, as the expansion of ties between China and America ushers in a new era in East Asia. The end of World War II was another such period, when America, Russia, and leading Chinese groups were maneuvering for position in the creation of a postwar order in the region. Then, as now, Americans argued about the nature of United States interests in Asia, the character of Soviet aims there, China's prospective role, and the appropriate response to the spread of Asian communism. To be sure, there have been basic changes in the political situation over a generation's time: a weak and divided China has become a rising power, and a conquered Japan has grown into a dominant economic force, while the focus of revolutionary ferment has shifted to Vietnam. But the main lines of debate a generation ago were strikingly similar to more recent issues: to what extent should America count on China as an ally? What was the meaning of communism in Asia for America's global goals? How best to cope with Soviet power in the Far East? Such questions have persisted because they represent important themes in twentieth-century American-East Asian relations. To explore the nature and outcome of the earlier China debate will be instructive as America seeks to define a policy for the post-Cold War Far East.

The 1945 debate centered on Sino-Russian-American relations and the postwar order. Racking the State Department first, the controversy became public after the defeat of Japan, when U.S. marines were dispatched to aid the floundering Chinese Nationalist regime of Chiang Kai-shek; the debate intensified in November 1945, when Patrick Hurley resigned as ambassador to China, openly attacking the U.S. Foreign Service as procommunist. The subsequent Senate Foreign Relations Committee hearings—the main forum for the debate—failed to clarify America's options in China before the Cold War narrowed her range of choices. Since the Senate played a crucial role in the foreign policy process, helping to shape the dialogue which culminated in the hearings and influencing both the general public and the policy-making elite which sought domestic support, this study emphasizes the interactions of the leading senators who addressed the issue. But it attempts to go beyond the senators, the Administration, and the diplomats, entering the realm of what one historian has termed the "diplomatic-intellectual-psychological history" of Sino-American relations.[3] It explores the formation of attitudes, the interrelationship between the legislative and executive branches, the role of public and pressure group opinion, and the aims of governmental leaders who set America on the path of anticommunist containment in Asia. Editors, lobbyists, businessmen, laborers, and infantrymen, as well as legislators, generals, and Cabinet officers, all participated in the China debate. The nationwide arousal generated by China exemplified the intellectual and political struggle of a pluralistic society to formulate a foreign policy at a time of crisis abroad and domestic uncertainty.

The underlying issue at hand was how America should respond to the Chinese Nationalist and Communist factions, then poised for a climactic power struggle after decades of intermittent civil war. Insightful Foreign Service officers urged an accommodation with the Chinese Communists before Russia could secure a foothold with them during their rise to power; this view also found favor among many liberal intellectuals and legislators, such as Senator Elbert Thomas, who feared an American commitment to the waning Nationalist regime would provoke a confrontation with the Soviet Union. But just as vociferous, although out of tune with prevailing opinion, were such pro-Nationalist arch-conservatives as Ambassador Hurley and Senator Styles Bridges, who challenged the loyalty of diplomats counseling a pragmatic connection with the Communists. Less preoccupied with loyalty, but just as anticommunist and outspokenly pro-Chiang Kai-shek, were many moderate conservatives like Arthur Vandenberg, the Senate's chief Republican foreign policy spokesman. Finally, among Administration spokesmen—such as Secretary of State James F. Byrnes, and Senator Tom Connally, chairman of the Foreign Relations Committee—Washington's stated goal of a Nationalist-Communist coalition held primacy; hence their efforts to dampen criticism from all quarters, in order to maximize American leverage on both Chinese factions for a compromise solution.

Highlighted by confusion and emotionalism, the dissension grew as the United States placed its troops in China after the Japanese surrender to bolster Chiang's position. American diplomats who had earlier warned against tying American power to the Nationalists became scapegoats of the conservatives' anger. Acting to combat right-wing criticism while assuaging widespread public resentment of its military intervention, the Administration urged a unified, bipartisan approach to China. But it failed to justify its policy adequately. Rather, it ridiculed Hurley's charges against the State Department, while insisting to the public (and to the alarmed Russians) that the American troops were in China only to help evacuate the defeated Japanese armies there. Important questions about China raised within the State Department, in the press, and in the political arena, remained clouded.

With the launching of a mission headed by the prestigious General George C. Marshall in December 1945, the Truman Administration succeeded in enlisting domestic support and official Soviet approval for its idealized coalition goal. But it was unable to reset America's course in line with realities in postwar China. Rebuffed by Washington in 1945, Mao signed a treaty in Moscow in 1950. America's failure then holds important lessons now, as we rebuild the shattered bridges to China.

I am indebted to a number of people for their assistance in writing this book. Akira Iriye as dissertation adviser helped me to develop a framework for analysis of American China policy. William H. McNeill and Eugene D. Genovese read the entire manuscript in its early stage, offering incisive suggestions for improvement. Walter LaFeber, Robert Dallek, Richard D. Challener, and John K. Emmerson gave useful advice and criticism. Among the archivists who facilitated my research, William Joyce, Stevens Hillyer, Alexander Clark, Wanda Randall, and Jack Haley were especially helpful.

I was fortunate to have studied as an undergraduate with Sam McSeveney and as a graduate student with John Hope Franklin; both are models of rigorous scholarship and dedicated teaching. My colleagues, Constance M. Turnbull and Alan Birch, encouraged me as I developed the manuscript for publication. My parents at all times have been a source of encouragement. The University of Chicago, the University of Hong Kong, and the Center for Asian Studies, University of Rochester, awarded funds to subsidize my research. I alone am responsible for any shortcomings in the book.

Dilemma in China

My deepest debt I owe to my wife, Ronni Singer Chern, who has provided constant love and support, while succeeding in her own career in homes as far apart as New York and Hong Kong.

Kenneth S. Chern
April, 1979

I AMERICAN IDEALS AND WORLD POLITICS

Doubting Republicans

When Franklin Roosevelt sailed to Europe for the Crimea Conference in February 1945, the Allied world hoped that he would not stumble as had Woodrow Wilson in his efforts to bring lasting peace and stability out of the ruin of total war. And, as Allied armies girdled the globe, smashing the remnants of the German and Japanese war machines, there was good reason for cautious optimism. The United Nations, and particularly the United States, Britain, and the Soviet Union, had cooperated impressively in the coordination and sacrifice of the war effort. If, at Yalta and thereafter, the major Allies could continue to act together with efficiency and trust, one could hope for amicable and stable political settlements both in Europe and in Asia.

The climate of American opinion was especially hopeful. On January 10, 1945, Senator Arthur Vandenberg climaxed his gradual transformation from prewar isolationism. On the Senate floor, he advocated a peacetime alliance among America, Britain, and Russia, to insure against a resurgence of German or Japanese militarism. Roosevelt was reported to be elated and bolstered; he took fifty copies of the speech to Yalta.[1]

Vandenberg, a Michigan Republican, had been one of the most respected exponents of isolationism—or "insulationism," as he called it—in the Senate before World War II. His beliefs had been shaken by Pearl Harbor, and he gradually came around to an internationalist viewpoint. During the presidential campaign of 1944 he had come to know John Foster Dulles, foreign policy adviser to Republican candidate Thomas E. Dewey and a New York lawyer with extensive experience in international affairs. Dulles and Vandenberg had found more common ground on foreign policy than they had expected, and they began collaborating. Their relationship was to blossom into a steadfast intellectual partnership and personal friendship.[2]

Internationalist ranks had been strengthened in 1944 when New Jersey sent to the Senate H. Alexander Smith, a devoted proponent of international cooperation. Among other Republicans, Styles Bridges was sharply critical of American foreign policy but cognizant of American international responsibilities. On the Democratic side, Tom Connally of Texas, chairman of the Senate Foreign Relations Committee, was a loyal supporter of Franklin Roosevelt's foreign policies, as were Chairman Elbert Thomas of the Senate Military Affairs Committee, liberal Floridian Claude Pepper, and others in positions of leadership.

Nonetheless, sturdy strains of isolationist thinking persisted in the Senate. Men like William Langer (Republican, North Dakota), Hiram Johnson (Republican, California), Robert LaFollette, Jr. (Independent, Wisconsin), and Burton K. Wheeler (Democrat, Montana) carried on the mistrust of foreign entanglements from the days of Lodge, Nye, and Borah. They put the weight of their considerable influence and seniority behind a skeptical questioning of the value to America first of international organization and later of loans and grants abroad. They remained a force to be reckoned with. In January 1945, the Republican Party reflected its ambivalence by adding to the Senate Foreign Relations Committee the very cautious and security-conscious internationalist Styles Bridges (to Dulles's delight) and, on the other hand, Alexander Wiley, a Wisconsinite of isolationist predilections.[3] At this time, too, Dulles expressed concern with the apparent lack of interest among many senators in postwar diplomatic collaboration.[4] Along the same lines, a bipartisan group including Tom Connally sponsored an informal Congressional meeting to stimulate interest in "developing contacts" with British parliamentarians.[5]

In this fluid political situation, Vandenberg's dramatic advocacy of a peacetime military alliance seemed to herald a new postwar internationalist consensus. His idea drew wide acclaim, and his influence would help to sway doubters and recalcitrants toward acceptance of international cooperation. As Allied armies rolled toward victory, the Roosevelt Administration continued to press enthusiastically for a postwar United Nations Organization for peacekeeping and collective security; and under Vandenberg's leadership, even the most suspicious isolationist and nationalistic senators came to support the United Nations idea.

There existed at the time of the Yalta Conference four major Senate factions: strong Republican nationalists, Republicans amenable to international cooperation, Democrats who fully supported Roosevelt's internationalist initiatives, and Democratic exponents of an even broader international collaboration than the Administration was willing to sponsor. Among all groups, particularly after Vandenberg's speech, there was widespread support for an essentially "internationalist" foreign policy. By this time,

17

most senators wanted the United States to make a firm commitment to the establishment and preservation of a peaceful postwar order, and they envisioned the framework for such an order in the prospective United Nations Organization, with America, England, and Russia the foremost guarantors of stability and justice. They commonly assumed that the rights of smaller peoples to democracy and self-determination—foremost public Allied war aims—would be protected through the mutual exercise of great power restraint within the mechanism of the world organization. Such an arrangement, they hoped, would provide collective security against aggression and war.

Disillusionment with internationalist ideals was not long in coming. In particular, the gradual leaking of the Yalta provisions on Poland and on United Nations structure gave many Americans pause, as did Soviet-American squabbling about the future of eastern Europe. As hopes for great power unity, international democracy, and self-determination were contradicted in practice, senators expressed a wide range of views about the emerging world balance of power. Conservative Republicans like Styles Bridges expressed fear of international social revolution and of Soviet encroachments against the West, while liberal Democrats such as Elbert Thomas worried lest America align herself with reactionary forces abroad and provoke a confrontation with Russia. Those at different points along the political spectrum—Vandenberg and Connally among them—variously attempted to resolve the tensions among competing social and political values in the world, and to define a satisfactory amalgam of Soviet and American power. The global policies advocated for the maintenance of international cooperation and for the preservation of commonly held internationalist ideals were accordingly diverse, as senators argued about the proper terms for Soviet-American relations. Thus did domestic political views entwine with American approaches to foreign affairs.

Security-conscious Republicans, like Bridges of New Hampshire, might be termed "nationalist internationalists," for they placed a high premium on the international promotion of American interests. Rejecting what they perceived to be threatening, illegitimate, and undemocratic Russian ambitions, they urged that America resist Soviet expansion; this was the only means to implement an acceptable postwar order in which European and Asian peoples would be free (indeed likely) to accept American influence and values. Long conscious of America's stake in global strategic developments, Bridges had warned, while America was still at peace, against the dangers of an Axis-dominated world. Although an arch-conservative anti-New Deal senator, he had sided with the Roosevelt Administration against the arms embargo legislation of 1937, had supported Selective Service and lend-lease to Britain in 1940, and had participated in the drive to repeal neutrality legislation.[6] In 1941, he argued for aid to Britain and Russia in a common fight against the Axis "thugs," but even after Pearl Harbor, his basic animus against the Soviet Union remained strong.[7] He foreswore any postwar friendship with the Russians, and in 1944 opposed the transfer of a cruiser to them.[8]

Cautiously supporting American initiatives for the United Nations and for great power cooperation in 1945, Bridges nevertheless remained suspicious of Soviet intentions. On July 28, 1945, he lauded the UN Charter as a great stride toward world peace, but he warned that the UN could not control the actions of large nations which were armed with the veto power.[9] Events in eastern Europe especially worried him. On April 4, the New Hampshire Division of the Polish-American Congress sent him a resolution protesting the Yalta decisions about Poland's postwar government and frontiers, and reminding him of the principles of the Atlantic Charter—the famous pledge by Churchill and Roosevelt of August 1941, later endorsed by Russia, to support national self-determination, equal access to trade, and a postwar

general security system.[10] Receiving a second letter from
the group urging Congressional action to save Poland,
Bridges responded on May 14 that Soviet Polish policy was
indeed "a very serious matter"; and he declared that America "and the Allies must stand up on this subject, not only
because of the tragic injustice to Poland, but also because it
involves the whole principle for which this war was
fought."[11]

During April and May, Bridges similarly followed reports
of Soviet penetration into contested areas such as Berlin,
Vienna, Czechoslovakia, the Balkans, and the Baltic
region.[12] On May 3, he urged that America secure information about Soviet-controlled eastern European areas where
"we have mutual interests," with the aim of "promoting
friendly relationships among the Allies."[13] Of course, the
Soviet Union was oblivious to such pleas for the same reasons
it ignored American pressure to loosen its control of the
Polish, Bulgarian, and other regimes near or touching its
hypersensitive and frequently-invaded western borderlands.

Bridges rapidly lost patience. On May 31, he noted that
in both world wars, America's great error had been her
"failure to use [her] enormous bargaining power in our relations with our allies" to support democratic principles and a
just peace for all nations.[14] And on June 11, he cautioned his
fellow senators against governmental and press reports announcing a great victory by President Truman's emissary to
Moscow, Harry Hopkins, on the issue of the veto in the UN
Security Council. No doubt disgusted with Hopkins's futile,
last-ditch effort to salvage a shred of the American position
on Poland as well as with Soviet insistence on rigid veto
powers over United Nations activities, he asserted that
Russia was creating new issues to blur pending questions:

> [Americans] have been hoodwinked by official
> comments ... by those who obviously want the
> American people to think that a trick played by

shrewd Soviet negotiators is a victory for the democratic way of thinking about the future International Security Organization.[15]

He expressed keen disappointment that American influence
was not exerted in behalf of small nations against the veto;
rather, America was "weakly giving in on great matters of
principle."

In tension with Bridges's hope for Soviet-American cooperation there existed a nagging mistrust of the Soviet Union
and an overriding impulse to translate democratic American traditions to the international sphere. As the pragmatic
terms of the Yalta postwar system came to light early in 1945,
he became progressively more disillusioned. Holding the
great powers to their wartime rhetoric of self-determination
and the protection of small states' rights, he time and again
drew attention to the contradictions between these principles, on the one hand, and Soviet domineering in eastern
Europe and the United Nations, on the other. International
privilege ought to be eschewed, he felt; those principles of
democracy and equality which prevailed in America, and
for which the Allies had liberated the occupied countries,
ought to be guaranteed for those countries as states, and for
the individuals within them. Yet Russia was threatening the
collective security, harmony, and equality on which the
postwar world depended. And, so long as America had the
overwhelming moral influence and military might she now
possessed, Bridges thought her delinquent in failing to
challenge Soviet bullying.

Implicit in Bridges's argument was the necessity of establishing a situation favorable to American interests in eastern
Europe, and to create a United Nations mechanism permitting anti-Soviet intervention in that area of the world. Yet,
quite aside from his insensitivity to Soviet concern over
border regions which had served as traditional staging areas
of anti-Russian attack, he never suggested how American

force might be applied to the extensive parts of eastern Europe occupied by the Soviet Army. By shying away from the military implications of his ambitious goals, he betrayed a basic flaw in his thinking: either a profound naiveté concerning the limits of American power in a part of the world so close to Russia, so important to her, and so dominated by the Red Army or, more likely, a cynical willingness to exploit foreign policy issues for partisan advantage. Pressure from Polish-Americans reinforced his impulse to reject any reasonable balance of power with Russia in Europe; if a "principled" demand for a curb on Russia and for international justice happened to be popular in a conservative state and among interested ethnic groups, such a stand would not be any more difficult for Bridges. This stand is especially significant in light of Bridges's prewar calculations of the unfavorable power balance America would likely face against a victorious Nazi Germany, and his consequent sophisticated decision to support England and Russia for practical strategic purposes. As with many ambitious public men, a principled stand on foreign affairs happily coincided with personal political profit. Indeed, Bridges's cryptic reference to official "hoodwinking" of the American people and the masking of Soviet trickery anticipated later partisan conservative charges, based on anticommunist "principle," that American foreign policy was threatened by Communist conspirators.

Somewhat more conciliatory toward Russia were Republican internationalists such as Arthur Vandenberg. As concerned as Bridges about American security and as skeptical of Soviet intentions, Vandenberg was more inclined to respect Soviet military power on the Eurasian land mass. He was torn between his ambitions for America and his knowledge of global power relationships. Calling for tough bargaining with Russia, he reluctantly admitted that the world had to live with expanding Soviet influence.

An enthusiastic proponent of the United Nations idea,

Vandenberg claimed that the genius of such an organization lay not in the use of military force, but in "the substitution of justice for force . . . of international law for piracy . . . of peace for war . . . [and] in the organization of these pacific mechanisms which shall stop future frictions short of the necessity for force."[16] As for Bridges, the big question mark in Vandenberg's internationalist concept was Soviet ambition. Regarding himself as a hard-nosed realist about the Russians, he was fond of noting that he had stood alone in the Senate against extending recognition to the USSR in 1933. By 1940 his habitual anti-Soviet animus had culminated in a demand during the Russo-Finnish conflict that the United States aid Finland and sever relations with Russia—despite his rigid isolationist position regarding the widespread Axis aggression of the same period.[17] His postwar alliance proposal, originally intended as an attack on Russian foreign policy, was modified to a positive suggestion in part, he later recalled, "to anticipate what ultimately became the 'Moscow menace' and to lay down a formula which would make postwar Soviet expansionism as illogical as it would be unnecessary (except for ulterior purposes)."[18]

The events of 1945 did little to ease Vandenberg's doubts about the implications of Soviet policy for world justice and (presumably identical) American interests. As the Yalta agreements trickled out to the public, it became apparent that great territorial and political concessions had been made to Russia at Poland's expense. And Russian policy in the spring of 1945 seemed to undermine even the slim support given Poland by the Yalta accord. To a Polish-American constituent Vandenberg wrote on February 13 that the agreed-upon Soviet-Polish boundary was "indefensible," and that "recognition of the [Soviet-sponsored] Lublin government is in net effect unjustified."[19] He expressed to Under Secretary of State Joseph C. Grew "deep disappointment" in the settlement as a symbol "of the general treatment to be accorded the smaller liberated nations."[20] In early March, he warned the Senate that the fate of Poland would greatly affect "the success of our ultimate plans for collective security and organized peace."[21]

Vandenberg worried also about Russia's efforts to maximize her power within the United Nations. On March 23, he decried the Yalta decision to award Britain and Russia multiple votes in the General Assembly, and rejected a tentative plan to similarly award America several votes as "deadly . . . to any further pretense of 'sovereign equality' among the lesser nations of the earth."[22] He was particularly irritated at Soviet efforts to extend the Security Council veto power from substantive questions (on which all major powers insisted) to include even discussion of international disputes.[23] Appointed by Roosevelt as a delegate to the San Francisco Conference to draft a UN Charter, he repeatedly stressed the need to defend American rights and world justice. "There is a general disposition to *stop this Stalin appeasement*," he noted on April 2. "It *has* to stop *sometime.* Every surrender makes it more difficult."[24] Disdainful of others' fears lest the Russians walk out of the conference, he was heartened when the American delegation held firm on limiting the veto and on other issues, forcing the Russians to compromise.

In turn, Vandenberg stood ready to compromise drastically the American position on some issues; and one of the concessions he was willing to make is enlightening. Among his major themes were equality of nations and international justice; he referred to the General Assembly as "tomorrow's Town Meeting of the World."[25] Yet, in the end, he was willing to face reality about the Polish issue, notwithstanding the agitated state of mind of his massive Polish-American constituency, a far more significant political factor in Michigan than in Styles Bridges's New Hampshire. In a revealing letter to the editor of the *Polish Daily News* in Detroit, an old friend, Vandenberg reluctantly concluded that an attack on the Yalta accord, and a quixotic crusade for Polish freedom, would simply leave Russia "in complete possession of everything she wants . . . [with] no hope for justice except through World War Number Three." It made more sense to weave Atlantic Charter principles into the UN Charter, and to provide the organization with "specific authority to examine . . . injustice . . . and to recommend correction."[26]

Underlying Vandenberg's resigned pragmatism about Poland was his perception of international power realities as they related to his hopes for the United Nations. Speaking on the Senate floor, he acknowledged charges that the Charter ensured world domination by the five permanent members of the Security Council, and more specifically by "a three-power military alliance between Russia, Britain, and the United States, since they will become its chief instruments of peace enforcement when the need for force arises."[27] Admitting that this held some truth, he argued that those three countries would predominate with or without a United Nations, and that the Charter was at least a curb on the great powers, which otherwise would determine their relations through military rivalry. Vandenberg earlier had assured a nationwide radio audience that his proposed great power security treaty was no substitute for, but rather an adjunct to, a general international organization.[28] He continued to feel that the UN, in which the powers exerted their authority under some controls, offered some hope for conciliation and world peace.

The presuppositions of Vandenberg's internationalism were similar to those of Bridges; national self-determination, equality of nations, and great power harmony were his watchwords. To these objectives, Vandenberg, like Bridges, perceived the greatest threat to emanate from the Soviet Union. But his response to the Soviet threat differed from that of Bridges; for he continued to hold cooperation with Russia, however limited, as essential. His expressions were highly ambiguous, carping about appeasement and fuming over Poland, while simultaneously admitting that little could be done to ameliorate Poland's condition or other problems except through inquiry, moral suasion, and hard bargaining. Vandenberg's ambiguity stemmed from contradictory imperatives: the need to salve public opinion and his own conscience, on the one hand, and the equal necessity to avoid a rupture with Russia if any decent peace, however imperfect, were to be salvaged.

In the final analysis, Poland was lost, not only because of American promises to Russia, but also because, as Vandenberg admitted, another war was unacceptable. He consciously reckoned with the Soviet military presence in eastern Europe, the preponderance of Soviet interest and influence which limited America's regional leverage to protests against trampled war aims and principles. To his mind, the only practicable policy was a continued vigilance for American interests and small nations' rights, and the constant use of American bargaining power and world opinion as restraining levers to modify Soviet behavior which threatened a just and peaceful world order.

Vandenberg's leadership at the San Francisco Conference accelerated his rise to foreign policy leadership. Influential Republicans followed his lead; John Foster Dulles accompanied him to San Francisco, and continued to work closely with him. After Roosevelt's death in April 1945, the Truman Administration continued to consult him, building the foundation of bipartisan policy making. With Tom Connally, he shepherded the UN Charter and implementing legislation through the Senate in the summer of 1945. Literally holding in his grip the Republican votes needed to achieve two-thirds Senate ratification, he delivered them, and his prestige rose to new heights.

Confident Democrats

In dealing with the Senate's Republicans, the primary foreign policy spokesman for the Roosevelt and Truman Administrations was Tom Connally, chairman of the Senate Foreign Relations Committee. A large, old-fashioned, white-maned Texas Democrat, Connally was strong-willed and hot-tempered; he could be crude in manner, and he was devastatingly sarcastic in debate. A conservative Southern New Dealer, he remained loyal to the national party through the Dixiecrat revolt of 1948, and to the end of his career. Democrats like Connally, who supported Roosevelt's foreign policy, had—like the Republicans—to reconcile internationalist ideals to the undeniable fact of preponderant great power strength. They sought to do so through the maintenance of Soviet-American harmony in mutual accommodation. In this way, they felt that the worst effects of raw power politics and international tensions might be mitigated, under a beneficent concert of powers within the United Nations. America, they reasoned, ought not to endanger the fragile Soviet-American relationship by too harsh a posture against Russian expansion.

Connally had long been a devoted internationalist. He had come to Congress during the Wilson era (1916), and had "admired Woodrow Wilson more than any man alive . . . [as] a fine statesman, a man of superb intellect and great courage." Elected to the Senate in 1928, he had worked with President Roosevelt to limit and eventually repeal the neutrality legislation of the 1930s; and he had supported the Selective Service Act (1940) and lend-lease to Britain (1941). In July 1941, he became chairman of the Foreign Relations Committee, and, during World War II, was instrumental in bringing senators of both parties into consultation with the State Department for wartime and postwar political planning. He was especially active in securing bipartisan support for American participation in a new international league to prevent war—the long-delayed fruit of Wilson's labors. Anxious that the United States demonstrate to Russia her sincerity in espousing a postwar league, he was gratified when the Connally Resolution (1943) put the Senate "on record in favor of United States participation in an international organization."[29]

Early in 1945, Connally voiced great hope for world harmony. On January 19, flushed with the climactic defeats of Axis armies in Europe and Asia, he termed Russia, Britain, and China "gallant and heroic Allies" against aggression, and he urged continued Allied unity in establishing a peaceful world order.[30] In February, he said that the Yalta agreements were "very helpful . . . reassuring," and "in the main highly satisfactory." He particularly extolled the decisions to give liberated countries the opportunity for democratic development under "their own systems of government," and to establish at San Francisco a collective security organization.[31]

At the same time, Connally echoed Roosevelt's desire to build rapidly the foundations of the United Nations Organization before tackling treaty complexities like those which had wrecked Wilson's efforts to bring America into the League of Nations. He urged that the "many vexing and irritating questions" arising from the war—allocation of territories, boundary demarcations, and the like—not be settled by unilateral or bilateral arrangement while the war still raged, but by representatives of the entire United Nations in the final peace treaty. He thus hoped, through a policy of postponement, to relegate to the future the knotty problems—such as Poland—about which Republican critics were already perturbed. On January 10, he warned Vandenberg that the greatest imponderable for America's allies was whether or not the United States would ratify a league charter, and he suggested that criticism and evidence of disunity at home would shake international confidence that America would stand by the fledgling organization. During

American Ideals and World Politics

the Yalta Conference, he similarly urged that "agitation and discussion of issues that may create dissension or division be withheld until the end of the pending meeting."[32]

Yet Connally's public statements were certainly more sanguine than were his private thoughts on developing great power tensions. On January 12—as he later recalled—he told Roosevelt that "for my own part . . . I was concerned about Russia's proposed partition of Poland." And, upon hearing from Roosevelt in March 1945 about the Yalta promise to allow the Soviet Union three seats in the General Assembly, Connally recalled: "Personally I disliked the idea . . . and told the President so."[33] These were precisely the same fears publicly articulated by Bridges and Vandenberg —fears which Connally at least partially shared, under his mask of optimism.

The reasons for Connally's mask are not far to seek: namely, his continued overriding concern both with domestic support for the UN and with Soviet-American accommodations as essential conditions for the postwar order. On the domestic front, the specter of the Senate rejection of Wilson's Versailles Treaty was never far from his mind. He warned Roosevelt on January 12 "that there was strong pressure for a large-scale Senate debate on foreign policy, especially on the postwar organization," and also "a desire on the part of individual senators to get into country-by-country debates on the floor."[34]

With the Russians, on the other hand, Connally first dealt intimately as a delegate at San Francisco, and he found them to be relatively flexible. Foreign Minister Molotov was "quite reasonable and conceded several points," such as the seating of the Soviet-backed Polish regime at the conference and the establishment of a great power veto over discussion of issues in the Security Council. In light of such Soviet concessions, it seemed particularly important to compromise in return. The denial to Russia of her three General Assembly votes would not have been

29

worth the inevitable fracas over the six British Commonwealth seats; for, as Connally emphasized, "without Russia
and the United Kingdom as members, the UN would be in-
effectual."[35] Furthermore, Connally noted in a radio address from San Francisco on May 9 that the effectiveness of
the UN as a peacekeeping body, stemming from the "wide
authority" of the Security Council to employ economic and
military sanctions, rested in the end on the material and
military resources of the great powers; they therefore ought
to retain a veto over substantive UN peacekeeping operations, notwithstanding the pained outcry of smaller nations
for equality of representation.[36] And on July 25, he lauded
the Charter before the Senate as a protector of small countries against unbridled military force, pointing out that "if
the five great powers, *or any three of them*, wish now, without any charter, to form a military and naval alliance for
the purpose of controlling the world, they can do so."[37]

Connally's message was clear: any international system
must recognize and channel the preponderance of great
power global strength, or else be worthless. In order to
avoid both a partisan rupture at home and a diplomatic
rupture with Russia, pending the establishment of such a
system within the UN, it therefore seemed necessary to mute
areas of Soviet-American conflict and to search for areas of
conciliation. Such a policy tied in with Connally's tactic of
postponing the public consideration of the thornier political
issues which might threaten at its inception the Soviet-
American concert essential to the functioning of such a
system.

Unlike his Republican counterparts, Connally resolved
the contradictions between idealism and power politics in
favor of a conciliatory stand toward Russia. A confirmed
Wilsonian internationalist, he nonetheless sought to dampen
and delay the inevitable American backlash to the inevitable continuation of traditional great power politics, in order
to get Soviet-American cooperation firmly on track at the

30

outset; thus might the coming disillusionment with unfulfilled wartime rhetoric be minimized. Leavened with pragmatism, Connally's Wilsonianism recognized the limits of international equality in the interests of a postwar concert of powers to keep the peace. Only Soviet-American harmony, within the democratic forum of the UN General Assembly,[38] might serve as a brake on great power recklessness, keep world order, and give small nations a reasonable chance to air their views and participate. Contrary to the Republicans' rejection of great power spheres in Europe, Connally's view implied an acceptance, however reluctant, of Soviet hegemony in eastern Europe. And beyond vague hopes for great power unity and good will, it held no guarantee of success. Yet, as the San Francisco Conference ended, Connally rejoiced at the bipartisan representation in America's delegation, and asserted that large areas of agreement had been found with the Russians. He concluded that, "all things considered, a splendid beginning has been made."[39]

One of Connally's strongest collaborators in developing American postwar foreign policy was Senator Elbert D. Thomas, of Utah. An ardently liberal New Dealer, Thomas was a man of broad vision and keen intellect. A Mormon missionary in Japan in his youth, he had been professor of politics at the University of Utah for ten years until his election to the Senate in 1932—the year Franklin Roosevelt was elected president.[40] A prolific writer and speaker, he authored four books; and while his professional specialty was the Far East, he tried to integrate his thinking on domestic and international affairs into coherent liberal patterns, always emphasizing the goals of widely based prosperity and world peace. A dedicated internationalist, he had been a strong advocate of collective security in the 1930s, had sponsored legislation aimed at arming the president with a discretionary embargo of war supplies to aggressor nations, and had collaborated with Connally and

31

others in the Senate floor fight of 1939 that led to the repeal
of neutrality legislation.[41] During World War II, he served
as vice-president of the American Society for International
Law, and represented the United States at several International Labor Organization conferences. In the Senate, he
chaired the Military Affairs Committee, simultaneously
serving on the Foreign Relations Committee.[42]

Among extremely conciliatory internationalist Democrats
like Thomas, the prime postwar objective was continuing
American cooperation with Russia, based on American
recognition of legitimate Soviet historic interests in Europe
and Asia; such cooperation, they reasoned, would virtually
force the rest of the world to fall into line, while its absence
would almost certainly doom any hope of a stable and enduring peace. Their views strongly implied the acceptance
of Soviet hegemony in large parts of the Eurasian land mass,
in sharp contrast to the aims of conservative nationalists
such as Styles Bridges.

Thomas made explicit his approach to foreign affairs in
The Four Fears (1944), a book which focused on American
misapprehensions that threatened to deflect American
foreign policy from its true course at the end of the war.
Carefully analyzing the "four fears"—of idealism, of entangling alliances, of England and Russia, and of revolution—he attempted to dispel each of them, and to suggest in
their stead, a constructive international program. Significantly, the most suggestive parts of his analysis concerned
Russia and revolution.

Treating the related problems of alliances, Britain, and
Russia, Thomas lamented the chronic American mispercep-
tion of world power relationships. Dismissing the traditional gospel which warned against entangling alliances, he
remarked that even the Founding Fathers had used them,
and he emphasized that technology had rendered isolationism obsolete. Alluding to Britain's traditionally negative image, he emphasized that a host of amicable Anglo-American

compromises and America's long dependence on the British Navy reflected a fundamental coincidence of interests which ought not to be obscured by ancient grievances.[43] But it was Russia which most interested him. Discerning a pattern of cordiality in Russian-American relations spanning more than a century, he traced the turning point to America's military intervention after the Bolshevik Revolution (1917), which had poisoned Soviet-American relations ever since. Thomas listed America's persistent fears of the Soviet Union—her dictatorship, her espousal of Communist revolution, her atheism, her disdain for private property—and argued that these traits of Soviet politics posed no threat to the United States, unless Americans had lost confidence in themselves or in their political system. Even now, in 1944, he lamented, though Russia had proven to be the strongest country in Europe, facing and beating Hitler's armies, distorted images of a wild, barbaric Russia in "a crazy reign of terror," persisted.[44]

Citing British and American uneasiness over Russia's tendency to occupy the political vacuum arising in territories conquered from Germany by the Red Army, Thomas argued that Russia legitimately sought to destroy her enemy and push him back into his own country. Urging that America recognize Russia's legitimate interests in eastern Europe, he warned against a repetition of the disastrous *cordon sanitaire* policy of ringing the Soviet Union with contrived independent territories. America, he reasoned, ought to recognize that Russia considered her interests as legitimate in the Baltic as did the United States hers in California, Texas, and Latin America. Although acquiescing in the Roosevelt Administration's decision to postpone specific territorial questions like that of Poland for the time being, he warned that Russia was clearly "here to stay," having earned her position in her valiant struggle against Germany. And he warned against the danger of destroying a prime condition of peace—a stable basis of postwar collaboration with

Russia.[45]

Thomas thus was willing to go to great lengths to secure the keystone of any future peaceful international order, a cooperative spirit between the emergent American and Soviet powers. In sharp contrast to the postures of Bridges and Vandenberg, he stood ready to sacrifice self-determination in eastern Europe to Russian security interests, and to create Soviet and American spheres of influence. In asserting that alliances were compatible with American interests, while stressing the absence of conflict with Britain and Russia, he strongly suggested a concert of powers, with each great power secure in its own "back yard," to guide the postwar order. Minimizing the implications of Soviet communism for the United States, he betrayed a deep anxiety lest emotional hostilities lead to open conflict between habitually peaceful and friendly countries, as a result either of irrelevant ideological considerations, or of unnecessary competition in areas of the world into which they might simultaneously expand.

Thomas's pragmatic and conciliatory approach to the Soviet Union seemed to contradict his professed concern with Americans' aversion to idealism. Calling upon the resources of idealism which, he claimed, had been instrumental in building America, he cautioned against the ever-present cynics and "realists" who, out of fear or ignorance, would try to sabotage the idealistic programs necessary for postwar progress. Indeed, he defended Woodrow Wilson's equitable plans after World War I against the criticism that they had been gullible.[46] He had somehow to bridge the gap between crude power calculations and the need to uphold ideals; he did so by advocating an integrated world economic and political program to alleviate international territorial and strategic rivalries. And to implement such a program, he reasoned, it was necessary to disabuse Americans of their fourth and most ominous fear—that of revolution.

Asserting that revolution was America's "oldest and

proudest tradition," Thomas lamented that, over the years, the United States had become a "stronghold of conservatism," shunning social reform at home, and hostile to the gigantic spiritual revolution of the twentieth century "against the theory of the western white man's divine right to run the world for his own benefit."[47] In Asia, he continued, Roosevelt's Four Freedoms were tantamount to revolution; and the three great revolutions in China, India, and Russia posed both great promise for the world and an unprecedented challenge to America's world leadership. The United States had to assume leadership in world political organization and economic reform—or else risk Asian unification in a "great unshakeable hate" against the West, quite possibly under Russian influence.[48]

Such leadership meant an active role in the institutionalization of international economic cooperation to alleviate want. Nations, America included, had to abandon their preoccupation with boundaries and territorial expansion and devote themselves to a more thorough exploitation of existing possessions, while cooperating to develop resources and markets to benefit all the people of a highly interdependent world. In particular, the powerful American economy had to be fully geared to eliminate want; for "the modern world cannot survive half fed, half starving." To these ends, Thomas reasoned, the system of international agreements toward which the Allies were working—the Bretton Woods plans for monetary stabilization and exchange management, the International Labor Organization, the Food and Agriculture Organization—were crucial. Governments had to cooperate in the rational production and distribution of goods to assure social welfare—the traditional socialist goal. Economic nationalism, tariffs, and cartels, based on outmoded ideas of scarcity and profit, must be abandoned. And producers would have to accept these restrictions in the interest of ameliorating the causes of modern wars. Man did "not have to conquer man," Thomas argued; he needed "merely to conquer his world."[49]

Thomas's program for a highly developed structure for economic development and amelioration rested squarely on Soviet-American cooperation for common peaceful purposes. And, since such commonality of purpose was a practical impossibility without acquiescence in the Soviet exercise of traditional geographic and historic interests on her European borderlands, Thomas strongly counseled acceptance of Soviet hegemony in that area as a legitimate parallel to traditional United States dominance in the Western Hemisphere. With such an understanding in effect, the two countries could jointly support an international structure of peace and development, notwithstanding their antagonistic domestic political systems. Thomas thus regarded a pragmatic acceptance of great power spheres as a prerequisite for his idealized economic cooperation. Far more than Connally, he turned Wilsonian idealism on its head, giving it a power base: acceptance of a Sovietized eastern Europe was not a necessary evil, but a positive, substantial part of a tolerant and realistic great power relationship on which to build. Implicitly, he assumed that with increased and widely based world prosperity, the subjugation of small nations within spheres would become less burdensome to them, less necessary to their imperial masters, and ultimately less prevalent, as economic coordination and opportunity reduced international political anxiety and competition.

The Four Fears found an audience. Reviewed in the United States and abroad, it provoked a sympathetic response, and it drew to Thomas a wide and sustained correspondence. One reviewer praised its exploration "beyond the surface of current problems" to expose "the principles, the prejudices and the passions that have to be reckoned with if the weight of public opinion is to be gathered to induce Congress to support an effective plan for a peaceful world."[50] During 1945, Thomas reiterated, in Congress and before the public, the themes he had developed in his book.

In June 1945, he termed great power unity the first step toward an effective peace; although it was four months after Yalta, and the political situation in eastern Europe was a source of anxiety to his Senate colleagues, he wrote:

> Of course, there will always be little problems and frictions to deal with, a boundary problem here and there—but if the people and the governments of the great powers are decided to solve these problems by common understanding, none of them can become a major danger to the peace of the world.[51]

He also continued to press for international economic cooperation, both in the United Nations, in world conferences on trade and employment, and in Senate approval of renewed Reciprocal Trade Agreements.[52] He continued to envision Soviet-American cooperation as the linchpin of a postwar order in which the transformation of world economic relationships might accommodate the Asian revolutions which were increasingly shaping world politics.

If Bridges, Vandenberg, Connally, and Thomas represented a cross section of Senate leadership in 1945, then the climate of opinion was mixed, varying according to deeply rooted perceptions of Soviet-American relations as the war drew to a victorious conclusion. All the senators were consciously aware of the Soviet Union as a critical constructive or destructive element in the new world order; the expansion of Russian capabilities and objectives amidst world wreckage was crystal clear. It was quite another matter to interpret the meaning of Soviet expansion for American interests and to fashion an American response. Interpretations ranged from the diagnosis of immoral and dangerous Soviet Communist expansionism in violation of wartime ideals, to a comfortable acceptance of apparently legitimate Russian territorial ambitions and normal great power behavior. If the Republicans saw in Yalta and its aftermath the confirmation of a deteriorating political situation in Europe and increasing Russian inflexibility which posed dire threats to American influence and to the principles for which the war had been fought, Connally and Thomas saw clear progress toward the building of an international organization, and hardly begrudged Russia her hardwon spoils. While the Republicans feared that appeasing Russia would tempt her to trample the Atlantic Charter and wreck the United Nations, Democrats worried lest American hostility toward Russia jeopardize Soviet cooperation which they deemed essential to the postwar system. Such dissension was closely related to Senate images of postwar China—images which were taking tangible form as the Pacific fighting approached its climax.

II WISHFUL THINKING
ABOUT CHINA

The Wartime Legacy

Early in 1945, the headlines screamed about the Battle of
the Bulge, the summit meeting at Yalta, and victory in
Europe. Later they proclaimed repression in Poland, the
birth of the United Nations, the atomic bomb, and victory
over Japan. As America breathed a sigh of relief at the end
of hostilities, and turned to grapple with the Russians in
Germany and eastern Europe, China was little on its mind.
With the elimination of Japan as an overriding threat on
which to focus common energies, national rivalries and
political revolution reemerged and threw China into chaos.
But to Americans who knew little of China and absorbed
themselves in the struggles across the Atlantic, these events
were faintly heard peals of thunder from a distant and
traditionally stormy land.

Chinese affairs in 1945 were conditioned not only by the

actions of the Far Eastern great powers—America, Russia, and (to a decreasing extent) Britain—but also by the long and bitter struggle for control of China between Chiang Kai-shek's Kuomintang Party, which controlled the Chinese Nationalist Government and Army, and the Chinese Communist Party, which dominated certain areas of northern China. America's initial policy after Pearl Harbor had been to encourage effective Chinese participation in the war against Japan, with the ultimate aim of China's emergence from the war as a strong and unified country, a stabilizing force in East Asia, and, as before, a friend of the United States. Toward these ends, the United States had attempted to upgrade the diplomatic status of China and had encouraged an accommodation between the Kuomintang and the Chinese Communists in the effort to repel the Japanese invaders. But the American effort was impeded by the low priority assigned China in Allied strategy, and was finally nullified by Sino-American discord regarding the deployment of Nationalist armies against Chiang's two enemies, the Japanese and the Communists.

In her wartime effort to build Chinese morale, invigorate the flagging Chinese military effort, and neutralize Japanese propaganda aimed at Chinese racial sensibilities, the United States undertook numerous symbolic gestures. In January 1943, America signed with China a treaty abolishing the decadent extraterritorial system under which Americans had been tried in United States courts for crimes committed on Chinese soil; a similar Sino-British treaty was concluded simultaneously.[1] In December 1943, Congress, encouraged by a highly organized lobby (including a dramatic cross-country tour by the eloquent Madame Chiang Kai-shek), repealed the Chinese Exclusion Act of 1924. This gesture, made possible by the gradual abatement of anti-Chinese prejudice, the growth of cultural interest in China, and the heroic wartime image of a China which, alone, had staved off Japan since 1937, set China's immigration quota at about one hundred persons per year.[2] At the same time, the Roosevelt Administration sought to instill among the Allies the notion of China as a great power by including her in the deliberations of the major Allies, notwithstanding the deep skepticism of the British and the Russians. China had been a signatory to the Declaration of the United Nations, along with America, Britain, and Russia, in January 1942. In November 1943, Roosevelt, Churchill, and Chiang met as "equals" at Cairo, and their joint statement included China among the "Three Great Allies." Moreover, they announced the policy (previously endorsed by Stalin for Roosevelt) of restoring to China all territories (Manchuria, Taiwan, and the Penghu Islands) earlier wrested from her by Japan.[3] This declaration coincided with the repeal of the Chinese exclusion legislation, and Roosevelt signed the bill upon returning from the conferences of Cairo and Teheran.

Yet, notwithstanding the wartime construction of an image of China as a great power, American goals for a vigorous Chinese effort against Japan and for the emergence of a strong and unified China from the war were frustrated by a combination of Allied military strategy and Chinese politics. More than a year before American entry into the war, Anglo-American military planners had decided to give the European effort against Germany top priority, in the event that the United States became involved; and after Pearl Harbor, this course was followed, leaving the China-Burma-India theater (CBI) meager manpower and material with which to protect British India, contain the Japanese threat to Burma and Indochina, and mobilize Chinese forces for operations against the Japanese in China. In January 1942, Roosevelt sent Lieutenant General Joseph W. Stilwell to China, to be Chiang Kai-shek's chief of staff and to command Chinese forces, with an eye to eventual joint Sino-American operations against Japanese-held areas of China and the establishment of air bases in China from which to bomb the Japanese homeland. Stilwell did the best he could with the scarce resources allocated to his program to reorganize the flaccid Nationalist armies. Simultaneously, airborne transportation over the Himalaya mountains was employed—a daring operation but quite limited in its carrying capacity—to keep China supplied, pending the destruction of Japan's coastal blockade. Also, General Claire Chennault, the air enthusiast, and his volunteer Flying Tigers were active in operations against the Japanese from bases in China.[4] These modest efforts in CBI bitterly disappointed Chiang who, after Pearl Harbor, naturally had envisioned China as the hub of a massive, coordinated Allied thrust against Japan. He was constantly frustrated in his attempts to secure from America more lend-lease supplies; for these he was in sharp competition with the British, who discounted China as a military factor and sought aid for Burma and India.

The military capability of China, under siege by Japanese armies in the north and east and virtually cut off from the south, was further dissipated by the internal struggle between the Kuomintang and the Communists. Ever since the late 1920s, when Chiang had abandoned his Russian orientation, civil war had raged intermittently between the two factions, with the Soviet Union alternately stimulating and dampening Chinese Communist militancy according to changing Russian needs. Since 1937, when Japan had attacked China from its stronghold in Manchuria, the Kuomintang and Mao Tse-tung's Communists had coexisted uneasily and had sought to expel their common enemy. The Soviet Union, smarting from the Anti-Comintern Pact (1936) between Japan and Germany, had supported since 1937 a common Chinese effort under Chiang against its major East Asian rival and potential enemy, and it continued to do so during World War II. Yet the factional truce remained that and nothing more; there was no military coordination and, after 1940, Chiang began to use his best military units to blockade and isolate the Communists in

Wishful Thinking About China

their base in north central China. The mutual mistrust and hostility—based on deep social and ideological cleavages within China—did not abate, and both sides awaited the end of foreign hostilities, when they would take up the cudgels for mastery of China.

By 1943, after six years of foreign invasion and much longer intermittent strife, the Chinese Government was sagging politically, militarily, economically, and morally. Inefficiency and corruption characterized the regime and the army, undermining Chiang's base of support among the people and crippling his military effectiveness. Wild inflation and black markets disrupted the nation's economy; morale ebbed in areas of Nationalist control.

In contrast, the Communists shrewdly instituted governmental, landholding, and military reforms, creating a massive base of popular support which augmented their highly disciplined political and military organization, and thus succeeded in controlling effectively substantial areas of northern and western China. By using guerrilla tactics and securing peasant support in areas behind Japanese lines, they thrived on the wartime disorder which was eroding Nationalist strength. Their base, estimated at several million in population in 1937, had ballooned to some 95 million people and a considerable portion of Chinese territory toward the end of the war, as the Kuomintang regime foundered and Japanese power waned.

Communist successes presented a mortal challenge to the potency and legitimacy of the Nationalist Government. The uneasy truce was severely strained by 1943—as were Sino-American relations—as Chiang continued to seal off the Communists to the north, thus failing to support the United States in turning back Japan. Moreover, Chiang exploited the wasteful and debilitating rivalry and corruption in the Kuomintang to maintain his own personal power, which was utterly dependent on an antiquated, ineffective, and competing group of warlord armies with personal allegiances to the Chinese ruler. He was, therefore, working totally at cross-purposes with his American chief of staff, Stilwell. Knowledgeable about China and militarily skilled, Stilwell endeavored to streamline the Chinese armies and to stimulate a national effort to throw China's full weight against the Japanese. His outspoken bluntness led to conflict with Chiang, who resented his interference in the structure of Chinese politics, upon which Chiang's power rested. Openly contemptuous of Chiang, Stilwell urged Washington to extract concessions from him—especially administrative and military reforms, and military collaboration with the Communists—in exchange for continuing American aid. Chiang finally demanded and secured Stilwell's recall in October 1944.

Soon thereafter, Roosevelt appointed Major General Patrick J. Hurley ambassador to China. An experienced but shallow wartime envoy, Hurley sought to harmonize Sino-American relations, keep China in the war, and secure a Communist-Kuomintang accord for the war effort and the peace to follow. His smooth manner and affability contrasted sharply with the demands of the perspicacious Stilwell; he soothed Chiang, and got on well with him. Although, in late 1944 and early 1945, he felt he was making progress with the Chinese factions, their respective objectives remained unchanged: seizure of the government for the Communists, and destruction of the Communists for the Kuomintang.

By 1945 Roosevelt and other policy makers had long realized that, whatever the outcome of her struggle, China would not be a great stabilizing force in Asia for years to come. With America's Pacific island-hopping strategy coming to a climax, they hoped merely that China would continue to tie down large numbers of Japanese troops otherwise available for battle with the United States. In 1943, the Allies had announced the policy of unconditional surrender, and analysts now envisioned a bitter two-year struggle, after the imminent defeat of Germany, as the Japanese fought stubbornly to preserve their imperial institutions. Unwilling to undertake massive military operations on the Asian mainland, the United States thus turned to the Soviet Union for aid in the Pacific theater; and at Yalta, Roosevelt secured Stalin's assurance that, within two or three months of Germany's surrender, Russia would enter the war against Japan. In return, Roosevelt and Churchill agreed to the cession of certain islands in the northwestern Pacific from Japan to Russia; the internationalization of the Manchurian commerical port of Dairen, with "the preeminent interests of the Soviet Union in this port being safeguarded and the lease of Port Arthur as a naval base of the U.S.S.R. restored"; and the joint Soviet-Chinese operation of major Manchurian railways, with preeminent Soviet interests safeguarded, yet with China retaining "full sovereignty in Manchuria." Roosevelt undertook to secure Chiang's concurrence in the agreement; and Stalin consented to make an alliance with the Chinese Government and to aid it in driving out the Japanese.[5]

The Yalta agreement on the Far East, highly secret, reflected Roosevelt's sense of the limits of American power in East Asia and the consequent need for Soviet aid—with corresponding concessions—in the Pacific war. By acquiescing in Stalin's demands for imperialist rights long craved (and sometimes held) by the tsars before him, Roosevelt contradicted America's traditional expressions of support for Chinese territorial and administrative integrity, and her wartime idealization of China as an emerging pillar of justice and stability in Asia. While the approaching climax of the Pacific war, and the political instability and military weakness of China, certainly justified some such reevaluation of East Asian power relationships as occurred at Yalta, America's continuing attachment to unconditional surrender maximized the need for Soviet collaboration, heightened American receptivity to Russian claims in Asia which

45

compromised Chinese sovereignty, and thereby weakened China's position regarding Soviet demands in Manchuria. Had the United States developed a more flexible policy toward Japan, and had she been more receptive to subsequent Japanese feelers for a negotiated peace, the reduced need for Soviet military cooperation would have eased the pressure on America to legitimize Soviet demands on China. Yet, even so, Stalin might have taken what he wished by marching without sanction into Manchuria when he felt strong enough to do so. Roosevelt at least had secured for Chiang a pledge of Soviet diplomatic and military support, and a limited definition of Soviet rights in Manchuria. These, it seemed, might serve as a basis for a Sino-Russian accommodation and as an inducement to the Chinese Communists to be flexible in the negotiations which Hurley was sponsoring for a Communist-Kuomintang settlement.

Thus, in 1945, China was a great power in name, but not in fact. Through the wartime machinations of the United States, she sat as one of the "Big Five" with a veto power in the Security Council, and she was treated in official pronouncements and public discussions of the United Nations as one of the major military and political factors in the just and harmonious international order envisioned for the future. While Hurley strove to prevent the Chinese political order from coming apart at the seams, and while Roosevelt yielded up Chinese rights to Stalin at a conference not even attended by the Chinese, American public policy assuming China to be a full-fledged global power offhandedly persisted. Public perceptions of China similarly persisted as vaguely optimistic expectations within the framework of wartime idealism, even as that idealism was threatened by the subjugation of Poland and the development of Soviet-American discord.

Wishful Thinking About China

Pro-Chiang Republicans

All through World War II, Congress had been keenly aware of China as a special and deserving ally. In his speeches before Congress, Roosevelt's references to China's bravery and heroism repeatedly drew unusually long and loud ovations. In 1942 and 1943, concerned representatives and senators of both parties pressed the Administration for the abolition of extraterritoriality, the repeal of Chinese Exclusion, and generally more aid and attention to China, which seemed neglected in favor of the European theater. Like most of the country, Congress was captivated by Madame Chiang during her long sojourn in the United States during these years. Charming, Christian, and Wellesley-educated, she successfully portrayed to congressmen, in public and in private, the plight and resolve of the Chinese people. Congress, it seemed, had little notion of the Chinese factional struggle, and generally assumed that Chiang would emerge from the war firmly in control of a China which would be ascendant in the Far East.[6]

The prevalent euphoria about China, a function of traditional missionary attachment, China's heroic wartime image, and intensive lobbying, began to break down toward the end of the war. As early as the spring of 1943, Stilwell, temporarily back in Washington to press his case for military reforms in China, had "two 'very satisfactory' sessions" with Senators LaFollette and Connally and other congressmen, in which he attempted to convey the truth about China's vast problems. In August 1943, the general showed five visiting senators around Kunming and Chungking, educating them to Chinese realities as an antidote to the charms of their hostess, Madame Chiang. He had some success; Senator Henry Cabot Lodge, Jr. (Republican, Massachusetts) urged that "sugary propaganda about China" cease.[7] Yet even during the war's concluding phase, when the harsh facts about China were filtering through to the

47

United States via officials, visitors, and the press, Congressional attitudes remained subject to the prevalent hopeful illusions in America concerning China's postwar prospects.

Significantly, the first effort to interpret Sino-American relations early in 1945 came not from any leading senator, but from Vandenberg's collaborator and Dewey's foreign policy adviser, Dulles. Speaking before the Cleveland Council on World Affairs in January, Dulles, a prominent lay Presbyterian, lauded America's "especial friendship and admiration" for the Chinese, which he attributed to Christian missionary activities. Explaining that protective policies for China—from John Hay's Open Door through the current war with Japan—reflected America's "determination that the 400,000,000 of China shall not become harnessed to the predatory designs of any alien power," he noted China's resulting "confidence in us." And he asserted that in 1937, Chiang Kai-shek had chosen "to rely on the ultimate support of the Christian democracies, notably the United States," rather than to become a Japanese puppet or to make concessions to the Communists in quest of Soviet support. Yet after four and one-half years of lonely struggle against Japan's entire might, the Chinese, expecting a quick victory with America's cobelligerency, had endured instead three more years of increasing economic and military desperation as American supplies went almost entirely into the air effort against Japan. Consequently, Dulles reasoned, the Chinese had lost confidence in their government, while the Communists, appearing to offer a shortcut toward desperately needed social reforms, had thrived. He now detected a growing demand by Americans "who advocate what they guess Moscow wants," that the United States recognize the Communists as the rulers of China, or force the Nationalists to coalesce with them. He warned that this seemingly "easy course," comparable to the courses Chiang had spurned in 1937, would be disloyal to friendly elements in China, would impair American prestige in the Far East, and would encourage the creation of "a solid oriental bloc" hostile to the white West, much as Japan had envisioned. Instead, he argued, America must support the Nationalists and thus encourage unified Chinese resistance against Japan. While the Kuomintang, like other regimes, might fall, Dulles chided that "it ought not to be our hand that pushes it under."[8]

In interpreting China's lone struggle and later collaboration against Japan as tokens of good faith in the West, Dulles did not see that Chiang's political interests allowed him no choice, since the other alternatives would have insured his overthrow or the virtual loss of Chinese independence. In attributing the Kuomintang's floundering to eight years of foreign war, he neglected preexisting factors in China which were exacerbated by such war, and which helped the Communist cause: economic crisis, chronic administrative inefficiency, demoralization of ill-treated armed forces, and the corruption and tyranny of the Chinese ruling elite. Warning America to deal only with her "friends" lest she discredit herself in Asia, he discounted the force and legitimacy of the Communist challenge. In effect, he urged that America pursue its interests in East Asia through the Kuomintang in light of an incipient Soviet-American struggle there. Since China was to be an intrinsic part of this struggle, it seemed senseless to deny the Chiang regime full diplomatic recognition and moral support against Soviet-backed insurgents. Only the Kuomintang, he reasoned, could unify China in war against Japan and against Soviet encroachments. Stressing the need to support Western values and American interests in China, Dulles presaged similar demands by Styles Bridges regarding America's response to Soviet encroachments in eastern Europe. And, like Bridges, he never suggested the use of military force to secure what he demanded. Yet, unlike Poland and the Baltic region, China had remained free (thus far) of Soviet occupation and, while Hurley strove toward an elusive factional coalition, Dulles could logically call for a policy supportive of Chiang's government.

Dulles's analysis of the Chinese situation hit a responsive chord in the internationalist wing of the Republican Party, and it drew praise from the president of the Council on World Affairs, among others. One correspondent, linking Dulles's presentation with Vandenberg's speech a week earlier, pointed out that Republicans were more able to speak their minds than were Administration spokesmen. Dulles himself, fresh from Dewey's bipartisan presidential campaign the previous autumn, spoke of developing "an area of common agreement" in foreign policy. He no doubt made his remarks on China in this frame of mind, for he, Vandenberg, and other internationalist Republicans clearly planned to play an aggressive (if nonpartisan) role in the development of postwar foreign policy, and they expected to reap their share of public recognition for their contributions.[9]

As the pivotal man in the bipartisan foreign policy system, Vandenberg at this time was primarily concerned with the United Nations, eastern Europe, and Soviet-American relations; but he had long been conscious of the Far East. As an isolationist, he had argued throughout the 1930s against a harsh policy toward Japan, stressing that American interests in Asia were not great enough to warrant the risk of war, and even suggesting an abandonment of the Philippines to avoid conflict. With American cobelligerency, Vandenberg's perspective shifted radically; now that China was an ally and Japan an unmistakable enemy, he took an active interest in Asia (no less than in Europe and Africa), with an eye toward victory and the postwar settlement. He supported symbolic American initiatives in support of China, and called for more aid to that country; at the same time, he quietly promoted for the 1944 Republican presidential nomination General Douglas MacArthur, and sympathized with the general's resentment at the low priority given his Pacific war effort.[10]

By 1944, China loomed far larger in Vandenberg's mind

than it ever had earlier. In April of that year, he lauded State Department plans for a United Nations grounded "virtually in a four-power alliance," with real authority vested in a council upon which "the Big Four"—America, Britain, Russia, and China—would always have representatives empowered with vetoes over the use of force. On the other hand, Vandenberg was suspicious of the secret wartime deliberations of the great powers. Concerned throughout the war with the implications of British and Soviet ambitions, he expressed pessimism in March 1944 about Roosevelt's secret commitments at conferences. "The so-called Atlantic Charter," he lamented, "has already been torn to shreds—so far as its promises to little countries are concerned." And in May 1944, alarmed by reports that at the Teheran Conference of the previous December, "Russia and Britain virtually agreed upon what they are to get out of the post-war world and that Roosevelt, by his silence, acquiesced," Vandenberg asserted that American policy sanctioned a virtual "three-power alliance (with China added as a pleasant gesture) to run the world." America would merely help to police a Soviet-British condominium.[11]

Thus, Vandenberg perceived discrepancies between "Atlantic Charter ideology" and the unrestrained selfishness of traditional great power politics. As a great power in name but not quite in fact, China would play a role conditioned by the development of one or the other alternative. In Vandenberg's idealized order, China would be part of a great power alliance so harmonious and strong, and operating to preserve so just and satisfying a peace, that the actual existence or lack of Chinese military power would not be critical to its operation. In his pessimistic premonitions of great power spheres of influence, the actuality of overwhelming Anglo-Russian-American power would leave China little more than a ceremonial ally with little influence or consequence. Hence China was not to be a critical factor *on her own*, but only in relation to other major powers in a

51

properly operating world concert of powers. Vandenberg's expectations for China in these varied contingencies squared well enough with America's continuing rhetoric about China as a postwar power and with China's simultaneous inability to legitimize her great power status either in battle or in self-government.

Vandenberg's worry over great power relationships persisted into 1945, and continued to influence his thinking about China. His highly publicized speech of January 10, offering an alternative to great power unilateralism in a peacetime military alliance, implicitly suggested a Sino-Russian-American concert in Asia, as well as an Anglo-Russian-American concert in Europe, to prevent a German or Japanese resurgence.[12] And when, with the pro-Chiang Dulles at his side, he served as a delegate to the San Francisco Conference from April through June, he was increasingly concerned about the stubborn conflicts between Russia and the West, and also quite conscious of the coincidence of Chinese and American interests in these conflicts.

In his tussles with the Russians, Vandenberg relied on and appreciated the support of the Chinese delegates at San Francisco. Working in collaboration with T. V. Soong, the Chinese foreign minister, and with V. K. Wellington Koo, the Chinese ambassador to the United States, he repeatedly acknowledged their tactical and moral support in difficult negotiations. He noted the support of Soong (along with that of Britain's Anthony Eden) in carrying out Roosevelt's pledge to Stalin to seat White Russia and the Ukraine in the UN, obnoxious though it was to them all, and he acclaimed their unity (in the privacy of his diary, fortunately for Chinese sensibilities): "A picture of Anglo-Saxon nations *keeping faith*"![13] When the Russians insisted on Security Council veto power over the discussion of important matters, Vandenberg took comfort in the support of England, France, and China; and he expressed delight when Russia backed down and accepted free discussion in the Security

Council. Even when the British and French wavered on the protection of regional arrangements such as that in the Western Hemisphere, he could count on the firm and dependable backing of the Chinese. Reciprocating this loyalty, Vandenberg worried that the allocation of multiple General Assembly seats to America, Britain, and Russia would be unfair to China (as well as to France).[14]

As Vandenberg's vision of great power harmony and global justice was jeopardized by Russia, he was beginning to conceive of close Sino-American collaboration in Asia as an alternative to acquiescence in Soviet expansion. As a relatively weak country and an American protégé, Nationalist China naturally supported American democratic principles and the blocking of unilateral Soviet encroachments in the Far East. Hence there was a solid basis for cooperation with China in resisting illegitimate Soviet demands. When Vandenberg admitted to the Senate in June 1945 that the UN Charter in effect sanctioned a dominant alliance of China, France, Britain, Russia, and America, in which the latter three would provide the real muscle, and when he argued that the best way to handle their preponderance of power was precisely through the United Nations as a brake on their actions, he had at the back of his mind still a Sino-American combination which Russia must respect in her approach to Asia. Consistent with his larger goal of hard bargaining with Russia, he assumed that the most successful means of balancing Soviet land power in Asia lay in common Sino-American policies resisting at least those demands which Russia would not back up with military force. Vandenberg viewed Nationalist China as solidly in the American camp on issues of vital concern to the United States; in light of the uncertain drift of Soviet-American relations, such friendship was highly valued. For, weak though she was, China could serve as a stabilizer, a surrogate for American power in Asia, while the primary Soviet-American competition took place in Europe. Unaware of the Yalta agreement on

53

Manchuria, Vandenberg must have contemplated America's position in China with relative cheer; there were as yet no Russian military operations in China, there was therefore no Soviet foothold, and thus Stalin would have to bargain for position in China or risk a confrontation with the United States rather than presenting her with a *fait accompli*, as in eastern Europe.

The implicit corollary to Vandenberg's conception of a pro-American Chinese bulwark in East Asia was the need, articulated by Dulles, to support the tried and tested friends of America: the Nationalist Government. Vandenberg's gratitude for Chinese support on issues pertaining strictly to the Western Hemisphere, and his reciprocal loyalty, implied a general mutuality of world interests and constituted a specific example of the advantage perceived by Dulles in a policy of unequivocal recognition and diplomatic support for the Nationalists as the sole legitimate authority in China.

Metternichean Democrats

Like his Republican counterparts, Tom Connally was conscious of America's interest in Chinese affairs. Appalled on his first trip to Asia in 1935 by the enormity of Chinese poverty and by Japan's warlike industrialization, he had empathized with China after the Japanese attack of 1937, while supporting Roosevelt's efforts to adopt a stronger policy toward Japan. After American entry into World War II, he helped secure Senate authorization of a half-billion dollar grant to China, and he maintained a "special interest" in the neglected Pacific theater, particularly in China.[15]

But, in contrast to internationalist Republicans, Connally was coolly critical of the Kuomintang regime. When, before the Senate Foreign Relations Committee in 1943, T. V. Soong denied prevalent reports "that Chiang was holing up in Chungking," rather than fighting the Japanese, Connally credited the Chinese diplomat with "a knack for getting American aid," noting that every one of "Dr. Soong's little lectures on China . . . cost the American government money." The same year, Connally later recalled, he became acquainted with Soong's sister, Madame Chiang. Receiving Connally and Representative Sol Bloom (Democrat, New York), chairman of the House Foreign Affairs Committee, at her quarters upstairs at the White House, she "entreated us to get Roosevelt to increase military aid to China," pouted about the behavior of General Stilwell, and "expressed great fondness" for General Chennault, Stilwell's rival in China. Connally declined to interfere in "the delicate international priorities and allocation system our military advisers had established."[16] If Connally's recollection was accurate, his attitude toward the Kuomintang's ruling elite was, at an early date, far more skeptical than the loyalty felt by Vandenberg, and worlds away from Dulles's notion of China's brave Christian soldiers fighting America's battles in Asia. He displayed considerable sensitivity to the manipulative efforts of the Chinese aimed at steering American policies to maximize the financial and military interests of Chiang and his associates.

Notwithstanding any personal suspicions of the Nationalist Government, Connally continued to support Roosevelt's policy of propping up China with symbolic gestures. In January 1945, he publicly envisioned the full participation of China, among other "powerful Allies," in the final military operations of the war and in the maintenance of the postwar order.[17] Asked by a Chinese correspondent to write a brief message for the upcoming Nationalist Party Constitutional Conference, Connally on May 1, 1945, transmitted his gratification that, while the world met at San Francisco to draw up an international organizational charter, the Chinese were establishing their own constitution with the aim of political unity and democracy in the tradition of the late Chinese revolutionary hero, Sun Yat-sen. Chinese representatives promptly assured him that his message would encourage China to press on against Japan, and that China would "strive to play a worthy part" in the United Nations.[18] Whether or not heartened by Chinese assurances, Connally was certainly conscious of China's one greatest resource when, on June 28, he defended to the Senate the structure of the Security Council, arguing that the population of its five permanent members outweighed that of all the other UN members.[19] For in sheer population, China was equal to the rest of the permanent Security Council members combined.

Yet, large numbers and all good intentions notwithstanding, Connally was acutely aware of China's relative weakness, and he was profoundly conscious of the great strength of the Soviet Union in East Asia, as in Europe. Always sensitive to the overriding necessity of Soviet-American collaboration in securing a workable postwar order, he welcomed Russian cooperation in the final stages of the Pacific war. Ignorant of the secret Yalta protocol on the Far East, he hailed the conference as evidence of Soviet-American partnership. And on April 5, 1945, he expressed joy and relief at Russia's denunciation of her neutrality treaty with Japan—an event flowing partly from Yalta concessions to Russia at China's expense—and welcomed the action's effects "on the international relations of the entire world."[20] Clearly, Connally stood in hopeful anticipation of Soviet aid in what was then envisioned as a long and costly campaign to defeat Japan.

Mouthing Administration rhetoric about a strong China, Connally, like Roosevelt, was conscious of China's instability. As in his thinking on world politics generally, his idealized pronouncements about East Asia constituted a mask designed to acclimatize the American people to a postwar order which would be utterly dependent on Soviet and American power. As in Europe, Connally hoped to leave Asian political problems—currently muffled in comparison

—to UN deliberation after the war's conclusion. He assigned top priority to Allied military action against Japan; such action would advance the idea and practice of UN harmony without confronting nagging political problems which, in his view, might endanger at the outset the Soviet-American good will essential to the postwar system. Implicitly, he sanctioned a Soviet-American entente in East Asia, with China at best a junior partner. China, like all nations which were not *truly* powerful, must simply accept the partial erosion of the national equality principle, in order to forestall the international anarchy of great power conflict. But it seemed imperative to mute any infringement of China's rights—as Roosevelt effectively did at Yalta—until the American public had accepted a functioning United Nations system based on Soviet-American collaboration. Connally's view was in stark contrast to the vision of a loyal, pro-American China supported by the United States in what was conceived by Dulles and Vandenberg as essentially an adversary relationship with Russia in East Asia.

The Far East in general, and China in particular, were also on the mind of Elbert Thomas during World War II, as they had been for decades. Having spent five youthful years as a Mormon missionary in Japan, he attributed his "lifelong study in things Oriental" to his proselytizing experience.[21] His four books reflected an unflagging scholarly interest both in Asian politics and in international relations.[22] After Pearl Harbor, he strongly advocated aid to China, played a leading role in the Senate drive for the renunciation of extraterritoriality, and worked hard for the repeal of the Chinese exclusion law as "a master stroke of psychological warfare."[23] Proud of America's wartime record in China, he lauded the Allies' practice of mutual accommodation among equal nations, envisioned a new democratic era in international affairs, and noted that the West had given China "that equality which Japan, another yellow people, denied her."[24]

Late in the war, Thomas was far more conscious and outspoken about China than were other Senate leaders. In his idealistic world vision, where cooperative pursuits would replace destructive competition and territorial obsessions, Thomas suggested that the Chinese abandon important national claims. In *The Four Fears* (1944), he argued that the retrocession of Hong Kong "might not leave China so free as she would be without it"; hence continued British influence would be at least a temporary advantage. Furthermore, he argued that Taiwan, guaranteed to China by the Cairo Declaration (1943), should be retained by Japan. Discounting "emotional" considerations, he maintained that Chinese rule there had been troubled, that Taiwan's integration with Japan had been economically productive, and that China had no need of insular possessions with accompanying naval burdens. Instead, China should expend her energies "on developing her own mainland and the bordering continental areas"—Turkestan, Mongolia, Tibet, and Manchuria—while "a subdued Japan and an anti-imperial Russia, busy with her own reconstruction, will leave China unperturbed by conflict."[25]

More naive than his contemporaneous thoughts on Europe, Thomas's analysis of the Far East in 1944 reflected a paradoxical blend of idealism and power politics. He soundly argued that China ought to develop her natural and historical land strength, and that Britain might be a stabilizer in postwar Asia. His suggestion that Japan retain Taiwan, like his warning against Polish acquisitions of German territory, implied a Metternichean arrangement in which the losers would enjoy some status;[26] he evidently had in mind the dangerous power vacuum and the German irridentism flowing from the harsh Versailles peace. At the same time, his formula required of China such idealism, such courtesy toward her Japanese tormentors, as to topple any Chinese government endorsing it. And, while he condoned Soviet control in nearby parts of eastern Europe, he expected an "anti-imperial" Soviet Union to leave uncontested the long-troubled Sino-Russian borderlands—prime areas of enduring Russian imperialism. Finally, Thomas did not explore the connection between his vague plans for peaceful Asian development and the three great Asian revolutions (in China, Russia, and India) which, he emphasized, were shaping the destiny of Asia.

Since in 1944 the primary war effort lay in Europe, and neither Soviet nor American intentions in Asia were fully developed or apparent, it is not surprising that Thomas's conception of postwar Asia was fuzzy. But it is significant that, in 1945, as his postwar vision for China was contradicted by developments in Chinese domestic and foreign affairs, his logic grew strained. At times, he spoke much like Vandenberg and Connally, idealizing China as a pillar of a just and cooperative peace. Shortly before Germany's capitulation in May 1945, he wrote an essay stressing the future interdependence of Asia and America, asserting that America must prevent any country from dominating Asia, and expressing hope that China, "even with countless pitfalls ahead," was emerging "as a real democracy." On April 19, 1945, toward the end of the last desperate Japanese offensive in China, he hailed the "magnificent teamwork" of Chinese and American forces in repelling it. And early in July, he asserted that China's populace, ideals, economic strength, and long resistance against Japan had "earned her al place in the 'big five' in the Security Council."[27] Yet, asked by a Chinese editor to give "some positive suggestions" for future Sino-American collaboration, he responded on June 27 with a lame admonition that the years ahead would not be easy, and with "a prayer for the future." Pressed on network radio to define a China policy, he admitted on July 14 that "to me . . . China is the world's biggest problem." And he maintained that China's size, class exploitation, and poverty were her own problems to solve—albeit with American aid.[28]

In mid-1945, Thomas resolved his conflicting opinions about China in a manner far less solicitous of the needs of the Chiang regime than that of Dulles or Vandenberg. To be sure, as a well-known Asia expert, he felt the weight of conservative opinion. The American Association for China Famine and Flood Relief, based in Chicago, pressed upon him the need for humanitarian aid, lest China fall under Communist, Soviet, or Japanese domination; and Brooklyn lobbyist Maurice William, of the Sun Yat-sen Memorial Committee, emphasized to Thomas the valiant resistance of a united China under Chiang against "totalitarianism in Asia," in behalf of "our democratic way of life and . . . our traditional policy of the Open Door."[29] But Thomas's thinking was far to the left of these groups, more receptive to the native social forces that were energizing Asia for revolutionary change, and very much more sensitive to the transcendent importance of finding agreement with Russia for the future peaceful development of East Asia. As his thought evolved, it increasingly resembled a body of opinion which viewed the Kuomintang and its American supporters with contempt. Indeed, this point of view was forcefully expounded in an article written by Laurence Salisbury and commended by him to Thomas in April 1945.

Appearing in the current issue of *Far Eastern Survey* (which Salisbury edited), the article claimed that the United States was "supporting a repressive oligarchy" against the Chinese Communists, the minority democratic parties, the intellectuals, and others who had the purpose and vigor to defeat the oligarchy in the cause of freedom. The previous autumn, Salisbury maintained, the United States had almost wrested from Chiang a greater effort against Japan and a liberalization of his self-serving regime; but after Stilwell's recall, General Hurley had given an unconditional commitment to the Kuomintang, thereby emboldening Chiang to consolidate his reactionary grip. Since the Chinese Communists, like them or not, were "on the scene to stay," Salisbury feared that a civil war would simply push them toward the Russians, and thereby divide the country "into a progressive North China supported by the Soviet Union and a fascist South China," supported by the United States. Especially worried lest Russia, upon entering the Pacific war, begin arming the Communists, he urged that the Chinese Government be reorganized to include the Communists and other disaffected elements; that America arm "all groups in China" willing to fight Japan; that, to overcome the Communists' reluctance to submit their armed forces to Chungking's control, an American be appointed to command all forces in China, along with American officers to command Chinese troops; and that the United States try to develop a common policy with Britain and Russia, since they also had stakes in China. Additionally, Salisbury warned lest America side with European colonialist governments against "the politically conscious Asian inhabitants" of dependencies which craved self-government. In particular, he noted that Britain might prefer a weak China in order to dampen Asian nationalism which might threaten European colonies; and he feared that in America's search for postwar stability in Japan, she would cooperate with the *zaibatsu* (industrialists and financiers) who had steered Japan toward dictatorship and aggression, and thereby discourage democratic movements in Asia.[30]

Despite Salisbury's suggestion that Americans serve with Chinese forces to assuage the Communists' fears of annihilation, his article represented a school of thought which may appropriately be termed "noninterventionist" with respect to China. This school—with numerous variations and nuances among the diplomats, writers, and politicians within it—generally deplored the unconditional support accorded Chiang by Hurley as, in effect, an intervention in Chinese politics designed to undercut the Kuomintang's opposition. Noninterventionists hoped that a nonpartisan distribution of supplies to all Chinese—including Communists—willing to fight the Japanese would rouse Chiang from his smugness and stimulate the political reforms needed both for military effectiveness and for governing China.

Critically important in noninterventionists' thinking was China's bearing on Soviet-American relations. Like Dulles, they pondered Soviet intentions in East Asia, but they operated on the opposite premise, that nothing inherent in the Chinese turmoil necessitated a Soviet-American confrontation. Indeed, their prime concern was to avoid such a confrontation by isolating the turmoil; hence the need to dissociate America from the repressions of a regime of questionable legitimacy. In the noninterventionist view, Soviet-American cooperation was vital for East Asia during and after the war, and, to this end, a common Anglo-Russian-American China policy seemed essential. This presumably would include an agreement to refrain from military intervention on behalf of any Chinese faction, and to support diplomatically whatever government evolved in China. Since Salisbury and other noninterventionists envisioned a great power acceptance of Asian nationalism and an end to colonialism, they implied as well a recognition by Russia and America of Chinese administrative and territorial integrity, which already had been secretly compromised by Roosevelt and Stalin. In seeking at Yalta to minimize Soviet-American tensions in East Asia, the United States had already gone beyond the acceptable limits of the noninterventionist framework which was, in essence, a Soviet-American concert of power recognizing Asian aspirations for independence and self-determination.

Elbert Thomas was a trustee of the American Council of the Institute of Pacific Relations (IPR), which published *Far Eastern Survey*, and he regularly received that periodical along with numerous books and pamphlets which the IPR, a small but influential organization, issued.[31] In late April and early May of 1945, Thomas was in Europe at the invitation of General Dwight Eisenhower, investigating German prison camp atrocities; so he did not immediately see the Salisbury article.[32] But whether or not he ever read it, he certainly embraced Salisbury's thinking far more than the notions of those who uncritically lauded Chiang Kai-shek. To be sure, he remained loyal to the Administration's foreign policy, and he neither impugned the character of the Kuomintang nor castigated Hurley's pro-Chiang policies. Yet his laudatory appraisal of Asiatic revolutions as movements toward the universal triumph of human rights was strongly suggestive of the Chinese Communists' struggle against Japanese conquest, and of their innovative political reforms and mass support in large parts of China. And, just as Salisbury perceived the squabbling Chinese factions as potential pawns in a Soviet-American confrontation and hoped for a great power concert to insure Asian stability, so Thomas consistently valued Russian-American coordination in the Far East; he called for "special postwar cooperation by the United States, Britain, Russia, and China, with the other United Nations."[33] On the other hand, as his suggestions for Hong Kong and Taiwan showed, Thomas did not share Salisbury's fears about a weakened China or a continued colonial presence in Asia. He thus far had stated only that America could not tolerate the domination of Asia by any one power; but his conception of the American, Soviet, and colonialists' roles in an East Asian postwar order became much clearer as the climax of the war laid bare Far Eastern political problems.

Thomas did not publicly resolve his indecision on American Far Eastern policy, nor did he elucidate the general objective of an Asiatic power balance, until the last weeks of the Pacific war. But by the summer of 1945, with American forces closing in on the Japanese islands, he may, as chairman of the Senate Military Affairs Committee, have had some notion of the impending use of the atomic bomb; and he began to voice radically altered opinions about American-East Asian relations. Asked about British, Dutch, and French possessions in Southeast Asia, he admitted that "the problems of those colonies are so complex that we can't deal with them at this distance," especially since the "colonial powers are our allies."[34] On July 29, he asserted that America had "less in the way of tangible interests [in Asia] . . . than China, Russia, France, Great Britain, Holland, or several other states"; and he argued that, having taken the major role in rendering Japan harmless, America had "already attained what should be our major objective."[35]

Finally, on August 2, Thomas wrote an article lamenting America's penchant for "militant crusading" around the world:

> The Russians know our strength on our own side of the ocean and also our weakness on theirs. They are not attempting to tell us what our policies shall be on our side in either North or South America, and we will do well to make up our minds right now not to talk, even among ourselves, about the use of force in dealing with them.[36]

China, he continued, posed the most serious threat to peace. For in Poland and other parts of Europe, America would do no more than criticize and protest against Soviet domination, "but over China we have worked ourselves up to a fighting attitude." He insisted that China, though in recent centuries decadent, was ancient, indestructible, and unconquerable from outside. And while America had been able to wage a successful war over China with a small island nation like Japan, he warned:

> If Russia impairs "the integrity and independence" of the so-called Republic and [the United States] attempts to guard it we can only

64

get ourselves into a third great war.[37]

In the face of Soviet power, Thomas had now abandoned his idealistic vision for East Asia. Articulating for the first time the probability of Soviet ambitions in Asia (as he had done all along in eastern Europe), he was prepared to acquiesce in massive Russian imperial thrusts there, and to rely on historic Chinese endurance to overcome them. Comparing China to Russia's European borderlands, he heavily discounted China's power, and contradicted his own calls for Sino-Russian-American collaboration in East Asia. Drawing back from the broad objective of utilizing American power somehow to prevent the domination of Asia by any country, Thomas would now strictly limit American interests and initiatives in the Far East, relying instead on the presence of imperial powers to stabilize the area. His was the purest of noninterventionist formulae: like Salisbury's, it recognized the necessity for Russian-American agreement on China, but rather than active American participation, it envisioned a power balance there based largely on Soviet (and other imperialists') terms. It was significantly more detrimental to China than was Connally's conception of a Soviet-American collaboration with China as junior partner, since the reduced American role implied a greater scope for Russian influence in China. Not even addressing the domestic Chinese political implications of such an arrangement, it was poles apart from the Dulles-Vandenberg conception of China under Chiang as an ally of the United States in containing Soviet expansion.

The End of the War

Even as Thomas was thinking through the Far Eastern puzzle and as Japanese power crumbled in the midsummer of 1945, no one expected the end to come so quickly. On August 6, the United States obliterated the city of

Hiroshima with a single atomic bomb. Two days later, the Soviet Union fulfilled its promise to enter the war against Japan. On August 9, Nagasaki was razed by a second atomic bomb and, assured that their emperor could remain "subject to the Supreme Commander of the Allied Powers,"[38] the Japanese accepted Allied terms. They formally surrendered to General MacArthur aboard the battleship *Missouri* in Tokyo Bay on September 2, 1945.

Relations among the Allies in East Asia were profoundly altered. The sudden victory in the Pacific caught Americans and Chinese alike unprepared, with huge Japanese armies in China and Manchuria waiting to surrender, and with large portions of China awaiting liberation and reconstruction. For the Russians, sudden victory brought into view the Yalta concessions; on August 9, the Red Army invaded Manchuria, and swiftly penetrated and took control of that region from the Japanese. In the coming months, the Kuomintang and Chinese Communists actively competed for control of China; and the Soviet Union, which signed a treaty of friendship with the Nationalists on August 14 in accordance with its Yalta obligation, began in the autumn to give limited aid to the Chinese Communists, while the United States came to the aid of the Kuomintang. These developments were deceptive at first, dimly perceived and then only gradually understood by the American public and the Senate, in the midst of many other, more pressing postwar issues.

In the summer and autumn of 1945, Vandenberg and Connally had their hands full in debating and steering through the Senate the implementing legislation for the United Nations Organization. Even Elbert Thomas, always conscious of Asia, was busy with the International Labor Organization, spending the better part of November in Paris attending a conference of that agency. Just as importantly, Anglo-Soviet-American tensions and their attendant publicity focused on the administration of Germany and eastern Europe. In contrast, the unilateral American occupation of Japan insured the attainment of at least some American goals with no consequences save the feeble protests of America's allies; while the persistently confused state of Chinese politics, combined with an uncertain Soviet policy in China, discouraged the focusing of Senate attention on the Far East.

Democrats Connally and Thomas, as chairmen of the Senate Foreign Relations and Military Affairs Committees, respectively, continued to give some thought to the East Asian situation. Both enthusiastically welcomed Russian entry into the Pacific war. On August 8, two days after Hiroshima had been devastated, Connally cheerily prophesied a speedy end to the war: "Russia should be able to drive the Japanese out of the mainland of Asia. The atomic bomb and our Navy will conquer the Japanese homeland."[39] The next day, as Russian troops poured into Manchuria, Connally, calculating the vast saving in American lives, was even more sanguine: "President Truman, in influencing Russia to enter the war against Japan, performed a gigantic service to the country and to the world."[40] Yet on August 14, with the end of the war, he noted that "Manchuria should be restored to China and the Japanese ousted from that territory and sent back to Japan."[41] At this point, he apparently envisioned no contradiction between Russian aims and military operations, on the one hand, and Chinese territorial and administrative integrity, on the other.

At the same time, Thomas was infused with new optimism for Soviet-American cooperation and for a Chinese resurgence, in the happy days following Japan's surrender. On August 9, flushed with America's demonstration of atomic power against Japan, he broadcast to the Japanese that the "mighty Soviet Union" had joined America, China, and Britain in standing "firm against aggression in the Far East."[42] In the ensuing weeks, he predicted that the work of Truman, Stalin and Churchill at the Potsdam Conference would "bear fruit in the continued co-operation yet to come"; and he urged that the occupation of Japan be not exclusively American, but include Chinese, British, Russians, and people of smaller nations in the Pacific war.[43] He also asserted that the Cairo Declaration of 1943 (which guaranteed the retrocession to China of Taiwan and Manchuria) had been given "added force" by the entry of Russia into the Pacific war; and he reaffirmed that, with Japan beaten, "certainly China will regain her lost sovereignty in Manchuria."[44] In this optimistic mood, Thomas similarly looked ahead to Asian reconstruction, envisioning Japanese manufacturing industries producing for export in exchange for food from other parts of the continent.[45] And on September 17, he reaffirmed his thesis that "the three greatest social, political, and economic revolutions of the world's entire history, the Chinese, the Indian, and the Russian," were "ushering in a new era," hopefully a dawning acceptance of the rights of man on a universal scale.[46]

In light of his recognition, weeks earlier, that Russia would probably expand into Asia, Thomas's assumption that Soviet military operations and political objectives in China were compatible with the restoration of Chinese territory and dignity seems naive. But the nagging realities of Chinese weakness and Russian power were firmly planted in his mind. He received from a Chinese diplomat the suggestion that surplus Chinese manpower be utilized under American-trained Chinese officers and American officers for occupation purposes, in order to fill the gap created by America's impulse for demobilization.[47] Clearly aimed at associating America militarily with the Nationalist Government, this proposal sought to bolster the illusion of Chinese power at a time when the Nationalist regime could not even control its own countryside in competition with the Communists. Thomas replied on October 31 that he had "always recommended the use of Chinese, Hollander, Commonwealth, and Philippine troops along with ours" in Japan, to represent "the new world of cooperative action."[48] Couched in idealistic terms, this was a shrewd evasion of the Chinese proposal, and it demonstrated Thomas's low opinion of China's prospects as a great power. Coupled with his sensitivity to Asian revolution and his enthusiasm for Soviet cooperation and responsibility in a Far Eastern settlement, it reflected Thomas's inauspicious appraisal of Nationalist China's prospects in her relations with Russia and in her contest with the Chinese Communists.

Thomas favored a continuation of Soviet, as well as Western colonial, interest in Asia, in order to help stabilize the area. Hasty colonial retrenchment would create a power vacuum in which revolutionary violence and great power rivalry would run rampant. He seemed to feel that in the complexity and turbulence of Asian politics, continued imperialist participation, if on a smaller and less oppressive scale, would create a power balance within which the social and political changes he welcomed could mature in somewhat orderly fashion, without being exploited by any faction or country. In any event, he perceived American interests in Asia to be less vital than those of other nations, and he viewed the risk to America of conflict with Russia in her Far Eastern borderlands as far outweighing any possible advantage to America in contesting with her the fate of China.

Such was certainly not the view of those who supported a strong Sino-American bond. On August 18, Senator H. Alexander Smith (Republican, New Jersey) relayed to Assistant Secretary of State Dean Acheson the apprehension of a former New Jersey senator at press reports of

> a secret agreement . . . reached before the Yalta conference, between Stalin and Roosevelt, whereby Russia was to reacquire the Chinese Eastern Railway, Outer and Inner Mongolia was to be united into a single republic within the sphere of Soviet economy and foreign policy, and

that Manchuria was to become an independent
republic within the Soviet Zone "of occupation."[49]

Smith, a strong internationalist who favored a Sino-Fili-
pino-American occupation of Japan, expressed concern lest
these reports presage "a partition of China and the Balkani-
zation of the Chinese people"; Acheson responded by discounting the "considerable confusion and speculation in the
press," and asserting that "apprehensions would appear to
be unfounded."[50] Whether or not this had the desired calm-
ing effect, it is clear that leaks about the Yalta settlement
exacerbated fears of Soviet expansion in Asia contrary to
Sino-American interests.

Yet, aside from Smith's query, leading Republicans were
virtually mute on Chinese affairs at the war's end. Vandenberg and Bridges variously concerned themselves with the
UN, atomic energy control, eastern Europe, Russia, and
communism in general. Even in the debate, late in
September, concerning the relative powers of the Truman
Administration and of General MacArthur in administering
the Japanese occupation, Senate Republicans limited
themselves to criticism of policy toward Japan, leaving out
China altogether.[51] It is significant that John Foster Dulles
wrote congratulatory letters both to William F. Knowland,
the replacement for deceased Senator Hiram Johnson of
California, and to Dean Acheson, the incoming under secretary of state, late in August.[52] For Knowland and Acheson
would be principals in the fierce partisan debates which
tore at American China policy from 1949 to 1952. But, for
the time being, the China problem seemed tame enough
compared to events across the Atlantic, and Dulles was
pleased that two able internationalists were coming into important executive and legislative jobs.

Through mid-autumn of 1945, China was at the periphery of the minds of most leading United States senators.
While Elbert Thomas was highly aware of the Far East,

most others were absorbed in other foreign policy problems, and China remained a backwater area in American diplomacy. To the extent that they spoke publicly about China at all, the senators talked generally in terms of Chinese equality with the great powers in achieving a cooperative East Asian order within the UN framework; this was in line with Washington's wartime rhetoric emphasizing China's postwar role as a power and the general world adherence to principles of national self-determination and equality of nations. But behind the rhetoric, there was a spectrum of thought varying according to several perceptions of troubled Soviet-American relations.

Just as American policymakers tried to cope with Soviet power and Chinese instability through Hurley's well-known efforts to heal China's political rift and through secret concessions to Russia at China's expense, so senators, writers, and other observers came to their own conclusions about America, Russia, and China. To Dulles and Vandenberg, China stood as a bulwark of pro-Westernism in the Orient against the dreaded expansion of Russian influence in Asia at America's expense. In Connally's view, China would be a valuable partner, along with Russia, in forging a workable international organization and in restoring in the Far East the order which Japan had wrecked. And Elbert Thomas, ambivalent about America's capacity or need to actively seek a strong, unfettered China at the expense of Soviet-American friendship, hoped for the emergence of a healthy China, yet would sacrifice Chinese territory and sovereignty to Russia's appetites in Asia in order to preserve the cooperative framework essential to world peace. To a far greater extent than the others, he faced the fact that China was a very, very junior great power and, much more than they, he was willing to remain passive as Russian power swelled to fill the turbulent Far Eastern vacuum. If John Foster Dulles was horrified by the prospect of Asian revolution and of expanding Russian power in the Far East, Elbert

Thomas regarded both as the wave of the future. It remained to be seen how this dissension would be expressed in the months ahead, when China exploded as a political issue.

III THE CONSERVATIVE CRITIQUE

The State Department Rift

"The astonishing feature of our foreign policy is the wide discrepancy between our announced policies and our conduct of international relations," stated Patrick J. Hurley in his jolting public resignation as ambassador to China on November 27, 1945. "We began the war with the principles of the Atlantic Charter and democracy as our goal. . . . We finished the war in the Far East furnishing lend-lease supplies and using all our reputation to undermine democracy and bolster imperialism and Communism."[1]

A conservative Oklahoma Republican, Hurley had served as President Hoover's secretary of war (1929-33) and later as attorney for Sinclair Oil in its settlement of expropriation terms with the Mexican Government (1938-40), before joining Franklin Roosevelt's bipartisan diplomatic system as a wartime envoy in many parts of the world. His last assignment, China, he termed "the most intricate and difficult."[2]

Long at odds with the professional diplomats at the State Department's Far Eastern office in Washington and at the American embassy in Chungking, he had been unable to fashion a coalition between the Kuomintang and the Chinese Communists after the defeat of Japan. In September 1945, ill and tired, he returned to the United States. Two months later, he quit, angrily blaming the Foreign Service for his troubles.

Hurley's stated objectives, allegedly defined by Roosevelt and supported by Truman, had been to prevent a Nationalist collapse, sustain the Chinese war effort, and "harmonize" Sino-American relations. But, Hurley declared, the career diplomats had "continuously advised" the Chinese Communists that his efforts did not represent American policy. Siding with "the Chinese Communist armed party and the imperialist bloc of nations whose policy it was to keep China divided against herself," these diplomats had "openly advised" the Communists to decline a military unification with the Nationalists barring Communist control. Even after the removal of offensive subordinates from China at his request, Hurley explained, they had been assigned to the China and Far East desks in Washington, or to advise MacArthur in Japan, and most had continued to support the Chinese Communist Party (CCP) "and at times . . . the imperialist bloc of nations against American policy." Consequently, America was being "sucked into a power bloc on the side of colonial imperialism against Communist imperialism." Principled American war aims, he reasoned, went unattained because of the secrecy which surrounded unhealthy State Department activities. He therefore urged that all of his reports, along with those of career diplomats dissenting from "promulgated American policy," be published; and he envisioned thereafter a State Department housecleaning from the bottom up.[3]

Hurley's allegations unleashed the first full-dress public debate on China policy after World War II. They were also the opening salvo of an intermittent but increasingly shrill and malicious attack upon American China policy and the State Department, culminating in the McCarthyite scourge of the early 1950s and haunting American diplomacy decades into the future. Hurley's attack, like those of his successors, was not unrelated to considerations of personal ambition and partisan political advantage. Yet it had its origins mainly in the confusion of America's aims and the frustration of her expectations in East Asia. Before the war had ended, the troublesome course of Chinese events had begun to pose stubborn and perplexing problems which, unsolved by the United States Government, caused discord within the State Department and presaged Hurley's accusations against the Foreign Service.

The conflict between Hurley and his subordinates derived from differing assumptions about the prospects of the Kuomintang, the nature of the Kuomintang-Communist rift, and Soviet policy in East Asia. Hurley was optimistic about the Kuomintang's ability to fight and to unite China under the leadership of Chiang, with whom he became close friends after being named ambassador in October 1944. He also drastically underestimated the Communist-Kuomintang rift, recognizing "the differences but not their depth, and he believed the hatred of Japan sufficient to overcome the mutual suspicions."[4] Cheerfully ascribing to the CCP a yearning for government "of the people, for the people, and by the people," he noted in February 1945 several "fundamental facts":

> The Communists are not in fact Communists, they are striving for democratic principles; and . . . the one party, one man personal Government of the Kuomintang is not in fact Fascist. It is striving for democratic principles. Both the Communists and the Kuomintang have a long way to go, but, if we know the way, if we are clear minded, tolerant

and patient, we can be helpful.[5]

Finally, he assumed—largely on the basis of Stalin's personal assurances to him—that the Soviet Union was ready to follow and support the American initiative toward Chinese unifica+ tion and unimpeded development under Chiang's rule. When, in the spring and summer of 1945, a Chinese settlement proved elusive, Hurley was certain that the revelation of Soviet support for Chiang, as embodied in the projected Sino-Russian treaty ultimately published in August 1945, would jolt the Chinese Communists into a more conciliatory stance regarding a coalition on terms favorable to Chiang—even though he continued to believe that they were not "real" communists but reforming democrats.

With Hurley's views America's career diplomats in Chungking—the "China hands"—profoundly disagreed. These diplomats were experienced in Chinese affairs, fluent in the language, perceptive, forceful, and articulate. Some of them Hurley inherited from the Stilwell mission, and a number, attached to the military, were not directly responsible to him. Prominent among them were John Paton Davies, Jr., John S. Service, Raymond P. Ludden, John K. Emmerson, and George Atcheson. The two most influential, Davies and Service, had served with Stilwell, regularly filing valuable reports on conditions in wartime China. Critics have stressed that both men, familiar with Chinese affairs but relatively ignorant of world communist history and practice, overemphasized the nationalist component in the Chinese Communist movement and correspondingly underrated the role of ideology; hence both allegedly overestimated America's potential influence over the CCP and grossly neglected the close bond between Yenan, the Chinese Communist capital, and Moscow. According to Tang Tsou and Russell Buhite, Davies and Service, although gauging more accurately than Hurley the relative strength of the Communists and the foundering Kuomintang, misunderstood the Leninist discipline, revolutionary aims, dictatorial aspirations, and pro-Soviet orientation of Mao Tse-tung and other Communist leaders. Confusing tactical political maneuvering employed to secure mass support with genuinely democratic development, Davies seemingly misapprehended the Communists as "backsliders" who welcomed class compromise and foreign investment. Service went even further, stressing that they sought "orderly democratic growth toward socialism" on the British model, rather than "violent revolution" or "an early monopoly of power."[6]

Indeed, Davies has since conceded that he underestimated the role of ideology in Chinese Communist foreign policy. He also has admitted his error in depicting the CCP as "democratic."[7] Yet this may not have been the glaring defect which critics have portrayed. As both men have indicated since, and as their on-the-spot reporting demonstrated, Davies and Service were proceeding on the accurate premises that Chinese communism was irrepressibly ascendent, and that America must somehow adjust to that reality, seeking always to protect its own interests no matter what might happen in China, while avoiding any commitment which might prove militarily hazardous, domestically unacceptable, or both. As Davies has observed, he was aware in 1944-45 of the Chinese Communists' tightening party discipline and continued Marxian internationalism, but was not principally concerned with such matters: "My attention was fixed on the issue of power"—as it was likely to be distributed in China—"and what the United States might do to attract Yenan away from the Soviet Union."[8] Similarly, after months of residence in Communist-held territory, Service reported in October 1944 that the Communists had mobilized the population in their areas through thoroughgoing reforms and thereby had effected active opposition to Japan; that any Nationalist attempt to eliminate them would merely strengthen their "ties . . . with the people" and ensure their victory; and that unless the Kuomintang reversed itself and matched their reforms, they would "be the dominant force in China within a few years." He also inferred from the social and historical context of the Chinese revolution, and from current CCP rhetoric and activities, that the Communists would continue to pursue a nationalistic foreign policy not excluding friendship with the United States if this suited their interests; they would not follow a strictly Soviet line, in view of "the overwhelming Russian presence so oppressively close," *unless* America foreclosed other options. He concluded that "two Chinas, neither an enemy, were at least better than a civil war, with one China an enemy and the U.S. committed to the losing side."[9]

Against the China hands' contention that the Communist revolution was nationalistic, peculiarly "Chinese," and therefore open to American influence, Tsou, Buhite, and other critics have cited the repeated prewar and wartime CCP policy shifts in cadence with "the twists and turns of Soviet policy," the persistent party contact between Yenan and Moscow, the dedicated Marxism of Communist leaders, and their habitual emphasis on Soviet support in a world divided between imperialists (usually including the United States) and antiimperialists. Communist hopes for American cooperation, gleaned by diplomats from firsthand contacts with them, allegedly represented a tactical shift designed to secure at least a benevolent American neutrality pending a Communist victory in China, following which the Communists' ideological antipathy toward America would inevitably emerge.[10]

Yet surely the interplay of ideology and pragmatism, of world revolution and national interest, is complex and subtle for any communist society, and particularly so for China, an Asian society in which communism had become firmly rooted and self-reliant after a long and troubled relationship with Stalin, who habitually had placed a premium on Russian security when it conflicted with communist revolution in China or anywhere else. Hence, the presupposition of a decisive bond between Soviet and Chinese Communist foreign policy in 1945 imputes a monolithic character to the international communist movement under Stalin's control which may seriously underestimate the flexibility of the Chinese Communists who, after all, were at a formative stage—self-sufficient survivors of a generation of adversity, rapidly gaining power in China, chronically uncertain of Russia's attitude toward them, historically on friendly terms with liberal elements among American intellectuals, reporters and diplomats, and currently fighting on the same side as the United States against the Japanese aggressor. They turned decisively against America only in 1946 and after, when convinced of America's continuing political and military support of their domestic enemies. They then turned more strongly toward Russia and to an ideologically "pure" foreign policy, never having perceived an opportunity to deal pragmatically with the United States.

This is not to deny that, given American neutrality or even friendship, the Communists might still have turned against the United States. But, in this connection, it is instructive to note their earlier and subsequent squabbles with their Soviet mentors, their eventual extrication from what Davies has termed "the possessive Russian embrace," and their ultimate, post-Cold War détente—surprisingly rapid and painless—with the hated Americans. Viewed in this light, it is possible to interpret much of their subsequent fiery rhetoric—attacks on Russia for too moderate a policy in eastern Europe, support of virulent Arab nationalism, charges of Soviet "revisionism" when Russia moved toward détente with the United States—as at least partly inspired by intense fear of their powerful and expansive neighbor and a compulsion to steer Russia toward involvement in the west, away from the chronically troubled Sino-Russian borderlands. One may even grant the saliency of ideology in much of Chinese Communist foreign policy, and the presence of recurrent internal conflict between foreign policy pragmatists and those who insist that Chinese Communist diplomacy remain ideologically pure.[11] In any event, it certainly behooved the United States in 1945—assuming the irreconcilability of the Communists and Nationalists, and in light of waxing Communist strength—to pursue a policy strengthening the position of those among the Communists who were open to a practical reconciliation with America and minimizing the effectiveness of the ideological purists in the formative years of Communist power.

Holding plausible, if unprovable, assumptions about the prospective foreign orientation of the CCP, the diplomats reasoned that a flexible policy was necessary, dealing pragmatically with all Chinese factions, and thereby taking Communist strength into account. This, they knew, might lead to a coalition government, a divided China, or a Communist victory. American actions, they hoped, would aim at a coalition, to secure traditional American objectives of Chinese unity and strength. But, just as they rejected Hurley's comparative estimate of Nationalist and Communist vitality, they were far more uncertain than he of the prospects for a coalition, particularly on Chiang's terms. More sensitive than Hurley to the depth of the Chinese cleavage, they pondered the contingency of unresolvable conflict. In writing about "two Chinas" and the necessity to woo the Communists, the China hands were suggesting a loose political-military coalition, a virtual truce in position, in which actual Kuomintang and Communist strength would be registered by the *de facto* division of administrative and military spheres between the factions geographically—a far less ambitious coalition than the fusion envisioned by Hurley.

The China hands deemed it especially important to adjust American policy for either contingency—loose coalition or outright civil war—as soon as possible; for with the expected end of the European war, Russia could be expected to intervene in the Far East, thereby coming in contact with the Communists in Manchuria and North China. Again at odds with Hurley, the China hands urged that a coalition must come *prior* to Soviet Pacific intervention lest Stalin face an uncontrollable temptation to exploit Chinese divisions. If no such coalition were forthcoming, then the United States must deal separately with the Communists as a rising force, lest they fall by default under Soviet influence. Davies recalls believing as early as October 1944 "that the balance of power in East Asia would shift against us when the Soviet Union moved eastward against Japan—unless we quickly countered by preemptive collaboration with Yenan." The next month, Davies urged that America "not indefinitely underwrite" Chiang's "politically bankrupt regime"; rather, she should increase her contacts with Yenan, preparatory to military collaboration under a coalition umbrella or, failing that, to the establishment of relations "with the regime which will probably inherit North China and Manchuria." While admitting that Soviet operations in North China would limit American leverage with the CCP, he argued that American aid could exert "considerable influence in the direction of Chinese nationalism and independence from Soviet control."[12] The continuation of such reporting in early 1945 caused great bitterness between the China hands and Hurley, who regarded the reports as pro-Communist efforts to undercut his mission. The diplomats in turn thought Hurley's posture rigidly pro-Kuomintang, alienating to Communists and liberal groups, and inciting Chiang to forceful suppression which would lead to a civil war and a CCP-Russian entente in hostility to the United States.

Policy differences were exacerbated by organizational disorder, personality problems, and the virtual absence of direction from the top of the Roosevelt Administration. Since Service, Davies, Ludden, and Emmerson had been attached to Stilwell's headquarters, and continued to serve with the military under his replacement, General Albert Wedemeyer, Hurley's control over them was tenuous. Using his delicate mission as justification, he imposed a censorship on all reports traversing the Chungking embassy enroute to Washington, along with a blackout on news stories unfavorable to the Kuomintang. He had periodic violent arguments with Davies and others who, he felt, were impeding his progress. The diplomats in turn scorned his obtuseness and arrogance, mocking the simple homilies and pompous style of the "Big Wind." Such internecine conflict extended to Washington, where the Chinese Affairs Division tried to keep some control over Hurley, or at least to keep track of his activities. A strong-willed and vain man, he enjoyed the confidence of Roosevelt, who had dispatched him to China in the summer of 1944 while Clarence Gauss was still ambassador, in typical disregard for normal State Department channels in favor of personal diplomacy-by-envoy. Even after replacing Gauss in October 1944, Hurley generally acted independently, carrying out his interpretation of his mission while the China desk endeavored in vain to steer him toward a less active and more evenhanded mediatory role, along the lines suggested by Service and Davies. All the while, Roosevelt and his advisers gave scant attention to Chinese politics. With their attention fixed on the climaxing European effort, they viewed China as a backwater area, a place to tie down Japanese troops while the United States conquered Japan from the sea and Russia attacked, hopefully, through Manchuria. With military considerations uppermost in the Administration's reckoning, the Chinese upheaval occupied a divided State Department.[13]

The Chinese Communists were frustrated by their inability to shake Hurley from his pro-Kuomintang posture, or to secure a higher priority from Washington. In January 1945, they made a bold gamble, transmitting to General Wedemeyer's headquarters in Chungking an offer by Chou En-lai and Mao Tse-tung to come to Washington for an "exploratory conference" with President Roosevelt, preparatory to expanded contacts with the Americans. But their effort to circumvent Hurley failed, for the ambassador saw their message. He angrily cabled Roosevelt about the offer, noting that it had resulted from the machinations of disloyal officers whose advice to the CCP was undercutting his mission for a unified China under Chiang. Couched in these terms, the Communists' offer angered Roosevelt, and no response was made to the initiative. Under different circumstances, the suggestion of such a journey would have had breathtaking implications for Sino-American relations; as it was, the episode further entrenched Hurley's position and augured badly for ensuing developments.[14]

A crisis erupted when Hurley went to Washington for consultations late in February 1945. By this time, the Chungking embassy staff was chafing under his restrictions. For months, the Communists had been suggesting joint military operations in the event of an American landing on the China coast later in 1945. Both Service and Davies—the latter recently transferred to Moscow to advise on Chinese affairs—had favored testing proffered Communist collaboration against the Japanese. And on February 28, assisted by the entire political staff at the Chungking embassy, Chargé George Atcheson wrote and dispatched an unusual, urgent message to Secretary of State Edward R. Stettinius, calling for a reversal of Hurley's policy. Noting Chiang's continued unwillingness to compromise with the CCP and China's consequent drift toward civil war, the message lamented America's failure to cooperate "with the large, aggressive and strategically situated armies and organized population of the Communist areas." It urged that while continuing aid to the Nationalists, America should "supply and cooperate with" the Communists and other anti-Japanese groups. She ought also to urge upon Chiang a coordinated and unified command, with an incorporation of Communist armies under the Nationalists through the command of American officers, each army operating in specified areas. Such steps, the message argued, would dispel America's rigidly pro-Kuomintang image, increase internal pressure on Chiang to be more reasonable, draw the CCP toward the United States, maximize the Chinese war effort, and "bring some unification which, even though not immediately complete, would provide the basis for peaceful future development toward full democracy."[15]

The Atcheson message may be criticized for unfounded hopes of genuine Chinese unity and democracy; yet, as in earlier Davies-Service memoranda, it was not so much internal Chinese politics as the foreign orientation of those holding power in China which concerned America's China hands. Judging by the tone of their arguments for arming the Chinese Communists, a genuine democratic coalition was not their primary consideration. As Service has retrospectively delineated the significance of the recommendation, if a coalition did not prove possible, so be it; by pursuing "an independent, uncommitted American policy," the United States could "adjust to and move with, rather than standing against, the tidal development of events in China."[16] Or, as Davies succinctly put it in an April 15 memo:

> A policy of aid to and cooperation with the Chinese Communist regime . . . will involve competing with Russian drawing-power rather than seeking to block it off, as would be the case were we to bolster Chiang as a balance and buffer.[17]

The geopolitical sophistication of the Davies-Service-Atcheson analyses reflected an understanding that a coalition, while obviously the neatest answer to America's needs, was by this time a doubtful outcome, and that America therefore had to treat with the Communists. In contrast, their references to democracy and factional unity seem oddly offhanded and naive. This suggests that the diplomats

were subject to the entirely human (and perhaps uncon-
scious) failing of larding their skeptical, hardheaded
judgments with doses of idealism demanded by America's
wartime internationalism, and by the time-honored rhetoric of American China policy. The Atcheson message, in
particular, would be read not only by Stettinius, but by
Hurley, Wedemeyer, and perhaps even Roosevelt. Hence
the standard homilies of American diplomacy stand side by
side with shrewd estimates of Chinese factional perceptions
and power potentials. Indeed, the China hands were
trapped between the *realpolitik* outlook induced by their
professional experience and knowledge of China, on the one
hand, and the missionary idealism of their country. In
defining revolutionary China in terms which they hoped
would be compatible with America's psychological
needs—interpreting the popular Chinese Communist
regime as democratic, and seriously pondering the possibility of Communist-Kuomintang unity when they really
suspected otherwise—they blurred the clarity of their
thought, compromised the integrity of their reporting, and
laid themselves open to subsequent demagogic political
attacks.

The immediate consequence of the Atcheson cable was
the complete vindication of Hurley. After acrimonious
debates with men from the Far Eastern and China desks,
Hurley conferred with Roosevelt. Near death, and preoccupied with the future of Europe, the president hoped that
China, with all its problems, could somehow be fitted into
the Yalta framework. Assured by Hurley of an imminent
Chinese coalition, he apprised his trusted envoy of the Yalta
Far Eastern agreement, and instructed him to help implement the Russo-Nationalist entente which the accord envisioned. Now in firm control, Hurley had the offending
diplomats removed from China by April. He journeyed to
London and Moscow, reaffirming Allied support for America's efforts to unify China under Chiang; when Roosevelt

died, he secured President Truman's support for his mission, and from April through August, he actively mediated in China, supporting the Nationalists' view that subordination of Communist armies and administration to the Kuomintang must precede any redistribution of power under a coalition—an imperative for Chiang, but clear political suicide for the CCP. He remained convinced—despite the earlier advice of the China hands and the recurrent warnings of the Soviet specialists in the Moscow embassy—that forthcoming Russian support to Chiang in a treaty held the key to Communist pliability.[18]

Hurley was not to see the attainment of his goal. Indeed, the sudden end of the Pacific war in August 1945 rendered the elusive coalition more distant than ever. Late that summer, it did appear that the Sino-Russian treaty—announced in August, legitimizing Russia's Yalta Far Eastern gains, and promising exclusive Soviet economic and military support to Chiang—might have a real impact. The Communists, perhaps stunned and certainly weakened diplomatically, temporarily softened their posture, bargaining during September for a division of China at the Yangtze River rather than the nationwide coalition they had previously demanded. But with the war against Japan over, both factions shifted their emphasis more and more toward consolidating their own power in the hope of destroying their rivals. As Nationalist and Communist armies raced to liberate vast chunks of occupied Chinese territory, political relations deteriorated, and sporadic armed clashes rapidly spread. The Nationalist military effort, woefully incompetent, was supported by a massive American airlift of Nationalist troops to inaccessible areas of North China, and by the emplacement in October of fifty thousand American marines to hold strategic areas in the region pending a Nationalist occupation. Emboldened by this support, Chiang rebuffed conciliatory Communist overtures and aimed at a military victory. The Russians, suspicious of American operations, gave limited logistical and military aid to the Communists in Soviet-occupied Manchuria after October, and did not cooperate with Nationalist efforts to occupy that region, as China became caught up as one focus of the growing mistrust between the United States and Russia late in 1945. With both Chinese factions receiving assistance from their sponsor powers, neither became any more disposed to negotiate a compromise settlement; their negotiations broke down. As American China hands had foreseen, the failure either to secure a coalition prior to Japan's surrender or to gain a foothold with the CCP had produced an American commitment to a foundering regime and a drift toward Chinese civil war.[19]

Hurley never quite understood these Far Eastern developments. Doggedly continuing to believe both in the utter dependence of the CCP on the Soviet Union and in Stalin's unconditional support of the Nationalist regime, he could not understand the failure of his policy, except in terms of subversion by career diplomats and "the imperialist bloc of nations." Back in Washington late in September for a long rest, he expressed anger about the reassignment of Service and Atcheson to advise MacArthur in Japan. With newspaper criticisms of his efforts, reports of his rift with the Foreign Service, and speculation that he would resign, his old fears of a State Department cabal against him were reinforced. This, he felt, tied in with the interests not only of the CCP, but also of the European colonialist powers hoping to regain their Asian territory and keep China impotent. Throughout his sojourn in China, he had suspected the motives of Britain (in Hong Kong), France (in Indochina), and Holland (in the East Indies), arguing that they were subverting the Atlantic Charter in order "to establish white imperialism over all the colored races." Alarmed by Truman's apparent reversal of Roosevelt's anticolonialist policy, he vainly had urged the use of economic pressure on America's European allies to secure wartime principles in Asia; and he associated the perversion of American policy with State Department treachery.[20]

The worsening news from China through October and November was supplemented by reports to Hurley from friendly State Department sources that Russia was obstructing the Nationalists and aiding the Communists in Manchuria. By early November, widespread criticisms of Hurley appeared in the press, and he was receiving a growing volume of mail protesting America's pro-Nationalist intervention in China. After much vacillation, he became convinced that intentionally damaging State Department leaks were providing left-wing publications and politicians with materials to attack and subvert him. He became convinced that he would never get vital departmental support for his mission. Particularly enraged by Representative Hugh DeLacy's speech—allegedly based on confidential materials —attacking his support of Chiang's "reactionary" regime, he issued his explosive resignation and indictment of the State Department on November 27.[21]

The Truman Administration, surprised and embarrassed, recovered quickly; the next day, the prestigious George C. Marshall, recently retired as wartime chief of staff, was appointed on a new mission to bring the Kuomintang and Communists under one roof. Marshall would be given a very flexible directive, allowing wide scope in pressuring or supporting both factions in his efforts. Although, in the pinch, America still would not abandon Chiang, Marshall might threaten such abandonment to induce him to compromise. Marshall's appointment inspired confidence.[22]

Nonetheless, Hurley's parting blast raised emotional and fundamental issues about Sino-Russian-American relations. It brought a volley of criticism from the Republican Party, and it stimulated concern in Congress, in the press, and among ordinary people across the country. Prodded by Senate critics, Tom Connally scheduled public hearings to allow Hurley and the Administration to make their cases before the Foreign Relations Committee. Here was an invaluable forum for testing Hurley's thesis that firm Soviet-American support for the legitimate Chinese regime was crucial to American interests as defined by wartime ideals, against the China hands' view that America had squandered her influence in China by rigidly backing a decadent regime, fomenting civil war, and alienating both the CCP and Russia. It remained to be seen how much Hurley and his supporters would contribute to the public's enlightenment.

Growth of Conservative Suspicion

While other Senate leaders variously commented on China throughout 1945, Styles Bridges remained silent until Hurley's resignation. Long conscious of America's strategic interest in East Asia, in the late 1930s he had opposed the exportation of scrap iron and steel to Japan, while advocating a strong naval program and the fortification of Guam; and during World War II, he heartily supported aid to the Chinese Nationalists.[23] But early in 1945, while forthrightly criticizing America's tolerance of Soviet dominance in eastern Europe, he made no comparable reference to Asia. No doubt he, like his fellow senators, felt Europe to be the critical arena of Soviet-American competition; furthermore, there was no Chinese ethnic lobby comparable to the New Hampshire Polish-Americans. Besides, Chiang had plenty of vocal support in conservative circles; John Foster Dulles, publisher Henry Luce, and Representatives Clare Boothe Luce (Republican, Connecticut) and Walter Judd (Republican, Minnesota), among others, portrayed the Kuomintang as a democratic base for a modernizing, pro-American China. Bridges thus far felt no compulsion to echo them.

But through the summer and autumn of 1945, Bridges collected a mass of documentary evidence attributing China's growing disorder to Soviet expansion and to a worldwide communist conspiracy with tentacles in the State Department. He saved a *New York Times* article of June 7, announcing the arrest of six persons for the theft of secret State Department documents for use in *Amerasia*, an outwardly harmless but Communist-connected periodical specializing in Asian affairs. Those arrested included Philip Jaffe and Kate Louise Mitchell, coeditors of the periodical; Lieutenant Andrew Roth, formerly of Naval Intelligence; Emmanuel Larsen of the State Department's China Division; correspondent Mark Gayn of the Field publications *PM* and *Chicago Sun*, which later printed the reports that aroused Hurley's suspicion about leaks; and, ominously, John Service, who, upon returning to Washington in April, unjudiciously but innocently had shared with Jaffe some of his reports as background material.[24] Bridges similarly saved letters from Secretary of State James F. Byrnes and Under Secretary Joseph C. Grew to Service—as publicized in the State Department *Bulletin* of August 26—expressing pleasure with Service's vindication by a grand jury and lauding his reassignment to the Far Eastern desk where he had maintained (in Byrnes's words) "an enviable record for integrity and ability."[25] Along with other senators, Bridges received in September from the Republican National Committee a copy of a recent American Communist Party resolution warning, among other things, that

> powerful circles in Washington and also London are pursuing the dangerous policy of trying to prevent a strong, united and democratic China; . . . they bolster up the reactionary, incompetent Chiang Kai-shek regime and . . . harbor the idea of a compromise peace with the Mikado in the hope of maintaining Japan as a reactionary bulwark in the Far East.[26]

Always quick to suspect government servants, and quite

conscious of a Communist threat to his conception of American security, Bridges still said nothing about Far Eastern policy. On September 24, during an acrimonious Senate debate on Assistant Secretary of State Dean Acheson's alleged attempts to curtail improperly MacArthur's powers in Japan, he equivocated. While Kenneth Wherry (Republican, Nebraska) attacked Acheson and Connally defended him, Bridges expressed admiration for both MacArthur *and* Acheson, expressing support for the latter's pending promotion to under secretary of state.[27]

But a response to Far Eastern problems was already taking shape in the minds of Bridges and other anticommunist ideologues—legislators, businessmen, lobbyists, and editors who later formed the core of the powerful "China Lobby." Bridges kept a speech draft by arch-conservative Representative George Dondero (Republican, Michigan), scheduled for delivery in the House on October 10; the speech charged that the "pro-Soviet press" had vilified MacArthur, had lobbied for a four-power control of the Japanese occupation in pursuit of Soviet interests, and had defended the *Amerasia* suspects, ultimately securing the dismissal of almost all charges. According to Dondero, Service had been assigned to help supervise MacArthur, while Grew, who had pressed for prosecution of the *Amerasia* case, had later publicly apologized to Service, and had then been replaced by Dean Acheson. Among the suspects, Dondero detected a pattern of affiliation with Communist fronts and Soviet-oriented organizations. He cited Service's favorable reports from Yenan, Jaffe's earlier sympathetic contacts with the CCP and other unsavory associations, and the connections of Service, Jaffe, Mitchell, and Roth with the Institute of Pacific Relations. Charging them with "outright espionage" for Russia and "international communism," he demanded a Congressional inquiry.[28]

Other anticommunist ideologues voiced similar thoughts at about the same time. Alfred Kohlberg, cited with approval by Dondero, was in the midst of a mounting campaign against the IPR. A New York based textile importer long preoccupied with Chinese politics, Kohlberg was destined to energize, even embody, the China Lobby in all its glory—editing magazines, organizing pressure groups, repeatedly memorializing government officials against abandoning Chiang, and forming close ties with Hurley and Bridges, among others. On August 31, he charged that the IPR, of which he was a disaffected member, had an "almost 100% Red" staff, and that its publications were "connected with and censored by Soviet agencies." In November, he obligingly sent to Hurley the critical newspaper reports which seemed to be based on malicious State Department leaks.[29] Along the same lines, the arch-conservative William R. Loeb—currently a Vermont publisher, and soon to edit the Manchester (New Hampshire) *Union-Leader* as a close ally of Bridges—wrote anxiously to Dean Acheson on October 6 about Service's reinstatement and the promotion of John Carter Vincent to head the State Department's Far Eastern Office. Claiming that communism had deeply penetrated the nation's media and government, and suggesting in particular that Vincent was "strongly sympathetic to the Communist and Russian viewpoint," he warned:

> Nothing of course could be more desirable from the Russian viewpoint than to place a keen sympathizer in the Far Eastern Division of the State Department and another sympathizer in the retinue around MacArthur.[30]

The right's preoccupation with domestic subversion reflected its perception of an inherent and ideological Soviet-American competition, in China and elsewhere. These conceptions were no doubt strengthened in the mind of Bridges, who had voiced similar ideas all year long regarding Europe, the United Nations, and Russia. Yet the evidence adduced for charges of betrayal was more hearsay than substance. Service pragmatically hoped to maximize American influence with the CCP, not to conspire with it against America; and Dondero neglected to state that Service alone, of all the *Amerasia* suspects, had been exonerated unanimously by the grand jury.[31] Loeb's innuendo against Vincent was based on alleged "reliable sources," but was unsubstantiated. Kohlberg's attack on the IPR was based on sentimental attachment to Chiang and blind opposition to communism, anywhere and in any form. The IPR leadership, sure he was out to destroy the organization, challenged his charges as biased, poorly documented, and distorted; it suggested an investigation by a committee including one of its members, a law partner of John Foster Dulles.[32]

As Bridges, among others, reflected on the apparent subversion of Far Eastern policy, he received a more dispassionate appraisal of the relationship between China's crisis and the Soviet-American contest in Asia. He somehow obtained a secret analysis of the Chinese Communist movement prepared by the War Department in July 1945. It was a précis of conclusions derived from an exhaustive report on the "Chinese Communist Movement," prepared over the previous six months by civilian and military analysts. Authorized by Colonel Alfred McCormack, the analysis was prepared in the name of General P. E. Peabody, chief of the Military Intelligence Service. Limited in circulation, the *Peabody Report* was distributed mostly within the armed services, with a few copies going to the White House and the State Department.[33]

On the nature of Chinese communism, the tone of the *Peabody Report* was ambiguous. On the one hand, it termed the CCP "the best led and most vigorous of present-day organizations in China," and noted its "high morale," relative self-sufficiency, popular support, and effective control of one-fifth of China and seventy million people. On the other hand, the report stated that although the CCP

currently talked of transforming a semifeudal society into a
"'bourgeois' (or capitalist) democracy," its ultimate aim was
"a one-party controlled 'democracy,'" on the pattern of
Russia rather than of England or America, suppressing opposition to Communist rule. Its "military strategy, diplomatic orientation, and propaganda policies," although
"adapted to fit the Chinese environment," were said to follow the Soviet line and international "Marxism-Leninism-
Stalinism." The report added that the Communists' ties to
Moscow did not preclude a friendly posture toward America and other "capitalist democracies" which might aid
them in their two-stage revolutionary aims; they would wel-
come American support against both Japan and the Nationalists.[34]

Going over the troubled history of Kuomintang-Communist relations, the *Peabody Report* discounted the impact
of the Communist guerrilla effort against Japan, arguing
that the Nationalists had done more fighting, and that the
current Communist military capacity was "small." The
report envisioned three alternative settlements for China.
Chiang, it stated, had stressed the war on Japan and had
tried to avoid a rupture with the Communists; he now
favored a National Assembly plan, with a view toward
democratic, constitutional government—provided that the
CCP, which repeatedly had violated the united front
against Japan, subordinated its armies to the Kuomintang
prior to a political settlement. In contrast, the Communists
were said to favor a division of China into two or more sections, united "in a loose 'federation'" of all parties, but with
the Kuomintang and Communists maintaining separate
armies and administrations within the coalition. This plan,
warned the report, would preclude genuine Chinese unity,
and leave the Nationalists open to continued Communist
penetration, legal and illegal. And the report noted the
widespread expectation of the third possibility, a civil war.[35]

The *Peabody Report* predicted that if Russia gave active

economic or military support to the CCP while America threw its weight behind Chiang, the two powers would collide head-on. It noted that Russia and Japan had both become leading Asian powers by virtue of their incursions against China, and predicted that after Japan's defeat, Russia would emerge "as the sole military land power in Asia." Soviet aims were characterized as uncertain. On the one hand, Russia currently (July 1945) seemed to support the Communist plan for a loose Chinese coalition, envisioning Soviet domination of borderland areas and perhaps North China proper through the CCP. On the other hand, Russia might try to reach an accommodation with the Nationalists on the basis of a Chinese "united front" which, the report stated, always had favored the CCP, in vivid contrast to Communist reverses during civil war; an entente with Chiang would also minimize the danger of a confrontation with America. In any case, the report stressed that Chinese independence and administrative integrity should continue to be the aim of American Far Eastern policy, as it had in the past, for China was the keystone of Asian affairs. It urged a common Russian-American policy in the postwar Far Eastern vacuum, looking toward internal Chinese unity. It warned that "prevention of a repetition of the 'Polish situation' in Manchuria and Korea is essential to post-war stability in the Far East." For with Russia coming into the war against Japan, a partition of China, as of Europe, into Anglo-American and Soviet military zones would stimulate the development of an exclusive Soviet sphere of influence, leave the Nationalists without the raw materials of Manchuria and North China crucial to the development of "a strong and stable state," and strongly favor the loose coalition envisioned by the CCP. The War Department analysis concluded that it was necessary for American, British, Chinese, and Russian forces to cooperate on equal terms in occupying North China, Manchuria, and Korea, in order to achieve a settlement conducive to Far Eastern peace and "the long range interests of the United States."[36]

Prepared with the Pacific war in its concluding stages, the *Peabody Report* provided a sophisticated interpretation of Far Eastern international politics. To be sure, it may be criticized for insufficient attention to the alternative of an American accommodation with the CCP, and for advocating an extensive occupation of China without exploring the consequences for America or the reaction of Russia. But it certainly provided an interesting counterpoint to the Davies-Service view, laying more emphasis on the historic and ideological bond between the CCP and Russia, stressing the distinction between Western conceptions of democracy and the popular support of a totalitarian movement, arguing that the Nationalists were willing and able to unify China with American support, and explaining the danger of dividing China as the China hands had suggested.

Exactly when Bridges became privy to the report is unclear. He was at least aware of its existence, its classification, and its limited distribution by the time of the Senate hearings on Far Eastern policy in December 1945.[37] Whether or not he understood its contents or even read it, the *Peabody Report* stood in vivid contrast to the other materials which he was accumulating and absorbing at the same time. It raised fundamental questions about Nationalist and Communist aims and strength, Soviet intentions, and American military priorities in East Asia, generally in a light favorable to conservative strategic aspirations. Its contents were at the heart of the State Department rift about the future of American policy. Although in fundamental disagreement with Hurley about Soviet aims, the report envisioned, as did Hurley, a coalition on Chiang's terms, bolstered by American military intervention if not by Russian good faith. It did not, as did Dondero, Kohlberg, Loeb, and Hurley, muddle the issue by impugning the loyalty of those who counseled a different strategy in Asia. It would not be long before Bridges chose his ground on the issue.

Bridges's Crusade

In the days following Hurley's resignation, debate broke out in Congress, in the press, and among the public. In the ensuing weeks, Hurley closely cooperated with Bridges, who was finally impelled to bold action. They dined together on the day of the resignation, and Hurley, who originally had planned to cite the Yalta Far Eastern protocol "as the blueprint for the Communist conquest of China," later recalled that Bridges "advised me to shoot the works," and release the document. Although Hurley was loath to leak top secret materials, he was undoubtedly heartened by Bridges's support. Moreover, Hurley's attack seemed to reverse the tide of adverse mail; in the following days, favorable letters and telegrams came "pouring in."[38] In addition to allies like Claire Chennault and William Loeb, hundreds of strangers congratulated him on his "courageous criticism," his "excellent" judgment, and his "contribution to Americanism"; he had, among other things, publicized Communist infiltration of the government, stood against "unAmerican activities," and unveiled the "dirty skunks in the State Department." Numerous admirers touted him for president.[39] Encouraged, and oblivious at first to the persistence of sentiment against him, Hurley reiterated his charges of Foreign Service subversion before the National Press Club on November 28.[40]

Bridges enthusiastically joined the fray. He composed a speech, intended for November 28, lamenting "the unfortunate state of American foreign policy," and citing bipartisan Senate dissatisfaction with its drift, indecision, and improvisation "without regard to principles or 'harmony.'" Citing Hurley as an unimpeachable source, Bridges echoed his allegations: America's allies paid "eloquent lip service to the

97

principle of democracy," but used America's supplies and reputation in the Far East to support imperialism and communism; high-level American policies toward China had been sabotaged by State Department career officers biased in favor of the CCP and the imperialist countries; and the saboteurs, reassigned to important posts in Washington, were protected by "the secrecy which has shrouded the State Department." In the interest of an enlightened public opinion, he urged a thorough Senate probe.[41]

On the Senate floor that day, the arch-conservative Kenneth Wherry beat Bridges to the punch; declaring that Hurley's accusations fell "very little short of treason," and making gratuitous references to State Department malfeasance in Latin America and Germany as well, Wherry introduced a resolution calling for the appointment of a special Senate committee to investigate State Department divergences from established foreign and military policies, particularly attempts to foster the establishment of communism abroad.[42] When Tom Connally belittled Hurley's attitude as "ridiculous," and mocked Wherry's concern about the State Department's "culprits," Bridges protested Connally's jesting manner, termed Hurley a "great American," and called for the appearance both of Hurley and of State Department spokesmen before the Foreign Relations Committee. Alluding to the many rumors afloat concerning the department's posture in China, he warned that there could not be "a great deal of smoke without there being some fire."[43]

The right-wing lobbyists had an effect, as national attention focused on the Hurley controversy. In the House of Representatives, an uproar of voices divided over China policy. George Dondero spoke on November 28, specifying one document passed to *Amerasia* as a detailed report on the military disposition of the Nationalist Chinese Army; he hinted that the document had found its way from its pilferer, Philip Jaffe, to the Chinese Communists by way of

a Chinese Communist delegate to the San Francisco Conference the previous spring; and he suggested that the
Amerasia prosecutors had been unaware of such activities,
with "some sinister influence" at work to quash the charges.
The same day, Representative Carl Curtis (Republican,
Nebraska) defended General Albert Wedemeyer's services
in China against attacks from some segments of the press,
and lent his support to Hurley. On the other hand, Washington Democrat Hugh DeLacy, whose suspiciously well-
informed speeches had been the immediate cause of
Hurley's walkout, attacked anew Hurley's policy of supporting a reactionary regime in the suppression of
democracy. And Republican Frances P. Bolton of Ohio expressed confusion at Hurley's charges, deprecated his judgment in comparison with that of career men who had served
long and loyally in the field, and pointed out that even
many Army men had differed violently with Hurley's
methods in China. Bridges heeded all of these comments; he
also kept *Washington Post* and *New York Times* editorials
calling for a more thorough inquiry into the whole affair.[44]

A week later, when the Foreign Relations Committee
began its hearings on Far Eastern policy, the controversy
was still in the news, tied in with further espionage charges.
Bridges kept copies of the right-wing *New York Journal-
American*, which editorialized its sympathy with the anticommunist crusade in its front-page news stories. On
December 4, the *Journal-American* boasted that its current
revelations of Russian atomic spying had "added new fuel to
the anti-Russian fire lighted" by Hurley's allegations of
State Department Communist infiltration; the same edition
publicized Wherry's reiterated demand for action on his
resolution, "now buried [presumably by Connally] in the
Senate Foreign Relations Committee." Over the next two
days, the newspaper headlined the existence of a "Red
Courier System" and "Soviet Ring" apparently relaying
atomic secrets, and touted Wherry's inevitable demand for

an inquiry. Indicating that Hurley's accusations against John S. Service had magnified Senate concern, it noted that Service's exoneration in the *Amerasia* case had been protested by the FBI.[45]

Amidst mounting public anxiety over China, Bridges and Hurley were part of a group sharing many assumptions, perceptions, and expectations about American China policy. Representing an indeterminate segment of American opinion, this group's articulate leadership was predominantly Republican, conservative, and nationalistic. Their concern about China reflected their general malaise about American foreign policy. To their minds, America had conquered expansionist fascism only to help nurture the equally aggressive and dangerous communist ideology. America seemed unable to cope with the communist threat centered in Russia; her impotence appeared to stem from a receptivity at home—most alarmingly, in the State Department—to an insidious, pro-Soviet spirit.

The consuming interest of these people in the ideological nature of the threat to America distorted their perceptions of the power-political problems attending Soviet-American conflicts of interest around the world. Hurley in particular would not even recognize any clash of national interests with the Russians; having dealt personally with Stalin, he refused to believe, despite all evidence, that the Soviet Union might oppose American aims in China; he stated that the Russians were keeping their word, following America's lead.[46] He saw no reason why the Russians should not acquiesce in a Nationalist China within America's political orbit; for him, the problem was entirely the actions of Americans who seemed more pro-Russian than the Russians. Hence his belated impulse to attack the Yalta accord as an American betrayal of China to Stalin, only months after he had helped to implement it. How else could he explain the breakdown of his program?

Unlike Hurley, most of his conservative supporters

acknowledged an active Russian menace; they construed Soviet ambitions in Manchuria, in China, and in eastern Europe as a dynamic totalitarian expansionism threatening wartime ideals and American interests alike. Postulating an all-or-nothing struggle between totalitarian and democratic ideologies, they found in the emerging Asiatic power balance a barometer of that struggle. Yet they, too, seemed to regard Soviet appetites as almost secondary when compared to attitudinal problems at home which were neutralizing the material and moral advantages which otherwise might be applied against Russia. Bridges's eagerness to expose Yalta's Far Eastern treachery stemmed from his preoccupation with ideological subversion. For anticommunist ideologues, it was not so much the political, military, or geographical situation in China as their own images of conflicting American and communist values that determined their perceptions of Chinese affairs. Viewing China as an abstraction defined by this global conflict, they were insensitive to its peculiar problems. In demanding a strongly pro-American Nationalist China, they could not begin to unravel the subtle relationship among Chinese social cleavages, world communism, and Soviet national interest, observed dully for so long firsthand by Hurley, and accessible for examination by Bridges in the *Peabody Report*. In a crusading mood, Bridges took the opportunity presented by the Senate hearings to spearhead the first postwar assault on American China policy.

At the hearings—open sessions chaired early in December by a reluctant Connally in response to public pressure—Bridges closely questioned Hurley and Secretary of State James F. Byrnes. He vocalized, clarified, and elaborated on the ideas which had taken shape in his mind. Exhibiting staunch nationalism and a strong sense of loyalty to the Kuomintang regime, he used Hurley's charges as a starting point to defend Chiang's cause, scrutinize American policy, and attack the State Department as procommunist.

At the session of December 6, Bridges asked Hurley if, to his knowledge, Chiang repeatedly had spurned Japanese peace feelers "and did loyally maintain his ties to the United States and the other Allies" in carrying on the battle against Japan. Hurley replied that, notwithstanding legitimate faults in Chiang's war policies and choice of cohorts, the Chinese leader had fought the Japanese alone at a time when they had been offering him great advantages to desist; having resisted such blandishments when Japan "appeared to be victorious and we were not in the war," Chiang would hardly have come to terms when Japan's "defeat was inevitable" and when China was receiving massive economic and military support from America.[47] Bridges rhetorically asked:

> If it is a fact—and it is, I might say—that for years the United States supplied the munitions of war, equipment, scrap-iron and steel to Japan, while Chiang Kai-shek and the Republic of China were fighting on against Japan, and if it is further true that Chiang Kai-shek had opportunities to settle the war with Japan on a very favorable basis, but his loyalty to the United States and to the Allies made him and the Republic of China fight on, do you or do you not think that we have a very great obligation to both himself and the Republic of China today?[48]

The next day Bridges asked Byrnes whether he felt that America "has had through the war some very definite moral or ethical obligation to Chiang Kai-shek and the Republic of China, inasmuch as they are a very loyal Ally of ours." He also wondered how Byrnes would have viewed suggestions to arm the CCP, "thereby bringing about a civil war in China." Byrnes replied that the United States had demonstrated its loyalty to the Chinese Republic by according it recognition at the San Francisco Conference, at the Council of Foreign

Ministers, and in the Japanese surrender terms. In the absence of a factional agreement, arming the Communists would have been out of the question, he added, and the Administration sought unity, not division, in postwar China.[49]

Bridges simultaneously probed the implications of great power settlements for America's Nationalist ally. On December 6, he teased Hurley: was there, to his knowledge, "any agreement made at Yalta involving China"? Hurley admitted that he knew "what transpired," but—afraid to divulge classified material, and on the advice of other senators—deferred to the secretary of state as a better authority.[50] The next day, Bridges asked Byrnes the same question. Byrnes, who before his appointment as secretary had accompanied Roosevelt to Yalta, tried to remember the gist of the published communiqué. Bridges prodded that it was

> very important to know whether there was an agreement made at Yalta relative to China, and whether that agreement was made . . . between the heads of the three great Governments, the strong, large Governments, the United States, Great Britain, and Russia, without the knowledge of China, . . . until later.[51]

He termed it "rather peculiar" to reach an accord "involving the life or death or [sic] seriously affecting China" in the absence of a Chinese representative. When Byrnes claimed no knowledge of any such agreement, Bridges assured him of his right not to reveal it.[52]

Failing to expose the alleged Yalta treachery, Bridges also voiced suspicion of current China policy. He asked Hurley whether or not Marshall had been instructed to implement the same policies earlier prescribed for Hurley. Stating that Marshall was probably under similar orders, Hurley maintained that a recent American policy declaration had publicly clarified the situation, and predicted that Marshall would secure a Chinese coalition. Unsatisfied, Bridges pressed Hurley as to whether he would be surprised to learn that a new directive enjoined Marshall to tell Chiang "that certain concessions must be made to the Chinese Communists," or else "our military aid and perhaps credits and so forth . . . will be held up." Receiving no direct answer, he confronted Byrnes the next day with the prevalent rumor to this effect. Was Hurley's directive—to uphold the Kuomintang regime—"still to be carried forward"? Byrnes replied that he knew of no change in the policy, which had been reaffirmed in a memorandum intended for Hurley and drawn up just prior to his resignation.[53] Again failing to elicit politically damaging information, Bridges nonetheless indirectly accused the Administration of planning a further betrayal of the Nationalists.

To Bridges, acceptance of a divided China or acceptance of the CCP—policies advocated by diplomats who recognized Chiang's weakness and who frankly acknowledged America's unwillingness to undertake the military effort necessary to save him—was unthinkable. His mind ran not to judgments of power relationships, but to considerations of loyalty and values, and he was not the first American politician dangerously obsessed with the latter to the exclusion of the former, where communism and the Soviet Union were concerned. Yet, as in his strictures earlier in 1945 regarding Soviet domination of eastern Europe, his sincerity remains suspect. For, in the years before World War II, he knew well enough how to calculate the current and potential world power balance, and to sanction measures— rearmament, aid to Britain and Russia, and finally war—necessary to preserve a world configuration which Germany and Japan were trying to destroy. But in 1945, he complained of American weakness before Soviet onslaughts in Europe and Asia, while maintaining a peculiar silence on the specific means to meet these challenges.

In particular, Bridges never advocated the massive

military intervention in China which was the inescapable corollary of the pro-Nationalist stance that he demanded. On the contrary, he fell into line with the strong nationwide impulse for demobilization which troubled American policymakers after the war's end. In a speech of October 1, to the Concord (New Hampshire) Chamber of Commerce, he had planned to warn that *"there must be no undue delay"* in American demobilization. While omitting this statement, he had claimed familiarity with the problem as a member of the Senate Military Affairs Committee, and had apologized for the "slow start" made by the services. Noting the reduced estimates of occupation needs, he had cheerfully forecasted the repatriation of six to seven hundred thousand men per month by the end of the year, and had reiterated: "We long to have them home."[54] Hence a glaring contradiction: while goading the Administration toward ever more forceful a commitment to a faltering regime in the world's most populous country, half way round the world and adjacent to a wary Soviet power, Bridges glossed over the strategic implications of his argument. In fact, he pandered to the domestic sentiment which would have to be painstakingly altered if his proposals were to be implemented. The conclusion is inescapable: through some combination of ideological fanaticism and partisan cynicism, Bridges obfuscated the military issue, deceiving the public (and perhaps himself) by blaming American officials for events in China which lay beyond America's power and will to alter.

More strongly than even Hurley would allege, Bridges claimed that Service and George Atcheson had attempted "to undermine" American policies. Under his guidance, Hurley testified that the career diplomats had seriously interfered with efforts to uphold the Chinese Republic, that their objectives had "sort of tied in" with CCP objectives, and that their plan to arm the Communists would have insured a Nationalist collapse. Bridges also went beyond Hurley in arguing that "final blame" for Foreign Service sabotage lay "at the top"—with Truman and Byrnes—for not dismissing those who had undercut Hurley. Bringing up the *Amerasia* arrests, the abortive prosecution, and Byrnes's subsequent congratulatory letter to Service, he termed the sequence "most weird":

> If that in itself, combined with the testimony of General Hurley, does not warrant a thorough and complete investigation of the State Department, I do not know what does.[55]

He asked whether Byrnes could "by any stretch of the imagination justify" his "very amazing" letter to Service; and he termed the reassignment of Service and Atcheson "to advise General MacArthur on all our Eastern policy . . . the most ridiculous thing I ever heard of." Ignoring Byrnes's citations of Service's innocence, intelligence, and character, Bridges brought up a "secret telephone call from a very-high-up in this Nation" to the Justice Department insisting that it "'lay off Service'"; soon admitting that he had no proof, and brushing aside Byrnes's and Connally's objections to the innuendo, he called for State Department loyalty investigations to weed out subversives.[56]

Nor did Bridges confine his suspicions to the China Division and the Far Eastern Office. Conspirators seemed to lurk everywhere. At the session of December 6, as Connally tried to discredit Hurley's charges against the Foreign Service by asking him about its cooperation on his many missions around the world, Hurley seized on Iran as a country where diplomats had "destroyed the American policy." When Hurley named Dean Acheson as the principal subverter of the Hurley-Roosevelt efforts at fostering Iranian free enterprise (in favor of British imperialism), Bridges asked for more information to clarify the need for an investigation.[57] At the same session, Bridges cited a recent newspaper article by Hugh Grant, a former American minister, charging "much the same thing" as Hurley. Grant stated that low-level sabotage was nothing new to the Foreign Service; in Thailand during 1940-41, members of his legation staff had opposed the American policy, collaborating instead with pro-Japanese elements and "the same imperialistic forces" which had thwarted Hurley.[58]

Finally, Bridges questioned Byrnes about the appointment of Colonel Alfred McCormack—the very man, in Military Intelligence, who had authorized the circulation of the *Peabody Report* on the Chinese Communists the previous July. Informants had recently told Bridges that Mc-Cormack had suppressed the *Peabody Report*, intended for use by Truman, Byrnes, Hurley, and others. He had, they added, led a "pro-Communist group" within Military Intelligence which interpreted events "in the light most favorable to the Russians"; he had killed or ignored valuable reports, especially on "Communist or Russian activities"; and, after his separation from the War Department, he had been appointed (through Dean Acheson's influence) to the State Department, where he now increasingly threatened the Administration's intelligence network. When Byrnes claimed no doubtful information on McCormack, Bridges retreated, neither accusing the colonel of anything, nor adducing his evidence in hand.[59] But it is ironic—perhaps inevitable—that the *Peabody Report* was used by the conservative ideologues not for its valuable content on China, but to impugn as unpatriotic the motives of the man who allegedly suppressed it.

Vandenberg's Futile Probe

For Arthur Vandenberg, it was a very hectic autumn. Having helped to steer the United Nations implementing legislation through the Senate during the summer months, he now sought to secure international atomic energy controls compatible with American security, to achieve a harmonious working relationship with Byrnes (who had replaced Stettinius as secretary of state in July 1945), to help lay the groundwork for the upcoming meetings of the foreign ministers (in Moscow) and of the General Assembly (in London), and to study the merits of an important but unpopular proposal for a billion-dollar loan to sorely pressed Britain. Preoccupied with these problems, he was silent from July through November on the less immediate issues raised by developments in China.[60] But on November 15, he delivered a Senate speech urging worldwide freedom of information, in the interest of harmonious world relations. That day, he and Connally had been summoned to the White House to be told of a secretly negotiated Anglo-Canadian-American atomic energy agreement, just as the agreement was made public. He therefore complained that an "iron curtain of secrecy" surrounded not only Russian activities in eastern Europe, but also the negotiations of great powers. In Vandenberg's view, America was sometimes to blame for the resulting frictions:

> We certainly shared responsibility for the iron curtain at epochal Yalta, where global decisions were made which will affect destiny for centuries to come and which were never fully and frankly exposed to our people. I doubt we yet know the whole truth.[61]

Pondering the implications of secrecy for Soviet-American "friendship," Vandenberg evidently viewed the speech as an important commentary, and it secured national news coverage.[62] However, he gave no hint about the nature of the secret Yalta accords, in China or elsewhere. Indeed, he was instrumental in preserving the secrecy of the Far Eastern settlement when Hurley resigned. For Hurley originally had planned, with Bridges's prodding, to publicize and attack the settlement. However, Vandenberg insisted that Hurley expunge from his statement the reference to Yalta. As Hurley later recalled, Vandenberg "was to be an important member" of the Byrnes delegation to the upcoming Moscow Conference. According to Vandenberg, the delegation would "correct the situation," and the accord would be publicized and fully explained at the end of the conference. Appealing to Hurley's patriotism, he warned that an exposure of the agreement would wreck the conference and badly injure American foreign relations. Fearful also of prosecution for revealing classified materials, Hurley acquiesced and did not cite Yalta, either in resigning or in testifying at the subsequent hearings.[63]

Vandenberg took no part in the public debate which raged for a week after Hurley quit. His thoughts continued to be reflective and troubled. On December 3, he read to the Senate a London dispatch indicating that British Foreign Minister Ernest Bevin, evidently on the word of British diplomats in Moscow, believed that "American control of Japan, rather than the atomic energy secrecy, is responsible for Russia's recent cooling toward the western powers." The article added that the Soviet media's emphasis on the persistent authority of Japanese industrial and military elements tended to corroborate Bevin's analysis:

> Alleged United States failure to encourage the weak progressive forces in Japan, combined with Russia's exclusion from a share in shaping Japan's destiny, evidently has been stimulating Soviet fear that Japan is to be prepared as a potential outpost against Soviet Russia.[64]

But, glossing over this insight into Far Eastern tensions, Vandenberg dwelled on persistent "Soviet fear" of an "ultimate resurgence of Axis aggression"; and he harked back to his speech of January 10, 1945, proposing once

109

again that America, Britain, and Russia take "collateral action" to assure an effective United Nations and a workable great power partnership for peace and security. Just as Russia now feared Japan, she had feared a resurgent Germany nearly a year before, Vandenberg noted; such fear "then and now seems to be either the reason for Russia's difficulties with us or at least the excuse," and the proposed treaty would "prevent the misunderstandings which are plaguing our international relationships today, if it be in fact true that the fear of this resurgence is to blame for our difficulties."[65]

Thus, as 1945 drew to an end, Vandenberg still talked in terms of freedom of communication and collective security pacts to improve great power relations. But he could not deny the possibility of deep-seated problems arising from veiled Soviet ambitions and animosities. In assailing sinister Yalta deals and in hinting at ulterior Soviet motives in the Far East, he was edging, haltingly, toward a condemnation of Soviet policy in China. Insensitive to Soviet displeasure with America's policy in Japan, he obliquely questioned Soviet obstruction of the Nationalists and connivance with the CCP in North China and Manchuria, in violation of Russia's treaty pledge to the Nationalist Government. For here, it seemed, was a flagrant case of Soviet bad faith toward a recent wartime ally, which could only reinforce Vandenberg's hope for a unified, pro-American bastion in Asia to offset Soviet power.

A question arises. Why did Vandenberg, suspicious of the Russians' motives, still seek new agreements with them? No doubt, his seemingly naive remarks about all-healing treaties reflected not so much an unrealistic hope as an effort, as he liked to put it, "to keep the record straight"—in this instance, to challenge the Russians' alleged concern with an Axis resurgence by offering a binding guarantee against it, thereby exposing the root of Soviet behavior: hostility toward the United States and ambitions contrary to

American conceptions of world stability and American security. But his reservations about Russia were general—encompassing Europe and the Middle East as well as East Asia—and he never specified the Chinese problem, which possibly had not yet taken concrete shape in his mind. Much as he loathed it, he was certainly unwilling for Hurley to expose the Yalta Far Eastern settlement, and thereby to doom Soviet-American accommodations which he continued to regard as a worthy, if elusive, goal.

At the hearings, Vandenberg lent a sympathetic ear to Hurley's complaints about the State Department. He asked "who did what, that you object to; and when he did it." Hurley replied that the previous February, he had been "confronted in Washington" with the Atcheson cable recommending that America furnish lend-lease supplies to the CCP. Supported by every American official in Chungking, the cable sought to contravene Hurley's refusal to arm "belligerents against the [Chinese] government," and in Hurley's view reflected the diplomats' intention "to destroy" that government. Vandenberg later asked who had assigned Atcheson and Service to supervisory positions and then to advise MacArthur, after their removal from China. He expressed puzzlement to Hurley that Truman and Byrnes were supposedly "standing behind you all the time, and yet within their jurisdiction things were happening to the contrary." Still later, Vandenberg admonished Byrnes that Atcheson had "taken advantage" of his "very first opportunity" to trumpet his disagreement with Hurley and to urge a change in policy. He established that Byrnes had approved Atcheson's ultimate assignment to Japan. He termed it "rather curious" to back Hurley by immediately reassigning objectionable officers like Atcheson and Service to the same theater as Hurley. And he generally warned that Hurley's charges applied not only to underlings, "but . . . very definitely . . . to the higher echelon," despite Hurley's "compliments to them."[66]

Vandenberg also expressed more general apprehensions over the conduct of American China policy, alluding particularly to suspected State Department leaks to the CCP and its sympathizers. The heart of Hurley's charge, he noted to Byrnes, was that the career diplomats had told the Chinese Communists that Hurley "did not speak for the United States." Referring also to Hurley's complaint that the DeLacy speech of November 26 had used State Department sources, Vandenberg cited Clare Boothe Luce's charge that DeLacy was echoing a Communist party line about Kuomintang ineptitude and Chinese Communist achievements; and he asserted that if Mrs. Luce were correct, then "it would scarcely be complimentary to the State Department" if the speech were "based on information" from it. Yet he remarked drily to China correspondent Theodore White that "if the State Department was as secretive out there as it is here at home, I would not have thought you saw very much" vital material on China policy. Vandenberg thus implied what Hurley and Bridges stated more boldly: that governmental secrecy was cloaking the absorption and transmittal of communistic ideas in the making of American foreign policy.[67]

Yet Vandenberg never became so obsessed by conspiracy as did his more unrestrained colleagues. Indeed, he intelligently challenged the defense of the China hands by Theodore White, who testified in behalf of other correspondents that the accused men were motivated by "complete integrity and conscientious devotion to American interests," all serving the country "nobly" in the midst of extreme wartime hardship, "all . . . reporting the truth to the American Government as they saw it." Commenting on White's denial of any possible cabal among the China hands unknown to the Chungking press corps, Vandenberg suggested that "it might not be a conspiracy" but instead "a difference, a very fundamental difference of opinion" whether or not to arm the Communist forces of northern China. "A man," he argued, "might have a perfectly honest opinion which could be deadly in its impact upon American policy" —such as giving lend-lease aid to the CCP, probably causing Chiang's government to fall.[68] This was an oversimplification of the situation of the previous winter, which had featured Hurley's aloofness from normal State Department channels and consequent hostility between Hurley and the China hands in Chungking and Washington. Yet Vandenberg did hint at an important factor cited by Hurley in the malfunctioning of China policy: the absence of clear direction from the top (at least until Roosevelt had sustained Hurley and the dissenting diplomats had been transferred), and the consequent division of the State Department against itself. This governmental abdication of responsibility regarding China Byrnes could not deny, for it had persisted and reached a crisis during the autumn, when civil war had erupted.[69]

Vandenberg thus went beyond considerations of personal malice and ideological subversion, suggesting as few others did that methods advocated by the anti-Hurley diplomats were very likely governed by the same long-range objectives cherished by Hurley and by American tradition: the establishment of a strong, united China susceptible to American influence, in the interests of American commercial and strategic security in East Asia. In making this point at the hearings, he was groping toward a public definition of the radically different alternatives in China perceived by clashing groups of informed Americans. This would have been the first step toward a clarification of substantive political and diplomatic issues in China and toward a more informed public appreciation of the dilemmas confronting the United States there. But his tentative effort was to no avail.

A few senators on the committee did haltingly move, with Vandenberg, toward an evaluation of the issues which had produced the State Department rift. Alexander Wiley (Republican, Wisconsin) asked Hurley whether the China hands had been motivated "by simply a disagreement as to the validity of the policy, or do you think there was back of their motives something else?"[70] Warren R. Austin (Republican, Vermont), a dedicated internationalist who along with Vandenberg had advised Hurley not to publicize the Yalta agreement, led Hurley to acknowledge that the CCP occupied "a large area in China," in fact about half of its territory, with military control "articulated in the armed forces" headed by Mao Tse-tung, and that the party was "unified enough" that its army "would be a great threat" to Chiang's unification of China.[71] And Henrik Shipstead (Republican, Minnesota), a staunch isolationist, asked whether the Communists had fought Japan "in good faith," whether the Nationalist Government was a republic in the sense of having a constitution and elections, and whether the Kuomintang-Communist rift was "ideological or political."[72] Yet, along with Vandenberg, these senators probed no further. Predominant attention focused on the State Department's formulation and execution of China policy. Although perfectly valid in light of the prevalent confusion about China, such attention became misdirected at the false issue of Communist conspiracy. Revealing inquiry into the diplomats' premise that American interests in China could best be secured through a more positive attitude toward the Chinese Communists was stifled by obsessive concern with the propriety and patriotism of the diplomats involved.

Vandenberg's fears about the State Department and China reinforced his apprehensions about the Yalta accords and his growing pessimism about Russian policies around the world, but they did not destroy his hopes for Soviet-American accommodation and open diplomacy. Concerned about a multitude of world issues whose resolution depended upon the Soviet attitude, he continued to anticipate some agreements and a reduction of tensions at Moscow. He apparently feared that a domestic row over Yalta would jeopardize the meetings by giving Stalin provocation—or excuse—to sabotage them. His assurance to Hurley that the

Far Eastern settlement would be revealed reflected his advocacy of public moral pressure on Russia to honor her commitments—in this case, at least to stick by her guarantee of exclusive support to the Chinese Nationalists, and thus to end her connivance with the CCP. Vandenberg's thoughts about China thus continued to reflect his tension between wariness of Russia and consciousness of the necessity for Soviet-American negotiations to maintain a peaceful postwar system. Indeed, tension over China was by now widespread in the United States; but in contrast to the pro-Chiang Republicans, growing numbers complained that American Far Eastern policy was, if anything, too aggressive in the months following the end of the war.

IV THE LIBERAL CRITIQUE

American Troops and Chinese Strife

It should have been a restful autumn. The war was over; the world had survived, and America was never stronger. But as the American people attempted to demobilize their armed forces, turn away from global affairs, and devote themselves once more to their domestic enterprise, the world was too much with them. Unremittingly, Poland, Germany, the Balkans, Iran, Japan, and China forced themselves on America's consciousness as nagging obstacles on the road to a political settlement, in an atmosphere of growing mistrust among America, Britain, and Russia. As autumn deepened into winter, the particular problems presented by China and Russia in the Far East bedeviled policymakers in the Truman Administration. It was a time of deepening misgivings about China, after a long period of relative inattention at high governmental levels. For it was now clear that events in China were not working out through an internationally sanctioned Kuomintang-dominated coalition, as Hurley had envisioned and American policymakers had vaguely hoped the previous summer. The Communist-Kuomintang talks since Hurley had departed in September had proved fruitless. As both factions contested liberation of Chinese territory from Japanese occupation, their armed clashes signified the active resumption of the civil war.[1]

The United States contributed mightily to the Nationalist cause between August and December 1945, with a spectacular sea and air lift which transported between four and five hundred thousand Nationalist troops from Chiang's base in central and southern China to important cities in the north and east. Moreover, fifty thousand United States marines were dispatched to North China early in October to supplement the sixty thousand American soldiers already in China at the end of the war. They occupied Peking, Tientsin, and nearby coal mines and railroads, pending the arrival of Nationalist troops. There is no doubt that this American aid was a critical factor enabling Chiang to reestablish his authority in substantial parts of Japanese-held China, particularly in the cities. Yet, as a result, he was emboldened to eschew negotiation with the Communists in favor of a military confrontation, to attempt an occupation of Soviet-held Manchuria which turned out to be beyond his means, and to solicit still further American military aid to these ends.[2]

Faced with the worsening Chinese turbulence, General Wedemeyer pondered the role of almost one hundred thousand American troops still under his command in China by November 1945. Their initial purpose, as defined in his directive of August 10 from the Joint Chiefs of Staff, was "to secure control of key ports and communication points in the China theater," support the Nationalist reoccupation of Japanese-held regions, temporarily accept local Japanese surrenders pending the arrival of Nationalist forces, and provide "the rapid transit" of those forces "to key areas in China"—all without supporting the Nationalists in any "fratricidal war." Wedemeyer quickly noted the inconsistency of this directive; and, as factional competition intensified during the autumn, he found himself ever more committed to the Kuomintang cause. Most Japanese forces in China—more than a million, excluding Manchuria—remained armed and in place, as the Communists hindered Nationalist movement and the Nationalists used Japanese forces (under Allied instructions not to surrender to the CCP) to contain Communist expansion. Sporadic fighting in North China involved the marines in several nasty incidents. During November, Wedemeyer resisted Chiang's repeated demands for aid in reoccupying Communist-infested Manchuria as the Russians evacuated; he reasoned that the area directly involved Sino-Russian relations and was clearly beyond Chiang's capacity to contest without jeopardizing the tenuous Nationalist position in North China proper. Indeed, he urged Washington several times that he had done all he could under his directive to facilitate the Nationalist occupation of North China, and recommended the rapid withdrawal of American forces, lest they be drawn further into Chinese strife. On November 23, he cabled the Army Chief of Staff that if America were henceforth to support the unification of China and Manchuria, then the United States must inevitably become involved in the Chinese civil war, and quite possibly in war with Russia; in this case, he would need far greater forces than he currently had, and an appropriate change in directive.[3]

Within and among the State, War, and Navy Departments there was much confusion and lengthy debate, during the critical days of November, about America's military intervention in China. John Carter Vincent, director of the State Department's Office of Far Eastern Affairs, counseled caution. In a memorandum of November 12 to Byrnes regarding a projected American military advisory group (MAG) to aid in the military restructuring and strengthening of China, Vincent warned against the development "of a *de facto* protectorate with a semi-colonial Chinese army under our direction"; he argued that American involvement in China's civil strife "would occasion serious difficulties for us without compensatory advantages." On the other hand, he forwarded to Acheson and Byrnes what he termed a "well-thought out" opposing analysis, written on November 16 by Everett F. Drumright, chief of the Division of Chinese Affairs. Drumright argued that the CCP, struggling to take control of North China and already entrenched in Manchuria thanks to Soviet aid, would destroy the short-range chance for "a strong and united China" if it entrenched itself securely in these regions. Such an eventuality, he reasoned, would invite foreign intervention, foster in North China a regime physically contiguous and ideologically attuned to Russia (and thus hostile to America), seriously impair traditional American security interests in East Asia, and probably result in a Soviet-American clash, perhaps even a world war. He therefore urged that America "resolutely and effectively" support a Nationalist recovery of China and Manchuria, pending the military renovation and economic reconstruction of China under American auspices.[4]

There was similar deliberation at the Cabinet level. At "State-War-Navy" meetings, Secretaries Byrnes, Robert Patterson (War), and James Forrestal (Navy), along with Under Secretary Acheson (State) and Assistant Secretary John J. McCloy (War), among others, struggled inconclusively to define America's posture in China, while the Army and State Department staffs hammered out the issues and alternatives. No one knew quite what to do.

Byrnes, like Vincent, was inclined to caution. Taking a broad view of the Chinese situation, he was conscious of the simmering Soviet-American dispute about Japan. In September, Washington had made it clear that MacArthur's occupation would be shaped entirely by American policy, subject only to the advice (not consent) of a Far Eastern Advisory Commission composed of Britain, Russia, China, and the United States. The Russians, envisioning a Soviet occupation of the northern half of Japan's northernmost island, Hokkaido, had insisted instead on a four-power control council to govern the occupation, subject to the rule of unanimity in order to protect Soviet interests. Mustering British support, Byrnes had stood firm on unilateral American control, and Stalin thus had declined to commit an army to Japan "like a piece of furniture," as if Russia were "an American satellite in the Pacific." Late in October, Ambassador Harriman in Moscow reported Stalin's indignation at the toleration of Japanese militarist elements and the persistence of Japanese anti-Soviet news stories; he warned that if Stalin continued to feel excluded from a fair part in administering Japan, Russia "would pursue a unilateral policy" in areas which she controlled.[5]

Byrnes was further worried by the tremendous rapidity of America's demobilization which, spurred on by popular demand, was impairing America's bargaining position around the world. At the State-War-Navy meeting of November 6, he dismissed MacArthur's request for occupation forces from other allies to bolster America's contingent, by calling attention to "the effect on the rest of the world," not just on Japan. Defending Stalin's reluctance to send forces in the absence of any Soviet authority, Byrnes argued that the presence of other allied troops in Japan would be an irritant, and quite possibly a step toward "two worlds and . . . another war"; for he well knew, to quote Feis, that "Soviet Russia could . . . greatly disturb the situation in China, Manchuria, and Korea if it chose." And at a meeting with Patterson and Forrestal on November 20, he lamented the enfeeblement both of American "fighting prestige" and of American national policy by current accelerated demobilization schedules. Expressing regret over Congressional insensitivity to the need for adequate military strength, and alluding to the scattering and retrenchment of American forces abroad, Byrnes concluded that "the situation in China worried him considerably more than that elsewhere." He hoped to deter Soviet military action in and about China by avoiding provocation of Stalin in Japan, at least until the dwindling of American military strength in China could be forestalled or offset through the development of a new China policy. What the nature of that policy might be, he did not yet hint.[6]

In contrast to Byrnes, Forrestal and Patterson envisioned a military solution in China, much as did Drumright's memorandum. Patterson, secretary of war since the retirement of the prestigious Henry L. Stimson in September, did on November 6 express agreement with Wedemeyer's recommendation against furnishing Chiang's armies with transportation to and within Manchuria. But on November 20, he told Byrnes and Forrestal that there was "no peril" in increasing America's commitment: "the 60,000 Marines who are there could walk from one end of China to the other without serious hindrance. Such incidents as there have been are merely comic opera fighting." He added that if America's presence incidentally supported the Nationalists, "so much the better," for America already had "a considerable investment in that policy." The same day, Forrestal noted to Byrnes and Patterson that there thus far had been no marine casualties, and warned against withdrawing in response to "Russian pressure." A week later he insisted to his colleagues that the United States could not "yank the Marines out of Northern China now," and he lamented the inadequate public understanding of the issue.[7]

Finally, on November 26, Forrestal and Patterson responded to Byrnes's inquiry with a memorandum expressing their fully developed views on China. Although they hedged, emphasizing the primacy of long-range political factors, they asserted that "the most important military element in the Far East favorable to the U.S. is a unified China, including Manchuria, friendly to the U.S." Arguing that Soviet policy did not currently appear to oppose such a unification, and that CCP strength had been "considerably exaggerated" in the press, they envisioned American transportation of additional Nationalist forces to occupy North China and Manchuria. They also envisioned substantial American aid in repatriating the half-million Japanese soldiers in North China, with the understanding that America would thereby probably contribute to Chiang's cause against the Communists. They urged American consultations with other powers, especially with Russia, to reach a political understanding consistent with America's aim of unifying Manchuria and China under Chiang. And they warned that if Manchuria were to come under Soviet control, "then Russia will have achieved in the Far East approximately the objectives Japan initially set out to accomplish," to the grave military disadvantage of the United States.[8] Sharing many of Hurley's assumptions about Soviet pliability, CCP weakness, and the need for a pro-Nationalist posture, Forrestal and Patterson were apparently oblivious to John McCloy's succinct warning of November 6 that if Russia in response actively supported the CCP, "then we are 'in a real mess.'"[9]

While this internal debate proceeded, the original plans to evacuate the China theater before the end of the year were abandoned. Although Byrnes was aware that Wedemeyer deemed it possible to begin marine withdrawals by November 15 and to deactivate the China theater by the end of the year, he also knew that the Joint Chiefs opposed deactivation until the establishment of the military advisory group. On November 20, he instructed Wedemeyer that "the Marines should remain in North China for the time being on the assumption they will play an effective role in the completion of disarmament and deportation of the Japanese forces in that area and who might but for their presence remain there." At the same time, Wedemeyer was asked whether an American presence in North China was "required or desirable" in removing the Japanese from that region and Manchuria, whether the Chinese would be able to pacify either region by themselves, and how much shipping was necessary to effect the Japanese repatriation.[10]

Indeed, the presence of Japanese troops was a complicating factor in an already confused and delicate situation. On November 6, McCloy had warned that these troops were "still very cocky," an "undefeated Army . . . quite different in morale from those in Japan or elsewhere." On November 23, Wedemeyer warned lest they give their arms to the Communists, "become an arrogant, independent armed force no longer amenable to Allied plans for their complete demobilization," or—if America withdrew— secure "the 'balance of power'" between the Kuomintang and the CCP. And on November 26, Patterson and Forrestal termed a Japanese repatriation essential to Chinese unification. Envisioning the use of "Japanese shipping plus any excess Allied shipping which happened to be available," to evacuate the Japanese from North China, they urged a rapid Nationalist assumption of responsibility for the operation, to facilitate an American "withdrawal . . . from the area."[11]

By this time, Washington had long been deprived of the services of the China hands who had predicted the consequences of an inflexibly pro-Nationalist policy the previous winter. Most of them had been transferred from China and dispersed by the previous April. And, as Davies has written, from those remaining in Chungking "there was no dissenting note"—regarding either Chiang's superiority or the wisdom of supporting him exclusively—"for the sufficient reason that Hurley had prohibited any such disagreement on pain of being branded disloyal."[12] When Chiang's efforts faltered, American policymakers thus faced a seeming dilemma: either expand assistance to the Nationalists while evacuating the Japanese, or effect a rapid Japanese repatriation without reference to Chiang's needs, thus leaving North China open to Communist penetration and American purposes defeated.

No voice called—as the China hands might have—for a more imaginative approach, a pragmatic recognition of the politico-military power distribution in China, and thus a policy conceding that Chiang Kai-shek could not unify the country under his rule. This would have meant concession to the CCP of its strongholds in North China and Manchuria. It would have cancelled America's blank check to Chiang, and perhaps would have dissuaded him from military adventurism far to the north. It would have enabled America to maintain her ties to the Kuomintang, while freeing her from an ever-deepening involvement in behalf of incompetent Nationalist efforts to occupy the whole country. In the event of renewed civil war, it would have enabled Washington to maintain her neutrality, pending a decisive swing of Chinese politics in favor of the Kuomintang or the CCP. Most importantly, such a policy would have afforded the Administration time to rethink its China policy in the absence of American involvement with combat in the north. And it would have cut short the one-sided military intervention which began to poison American-Communist relations late in 1945.

In particular, the United States might have undertaken a strictly defined program of aid to Chiang, including the massive airlifting of Nationalist troops to northern and eastern China as actually took place. Immediately thereafter, American planes might have repatriated the half-million Japanese troops in the critical North China region, just as they had transported a roughly equivalent number of Chinese troops from the south and west. Then, American forces could have been withdrawn on the valid grounds that their continued presence would constitute interference in Chinese politics. Having transported such a large Chinese army would amply have fulfilled the obligation felt by

Washington to aid her ally in recovering its territory. Deprived of subsequent American aid, Chiang would have been forced either to secure what he could against the CCP in the north, or to withdraw to the south. America would not have underwritten his campaign.

But such a policy would have constituted a redefinition of America's immediate interests in China in light of Chiang's inability to control China, the waxing Communist movement in the north, and the Soviets' aid to their surprisingly vigorous confreres in Manchuria. It would have been an adjustment to the phenomenon of Asian revolution, with an eye to maintaining American influence with all factions in China, while the fate of that country remained in doubt. If—as the China hands had suggested—the dream of a united, democratic China under Chiang was not to be, and if America could not afford to combat a revolutionary movement gripping China's masses, then at least the United States could have utilized its political influence and economic power to compete with Russia for position with the Communists, rather than pushing them through military intervention ever closer to a Soviet orientation. As Davies has observed, a neutral attitude in the event of subsequent civil war would have had "the *realpolitik* objective of creating conditions whereby the Chinese Communists might retain their independence and develop their own jealous interests as a natural counterweight to Soviet power in East Asia"[13]—as they since have done, in spite of their poisoned Cold War relations with the United States.

In the event, American policymakers could not adjust to the success of communist revolution in war-torn, peasant Asia. The time-honored rhetoric of the Open Door policy, the public wartime ideal of a united, democratic China, and the assumptions of America's leadership all militated against such an adjustment. Both public expectations and Administration goals reduced the range of policy options to a military dilemma: either abandon the Nationalists or

126

destroy the CCP. Through all of the rambling policy memoranda, discursive meetings, and bureaucratic buck-passing, uncertainty and indecision ran. The State, War, and Navy Departments each sought more guidance than they gave one another; all three craved the recommendations of Wedemeyer, who in turn gave choices, not answers. Feis aptly noted "a wish to postpone decision, possibly also a wish to try to define the problem as a military rather than a political one."[14] Finally, the outlines of a policy began to emerge. At the November 27 State-War-Navy meeting, Byrnes suggested a way out of the China trap: "to try to force the Chinese Government and the Chinese Communists to get together on a compromise basis, perhaps telling Generalissimo Chiang Kai-shek that we will stop the aid to his government unless he goes along with this." At the same meeting, Dean Acheson suggested the outline of such a policy, recently adumbrated by Vincent along with other alternatives, and currently under State Department consideration: keeping the marines in China for the present, preparing for the further transport and support of Chinese armies in North China, seeking a truce in disputed areas, and promoting a political settlement between the factions in part through pressure on Chiang to compromise.[15]

In its new policy, the Administration endeavored—as urged by the China hands a year earlier—to cancel the *carte blanche* which had underwritten Chiang's military adventures and stimulated civil war. But it tried to solve its dilemma by forcing a coalition—a sharing of political power—which Chiang could never permit, in the certain knowledge that the CCP would thereby destroy him. The Administration continued to underestimate the depth of the Communist-Kuomintang rift. It also ignored Russia's propensity to expand her influence among the Communists by aiding them, thereby maintaining her leverage in Manchuria and North China and preventing the entrenchment of American military power near her border. Forrestal

127

queried whether "we could not talk the matter over realistically with the Russians," and secure their support for Chiang. Byrnes in turn referred to Russia's assurances that she would not let the Communists enter Manchuria, tentatively suggested that America "assume Soviet good faith" in the matter, and even considered asking the Russians to stay in Manchuria past their scheduled withdrawal date early in December, in effect to have them preserve the region for the Nationalists against nearby Communists. Davies, Harriman, and Kennan could have told them that Stalin would not exert himself to save Chiang from his domestic opposition, facilitate the extension of American military operations in China, and help America to achieve a Chinese counterweight to Soviet Asiatic power. It is clear that American policymakers continued to nurse unreasonable expectations of a pro-American settlement in China with international legitimation. Forrestal even suggested that the fledgling United Nations Organization—then under strong American influence—be used to effect a solution in China. Of these ambitions, in the face of Chinese disorder and Soviet suspicion, America's bid for a factional coalition with Stalin's approval was a desperate expression.[16] And no sooner had the State, War, and Navy secretaries resolved to send Hurley on this uncertain new mission, than his angry public resignation exploded in their faces, the very same day. Only in the ensuing weeks, under General Marshall's influence, would the policy assume its full form.

In its public posture, the Administration stressed a mixture of traditional Open Door goals and idealistic wartime principles. On October 20, 1945, Vincent defined American interests and objectives in Asia before the Foreign Policy Association in New York City; the speech was prominently publicized, and frequently cited, by the State Department.[17] America, Vincent stated, would continue to aim toward a strong, united, cooperative, and democratic

China; and he hailed the efforts of Hurley, then home for consultation, toward a negotiated settlement among Nationalists, Communists, and other groups. But he noted that China's greatest need was for economic reforms—especially in agriculture, taxation, currency, and transportation—to increase farming incomes and provide a secure base for industrialization. Promising American financial and technical support for such a reform program, he envisioned Chinese and American commercial expansion "on a non-discriminatory and mutually beneficial basis"; he termed it "our policy to encourage [such] commercial relations" and to "facilitate the reestablishment of American business in China."

Internationally, Vincent asserted that China might "form a buffer or a bridge" in Soviet-American relations. Declaring that "the bridge concept is preeminently preferable," he maintained that Sino-Russian-American cooperation was essential to American interests; he stressed America's desire "for stability in the Far East"; and he disavowed any thought of cooperating with either China or Russia against the other. Acknowledging important Soviet interests in the Far East, he assumed Soviet recognition of important American interests in the region; and he emphasized the need to convince Russia that American objectives "are in harmony with the objectives of any peacefully inclined nation." Warning against the idea that the democratization and unification of China was "our private and exclusive job," he anticipated questions regarding the deployment of the marines in North China:

> They have been sent there pursuant to military directives to serve a specific purpose, that is, to assist Chiang Kai-shek in demobilizing and repatriating Japanese troops in the area. Their stay is temporary. They will be withdrawn when they are no longer required for the purpose for which

129

they were sent. Generalissimo Chiang has announced that the Marines would leave north
China as soon as they can be relieved by Chinese
Government forces. The process of relief is now in
progress.[18]

But these pious hopes for China fell upon a skeptical
public, a wary Soviet Union, and a progressively embittered
Chinese Communist leadership. The Administration, it
seemed, protested too much. Far from moving toward unity
and democracy, the Chinese were in conflict, torn between
a semifeudal dictatorship and a dedicated revolutionary
party. And, far from maintaining a neutral posture, the
United States was entrenching itself in contested areas, its
marines holding cities, mines, and railroads for the Nationalists and occasionally skirmishing with Communist troops
who were prevented from pressing their geographic and
organizational advantage. Vincent's soothing public stance
and his cautious departmental input were belied by the
ever-worsening news from China. There was a yawning gap
between American statements of objectives in China and
actual conditions there. Chinese disorder and an inconsis-
tent American policy gave Bridges, Hurley, Vandenberg,
and other conservatives reason to complain about America's
failure sufficiently to support the Nationalists in developing
a pro-American outpost in Asia. But it also gave a far larger
group of Americans reason to protest against Washington's
intervention in a civil war, contrary both to American interests and to the principles America had espoused throughout
World War II.

The Noninterventionist Groundswell

The prospect of growing military involvement in Chinese
strife, unexplained by the Truman Administration, aroused

widespread anxiety throughout the United States in the autumn of 1945. As a "noninterventionist" tide swept the country, people from all walks of life criticized American policy. Liberals and radicals were sensitive to Russia's interests on her Far Eastern periphery, and sympathetic with the revolutionary impulse all over Asia; they interpreted America's pro-Kuomintang posture as a challenge to Asian nationalism and Soviet security. People of varying views cited the Administration for violating the wartime principle of self-determination. Others, especially among those who were serving in the China theater or who had relatives there, were more particularistic; caring not at all for Asia, they deemed America's commitment there suspicious, wasteful, and dangerous. As the Chinese crisis deepened, and America's proclaimed policy of noninterference grew increasingly remote from reality, the domestic reaction spread.

Sporadic noninterventionist ripples made their way to the State Department not long after the war had ended. On September 16, an army lieutenant stationed in China wrote to his father back in Rhode Island, detailing the ways in which the Chinese—Communists, bandits, and Nationalist ("Chink") soldiers alike—were attacking, robbing, and even killing American soldiers, and generally treating them "like dirt." Complaining about "the policy that the Chinese are always right," he wondered why America did not "tell them where they get off." It was "degrading" and "humiliating," he argued, that American troops were carrying lend-lease supplies to them after the war's end, while Chinese personnel were not helping in their own cause. "We are 'suckers' to them," he concluded; for the Americans had "been reduced to servants of that rotten, stinking gang, many times over worse than the Japs." On October 11, the officer's father forwarded the complaint to Senator Theodore F. Green (Democrat, Rhode Island), a member of the Foreign Relations Committee; Green in turn forwarded both letters to Byrnes on October 17, suggesting that the soldier's account "demands an appropriate investigation." And, on a broader level, Dean Acheson was sent a note the same day from a friend, a St. Louis attorney, expressing concern with the "military control" of American China policy. The lawyer recounted a speech of the previous evening by Harrison Forman, a journalist and author of *Report from Red China*, claiming that the "so-called Communists of North Central China" had possession of that region except for the large cities; that they had a powerful army, popular support, and a more democratic outlook than the Kuomintang; that they were not in fact communists at all, and had no connection with Stalin; and that the American forces, in flying Chiang's troops into northern cities and enabling them to secure Japanese weapons, were taking sides with the Kuomintang against the CCP.[19]

These ripples of discontent conveyed an impression of the Kuomintang far different from the image of a loyal, deserving ally reponsive to American influence, as perceived by American conservatives. The impression was of Nationalist arrogance, xenophobia, viciousness, and illegitimacy. Sensing Chinese hostility and manipulation, people divorced in their minds American and Nationalist interests, viewed American military aid to the Nationalists as a reckless involvement in a foreign civil war, and sometimes took deprecatory views of the Chinese as a people.

Simultaneously, Congressmen began to question the State Department about the motives and implications of America's military presence in North China. On October 3, Hugh DeLacy wrote to Acheson expressing concern over the use of the marines. Acheson replied on October 9 that the marines were there to aid the army and the Nationalist forces in the Japanese repatriation; American forces were not in China to aid "any Chinese faction or group." A week later, Representative Mike Mansfield (Democrat, Montana) called on Vincent. Mansfield knew China; he had served there in the Navy, had taught Far Eastern history at the University of

Montana, and had undertaken a fact-finding mission to China at Roosevelt's request late in 1944. Now he confided freely to Vincent, an old acquaintance, his fear that the use of the marines to garrison North China, especially for a prolonged period, would be "most unwise." Unmoved by the same explanation given DeLacy, he warned that Russia, which recently had informed Chiang of its intention to withdraw from Manchuria by the end of November, "might reconsider" if the American marines stayed on. He therefore urged an American withdrawal by that date; for by then, he argued, American planes might easily lift sufficient Chinese troops to garrison the cities of North China and disarm and repatriate the Japanese troops on their own. Vincent apprised Acheson of Mansfield's misgivings the next day.[20]

As the Administration's dilemma sharpened with the spread of the Chinese civil war in November, public and Congressional concern mounted over the Nationalists' venality and America's seemingly unqualified assistance to their cause. Among other leaders, Elbert Thomas felt the weight of this noninterventionist pressure, and one of the sternest critiques of American policy came to Thomas from the Committee for a Democratic Policy Toward China. Based in New York City, this organization included a number of leading liberal and radical intellectuals and writers. The secretary of its information organ was Ilona Ralf Sues, a strong internationalist who had spent years in China and in 1944 had written a book sympathetic toward the CCP while critical of fascist tendencies in the Kuomintang leadership. Other members included Mrs. Edgar Snow, Frederick V. Field, Gunther Stein, Maxwell Stewart, Leland Stowe, and Arthur Upham Pope.[21] On November 2, the committee sent Thomas a memorandum charging that Hurley had supported Chiang's demand for Stilwell's recall in October 1944 and that, once rid of Stilwell, Chiang had reneged on his promise to increase his war effort against Japan and to seek an understanding with the CCP. Hurley, it continued, had censored from the reports of experienced diplomats "everything unfavorable to Chiang," had purged large numbers of knowledgeable Foreign Service and Army officers from his staff, had shut off American reporting from Yenan, and had armed only Kuomintang troops, who were then groomed by Chiang "for civil war" rather than for war on Japan.

The memorandum added that Hurley and Wedemeyer had aided Chiang in preventing the Communists from entering the major cities of North China, and that Hurley "threw all American power and influence on one side" at the factional negotiations. It warned:

> Civil war looms in China with the United States committed to one side. There are more U.S. troops in the country now than were sent there to fight Japan. If it had not been for their presence, Chiang Kai-shek would not have dared substitute military action for negotiations in his dealings with the Chinese Communists. The Chinese civil war, begun with American involvement, cannot continue without it. It creates a new, and major, area of danger for U.S.-Soviet relations and international peace.[22]

Consequently, the committee urged its audience, Thomas among them,

> to use your influence, before it is too late, to press for the recall of Ambassador Hurley and U.S. forces and equipment in China. This is the only way to halt the Chinese civil war and to clear the way for a new and better American policy which will help China to build herself up instead of tearing herself to pieces.[23]

Although Thomas neither criticized the Hurley-Wedemeyer policy nor passed judgment on the Kuomintang, he never wavered from his earlier expressions of encouragement for the transnational Asian social revolution; in his weekly messages to Japan, he dwelt on the transgressions of the discredited Japanese leadership, while envisioning the growth of liberal democratic movements and institutions in Japan. Regarding Russia, he wrote an article in November repeating his thesis, earlier presented in *The Four Fears*, that despite their mortal fear of one another, with each doing "everything imaginable to insult, antagonize, irritate, and thwart the other," America and Russia were bound together by strong common interests. He noted that when the crisis of world war revealed "real motives" and true interests, "Russia and America awoke to find themselves world partners." With their mutually offensive dogmas broken down by splendid wartime cooperation, Thomas concluded that the two countries could strive together toward peace, while recognizing their seemingly permanent difference in political philosophy. On November 7, the Russian-American Club of Los Angeles sent Thomas a warm acknowledgment of his message commemorating the twenty-eighth anniversary of the Bolshevik Revolution. Expressing its encouragement that "we have on our side in these menacing times men of such eminence and influence as yourself," the club declared that world peace "depends upon friendly and harmonious" Soviet-American relations.[24]

But Thomas took practically no part in the China debate which was erupting in November 1945. Something of a diplomatic troubleshooter for Truman, he traveled abroad on numerous missions; as a delegate to the International Labor Organization Conference in Paris, he spent the end of October and most of November in France and Italy studying the dislocated economic and financial situation in Europe. He was thus remote from the issues presented to him by the Committee for a Democratic Policy Toward China, whose memoranda lay unread pending his return.[25]

In the United States, left-wing concern about China was intensifying. On November 4, the Committee for a Democratic Policy Toward China, newly rechristened the Committee for a Democratic Far Eastern Policy, sent Truman a letter assailing American intervention in China as a violation of Truman's own recent Navy Day speech affirming the concept of freely chosen self-government for all peoples. According to the committee, Washington was giving "exclusive support" to the militarist dominated Kuomintang, while ignoring the democratic hopes of "millions of Chinese" in the CCP, the Democratic League, and even the Kuomintang itself. Fearing a "disastrous civil war" and perhaps a third world war, the committee urged Truman to withdraw all American troops and military equipment, and to condition future economic and military aid on peaceful, democratic development in China. Along the same lines, Harry Bridges, president of the International Longshoremen's and Warehousemen's Union, wired Secretary of War Patterson from San Francisco on November 10 to demand an immediate American evacuation from China. Claiming that "the 'big stick' of American might has no place in China," he asserted that American troops and arms which had defeated "Nazi Germany and Fascist Japan" must not be "used in the cause of the Chiang dictatorship's drive for civil war in China." He termed the marine landings and America's transportation of Nationalist troops an "unbridled attempt of imperialist interests to use American military might against the Chinese people." And the Communist Party of New York State on November 15 wired Byrnes a resolution of "25,000 New York Citizens, in mass meeting assembled at Union Square," demanding immediate cessation of American military intervention, a prompt withdrawal of all American armed forces from China, and a return to Roosevelt's policy for "unity of the Anglo-Soviet-American coalition and the United Nations."[26]

The ferment went beyond the left, as churchmen began

to speak up. The editor of *Protestant* was reported to have sent Truman a message "on behalf of 5,000 Protestant clergymen" expressing alarm at reports of American aid to one side in the Chinese imbroglio, in contradiction to the president's Navy Day rhetoric. On November 10, the United Christian Council for Democracy, based in New York, and claiming to represent "ten thousand liberal church leaders" across the country, conveyed to Byrnes its "strong opposition" to America's support of the "undemocratic and reactionary military and political clique" controlling the Nationalists. Worried by the "pattern of supporting old ruling groups against movements of the people toward economic and political freedom" in China and elsewhere, the Council called for a democratic policy encouraging the "achievement of free elections and a coalition government." On November 23, a Baptist minister from South Carolina warned Byrnes: "[W]e bet on the wrong horse in Russia in the last war. I certainly hope we are not going to repeat that mistake in China."[27]

Criticism of American military policy mushroomed in Congress, as well. Representative Albert Engel (Democrat, California) told the House that while on a recent fact-finding trip to China with an Appropriations subcommittee, he had been advised that American troops would be removed by December 15; after observing the low morale of the troops, he had been shocked to see Wedemeyer's prediction that they would remain on to aid in the Japanese repatriation. Declaring that the American people would "not tolerate" another war in the Far East, Engel admonished: "You cannot help to move troops in a country that is at war, and China does have civil war, without becoming involved on one side or the other." On November 14, Representative Ellis E. Patterson (Democrat, California) wrote to Byrnes, similarly voicing concern that the transportation of Nationalist troops "to battlefronts with the Chinese Communists" constituted "unjustifiable intervention" in China, "contrary to the established principle of self-determination." He urged that America instead support "peaceful negotiations . . . leading to a free national election" and constitutional government in China.[28]

Late in November, Congressional discontent reached a crescendo. On November 26, six representatives acted. Three were from Washington State, and three from California. They were variously left-of-center Democrats deeply influenced by the Great Depression and the New Deal, committed to government activism for public welfare at home, and in international affairs strongly conscious of the need for Soviet-American cooperation. In terms of geographic base, political background, and social philosophy, they were much akin to Elbert Thomas, but were without his expertise in military, diplomatic, and Far Eastern affairs. The six now introduced resolutions calling variously for the withdrawal of troops, marines, and munitions from China, for the common purpose of encouraging Chinese unity, democracy, and self-determination. The same day, DeLacy made the speech which was an immediate cause of Hurley's resignation. Charging that Wedemeyer had "authorized air attacks upon a tiny Chinese village" on a trifling pretext, he argued that American forces were suppressing the democratic aspirations of the Chinese people. Contrasting the censorship, crushing taxes, graft, and inflation of Kuomintang China with the "vigorous new democracy" of the CCP, DeLacy assailed Hurley's "blank-check support" of Chiang, urged in its stead American "pressure for a genuine coalition government" representing all Chinese groups, and warned:

> If America now continues to lend its great power to the establishing of anti-Communist bases in North China, that, too, will have its own logic. And that logic is not of peace and self-government for all peoples. It is the logic of the most reactionary of American big businessmen, wanting unre-

138

stricted economic exploitation of Asia. It is the
logic of a new world war, this time against the
Soviet Union, launched from great bases in the
Pacific, from anti-Communist basis [*sic*] in north
China.[29]

On December 5, Walter Judd and Clare Boothe Luce
attacked DeLacy in the House and defended Chiang's government against his charges. Luce termed DeLacy "Com-
munist-fed," and noted that he was following the party line
on China. Such reactions, along with Vandenberg's concern
about possible State Department dissemination of Communist materials, reflected a mounting conservative fear
about the possibility of Communist influence on American
China policy. And, not surprisingly, most of the suspect persons and groups were prominent noninterventionists, or
were otherwise perceived to be against a vigorous American
military policy in East Asia. Hence Dondero's attacks on
Acheson, on Service, and on Frederick V. Field (of the Committee for a Democratic Far Eastern Policy); Kohlberg's
campaign against the IPR; Loeb's doubts about Vincent; and
Bridges's innuendo against State Department officials, high
and low.[30] For their part, left-wing noninterventionists long
had been attacking those they regarded as the pillars of anti-
democratic, interventionist, or imperialist policies in China
and Japan. Their criticisms mounted after the outbreak of
the Hurley debate, prompting Bridges to remark to Hurley
in December that "the same crowd who have been sabotaging your efforts . . . in China are now pretty well centering
their attack on General Albert Wedemeyer."[31] The mutual
suspicion engendered was aptly illustrated by the hostility
between Kohlberg and the IPR board, each certain that the
other was trying to pervert American China policy.

Such recriminations suggest the depth of feeling about
China among conservatives and liberals alike. This depth of
feeling in turn suggests the enormous significance attached

by many in both groups to China's future, both for American interests and for world politics. Indeed, the progressive frustration of wartime ideals throughout 1945 heightened the clash of differing assumptions about the causes of the great power animosities developing in East Asia and elsewhere. Rather than the anticipated United Nations framework of democracy and international cooperation, Americans were confronted at the war's end with an impoverished, war-torn, revolutionary world, featuring numerous Soviet-American tensions. For China in particular, internationalist hopes died hard; for, as Thomas observed, China always seemed to inspire in Americans an especially aggressive loyalty. Thus conservatives who championed Chiang, liberals who denounced his crusade against the CCP, and policymakers who sought a Chinese coalition all saw in China a test case for their varying conceptions of an Asiatic order in keeping with justice and American interests. As the spreading civil war drew the United States toward involvement, Americans variously came to terms with the elemental facts of Asian revolution and Soviet power in the Far East.

Quite aside from the interest groups, professional organizations, and politicians that attacked military aid to a corrupt regime and warned against a confrontation with Russia, the American people were rejecting what seemed to be a risky and senseless military adventure. Anxious for the return home of American troops and hungering for an explanation of American methods and objectives in China, they deluged their representatives with inquiries and criticisms. On November 8, a state legislator wrote Byrnes that "the people of Montana cannot understand why American armed forces are practically participating in the Chinese civil war. Neither do we like," he continued, "to see American war materials being used to subjugate the peoples of the Orient, and hope that our country can refrain from meddling in the internal affairs of all peoples." Two days later, a Minnesota state senator apprised Truman of growing resentment "over the reported use of Marines" and lend-lease supplies in China, especially among "parents of the boys in the Corps." Alluding to the wide but inaccurate publicity being given China, he warned that the issues there were "little understood by the average citizen," and he urged the Administration to make a clarifying statement. On November 17, congressmen from Texas, Arizona, and California asked the State Department for comments on China, while relaying constituents' requests for clarifications of American policy there and in Pacific areas where colonial powers were clashing with native independence movements. On November 23, Representative William R. Thom of Ohio wrote Byrnes: "My mail is filled with demands for an explanation of why we are keeping Marines in the parts of China where a civil war is in progress." Confessing "that I do not understand" State Department policy, he was admittedly "at a loss" to answer anxious letters and telephone calls. The same day, Representative Louis Ludlow of Indiana wrote Byrnes that his constituent mail was "very critical of our government's policy," with information "requested almost daily." "How many fighting men do we have in China?" he asked. "Why are they there and what are they doing? How long is it intended to keep them there? Are our forces in China likely to be augmented or decreased?" On November 27—the day Hurley quit—Senator Hugh B. Mitchell of Washington warned that his constituents continued "to express grave concern over the ever worsening picture in China," and he asked:

> Cannot the Department on the basis of facts at hand choose some other instrument than the military in China? Cannot the Department take the position the American people demand and offer every peaceful assistance toward unity to a nation which has already suffered so much?[32]

Similar feelings persisted throughout the country until

and beyond Hurley's explosion at the end of November. Not only from New York and California—liberal, internationalist centers—but also from Illinois and Connecticut, Florida and Georgia, Louisiana, Texas, Colorado, and Hurley's native Oklahoma, came citizens' protests against American military involvement in China, and simultaneous Congressional puzzlement.[33] There was a deep sense of frustration and alienation from what was perceived to be an Administration posture of neutrality, thinly masking a purposeful military intervention. A constituent wrote to Senator Brien McMahon (Democrat, Connecticut) on November 16 that there currently appeared to be "an unnecessary amount of military equipment and personnel" in China, probably out of proportion to American interests there. Deriding the Administration's claim that these were needed to protect American property, he expressed his growing fear that "directly or indirectly we are using our force" to influence the course of the civil war.[34] On November 25, an Oklahoman wrote her Congressman, Jed Johnson, that if American troops became involved in the Chinese strife,

> any straight thinking person will know that it's entirely unnecessary. There's no reason in the world why our boys should be used in a war that absolutely does not concern us. Why should our boys die fighting with or for people who know nothing but war, and when they have just been rescued from one enemy begin fighting among themselves?[35]

Forwarding the letter to Byrnes, Johnson noted that it was "written from a small rural post office before the current controversy broke into print and obviously is not an inspired propaganda letter." He added:

> It may be that the writer has a relative in the armed forces in China—I do not know—but if so,

142

several thousand other Americans do also. I am submitting the letter chiefly because it would indicate that the American people will never be convinced that we have any business keeping American troops in China now that the war is over.[36]

There clearly occurred at this time a large groundswell of public sentiment intuitively sharing the assumptions which the conscious, professional, and organized noninterventionists were articulating in a more precise and informed manner. Some people expressed fears of a great power confrontation. One liberal Chicagoan, discerning an American pattern of "creating, stimulating, or inviting 'incidents'" in order to justify the use of "overwhelming force," wrote his Congressman: "We must get out of China. The Russians are leaving, we can too." Many liberals linked China with the efforts of the British, Dutch, and French to restore colonial administration in the East Indies and Indochina, and some specifically condemned the use of American loans and lend-lease supplies by colonial powers to suppress nationalistic revolutionary movements, in contradiction to wartime allied rhetoric. But if liberals regarded the Chinese situation as a bad regime set against an oppressed people with democratic aspirations, other Americans opposing intervention viewed the entire Chinese people in a rather ugly light. In contrast to the adulation of "the Chinese people" or their supposedly legitimate representatives by Bridges, Thomas, Vandenberg, and others, there persisted among Americans the old stereotype of a sly, manipulative, barbaric, warlike, or perpetually disordered people. These stereotypes formed part of America's traditional emotionalism about China, and very soon after the end of the war, the dominant euphoria about the Chinese which had been played off against the wartime derogation of "the Japs" had been sufficiently strained by America's postwar entanglement to let the seamy, racist side of America's love-hate complex for China emerge. To many a war-weary, frustrated, and angry American, noninterventionism might be grounded not in any idealistic hope for democracy and social justice, but instead in the view that the whole of China was so incorrigibly base as to be not worth saving. As one woman with a son in the marines wrote, her boy owed no allegiance nor any obligation to China, and she for one was unwilling to see him "risk his life or endure further suffering in that rotten country's defense."[37] Thus did the contradictions and risks of America's China policy stir undercurrents of a parochial isolationist sentiment.

In America in 1945, there was thus a great oversimplification and confusion in perceptions of China. The persistence of emotional duality among Americans of varying political biases boded ill for the development of an informed and limited objective in China. The continued reaction by Americans to oversimplified symbols—Chiang as the embodiment of virtue or vice, the Chinese Communists as pure nationalists or a sinister extension of Soviet power—restricted the range of choice in United States China policy, and heightened the emotional reaction to the ultimate failure of that policy.

For the time being, the Chinese struggle had not reached such a critical stage for the United States. More than anything else, Americans craved information; public ignorance about China demanded enlightenment. The craving intensified with the political uproar following Hurley's resignation. Senators Edwin Johnson (Democrat, Colorado), Richard Russell (Democrat, Georgia), and Brien McMahon, along with many representatives, prompted by constituent demand, queried the State Department. Soldiers and sailors, along with their relatives, continued to demand explanations; so did merchant marine crews, political clubs, the American War Dads, and many ordinary people.[38] On November 28, the editor-in-chief of a prominent publishing house wrote to Vincent:

> I am one of a vast number of Americans who wish
> to know why the Navy and the Air Forces cannot
> be used to repatriate the Japanese rather than to
> help supply the Chiang forces with arms and am-
> munition. Is there any answer to this question?[39]

The next day, Representative John H. Folger wired Byrnes
that "it would be helpful" to call upon Stilwell, George Atcheson, former Ambassador Gauss, and "many others having reliable knowledge of the situation and its history," for
"full reports and conversations" on China. A day later, a
Park Avenue physician wrote to Dean Acheson urging that
the State Department "appeal publicly to the people for
support" against Hurley, if necessary. And on December 5,
a constituent whose kid brother was stationed at Tsingtao
wrote to Senator McMahon, asserting that the marines' mission to disarm the Japanese had been accomplished, and
wondering "why we should invite any further trouble or ag-
gravation" by intervening in a bloody civil war:

> I am not averse to offering our diplomatic assis-
> tance in an effort to mediate China's internal
> strife, but I most vehemently protest and draw
> the line when it resolves itself into offering mili-
> tary assistance which might conceivably draw us
> into the struggle. Let our State Department clear-
> ly define the case![40]

Just as significant as the hue and cry from the public were
the reports coming to the State Department of foreign efforts to discredit Washington's China policy by appealing to
American opinion. The Chinese Communists, angry about
American intervention on behalf of Chiang, and the Russians, alarmed at the American military presence in North

China, were endeavoring to manipulate American sentiment to force a reduction of American aid to the Nationalists. Since the marines' deployment, the department had
been aware of Soviet interest in Congressional and public
criticism of Administration policy. And on November 4,
Washington received from the American consul general in
Vladivostok, O. Edmund Clubb, a revealing observation:

> Any rising tide [of] revolution in China generally
> would surely be viewed with deep sympathy in
> USSR. Moscow estimate of that revolutionary situ-
> ation would probably include belief that American
> opinion would not suffer extension direct U.S. sup-
> port Chungking with military supplies for use in
> civil war, especially if it were made to appear that
> U.S.A. was thus "opposing will of Chinese people"
> and that such policy, moreover, held danger of ex-
> acerbation U.S.A.-USSR relations.[41]

Chinese Communist efforts to limit American intervention were similarly noted. Reports indicated that while
American assistance to the Nationalists had a "profound"
impact on Communist attitudes toward the United States,
CCP hostility did "not extend [to the] American people
whose support [is deemed] desirable and to be cultivated";
confident of their ability to absorb northern China as soon
as the American forces evacuated, the Communists might
encourage "clashes with small U.S. units" in order "to influence American opinion and hasten withdrawal." And on
November 26, Wedemeyer warned:

> The Chinese Communists are doing utmost to in-
> timidate and to involve United States Forces in
> military operations that definitely can be con-
> strued as offensive in nature. They hope thereby
> to influence public opinion in the States and

abroad in their contention that the United States
is interfering with the internal affairs of China
and that our military forces should be removed
summarily.[42]

It was very clear that Americans reading and hearing
about the situation in China were ever more fearful of military ensnarement, and ever more insistent that the Administration explain itself, pull out, or both. The extent to which
purposeful CCP and Soviet policies toward this end were responsible for this insistence is not precisely measurable. But
the severity of the reaction indicated that, whatever the role
of alien influences, there was a strong enough indigenous
tide against intervention to be quite significant in its own
right, and that public opinion was sufficiently outraged to
become susceptible to the influence of skillful foreign propaganda. The State Department would have been blind to
miss the signals. On December 13, the department noted
that during the past weeks, it had "received hundreds of letters protesting against U.S. military participation in the
Chinese civil war, or urging the withdrawal of U.S. troops
from China." Analyzing incoming letters and telegrams for
one day, the department concluded that communications
were "practically unanimous in opposing" American intervention, and that such communications were "coming . . .
in large numbers." It further concluded that, while C.I.O.
unions and Communists were writing and wiring in such
large numbers "as to suggest an organized drive," the

> other communications are so varied and the geo-
> graphical spread is so great as to suggest that the
> protests represent a strong feeling among people
> who are acting, for the most part, spontaneously.
> In the light of this and other types of evidence,
> the conclusion is that the use of U.S. troops in
> China is unpopular with the American people.[43]

In the midst of growing foreign and domestic pressures, the State Department endeavored to clarify its goals and methods in China, as articulated by Vincent in his October speech. In a departmental *Policy Manual*, internally circulated and revised as of November 14, American China policy was outlined for use in the formulation of public statements for the period following December 1, 1945. Beyond the traditional objective of "a strong, independent, united and democratic China" contributing to East Asian peace and stability, the manual claimed:

> We believe that collaboration among China, the United States, Great Britain and the Soviet Union is essential for the peace and security of the Pacific area, and that such collaboration, within the framework of the United Nations Organization and otherwise, should extend to all legitimate fields of endeavor on the basis of equality of opportunity and respect for national sovereignty.[44]

The manual envisioned the use of American economic aid "to encourage concessions by the Central Government, by the so-called 'Communists', and by the other factions" to facilitate a broadening of the regime under Chiang with a view toward "developing democracy." But it declared that such a solution "depends primarily upon the good will of the Chinese leaders themselves," and it asserted that American forces were currently in China simply to facilitate the Japanese surrender as prescribed the previous August.[45]

Like the Vincent speech, the *Policy Manual* defined American objectives in terms of Open Door principles and wartime idealism. An important step in the genesis of the Administration's defense of its actions, it was designed to allay Soviet fear and CCP anger about America's military presence in China, to assure the American public that Washington did not contemplate an open-ended intervention, and to secure support for the Administration's developing coalition policy. The *Policy Manual* reflected the continuing illusions that a true political compromise was possible in China, that democratic institutions could flourish there in the wake of such a compromise, and that the support of Russia might be secured toward the end of a strong China. Additionally, the manual skirted the question being raised with increasing urgency among Americans: what was the current impact of the American forces on the spreading civil war, and where might the intervention lead?

Yet it is not surprising that the State Department failed to confront the China issue publicly, since that issue was currently a focus of hot debate within the Administration. If the traditional and idealistic definitions of American interests in China seem naive or dissimulating in light of the situation there, they can only be said to have reflected the contemporaneous confusion and uncertainty within the Administration as the War, State, and Navy Departments struggled to keep pace with events. If policy definitions were superficial in public, they were also vague within the government. On November 1, the War Department had asked the State Department for guidance:

> It would be most valuable to have a clear cut statement of minimum interests from which the U.S. will not retreat in the event of a clash of interests in the Far East, particularly concerning Manchuria, Inner Mongolia, North China and Korea.[46]

Refusing to make such a commitment, the State Department replied four long weeks later that it was not possible "to give any such statement which would be sufficiently reliable or certain to furnish the basis on which the War Department might determine in advance the military steps to be taken against possible aggression in the Far East."[47] Little wonder that during the policy debate, public statements were so general, and the people so confused.

The Strange Silence of Elbert Thomas

Amidst the national curiosity and public commotion of late November and early December 1945, nobody in government stood more qualified to articulate a knowledgeable noninterventionist critique of American China policy than Elbert Thomas. At a time when both liberals and conservatives were urging a return in practice to the lofty democratic principles still mouthed by the Administration, but were urging diametrically opposed policies in China in the name of those principles, Thomas might have spoken on the dynamics and potentials of Asian revolution. As chairman of the Senate Military Affairs Committee, a high-ranking member of the Foreign Relations Committee, and a respected expert on Asia, he might have collaborated with Vandenberg, who in stressing the disastrous implications of liberal policies, was moving toward a clarification of the issues in China. Had Thomas publicly stated his high priority for the satisfaction of Russia's border aspirations in the Far East, or posited the legitimacy of the Chinese Communist revolution, the conflict with the Bridges-Vandenberg vision of a strong, pro-Western China under Chiang would at least have bared differences in perception and objectives to close public scrutiny. Ideally, Thomas might have helped to educate the American people to the complexities of politics in China and to the limitations of American capabilities there. In the event, he did none of these things.

Late in November, Thomas returned from his European journey, having missed the buildup of American tensions over China. He met with Truman on November 26, just as the Administration was formulating its flexible new policy, and the day before Hurley resigned. At that meeting, and in summing up his thoughts at Truman's request on November 30, he dwelled on the significance of Soviet power:

> Economically and from the standpoint of money, Russia will be very, very strong and more like the old exploiting industrialist nations. From the standpoint of vigor and stability, Russia is the big winner of the war. She will accomplish her now generations old policy in regard to her "place in the Sun," to use the phrase so often used by Russian imperialists back in the early nineties.[48]

Urging that inevitable changes—such as Soviet acquisition of "free access to the Mediterranean"—be made peacefully, he warned that "Russia looms . . . large for the problem of the world."

The progressive American military involvement in China could not but have magnified Thomas's fear of the previous August that America's "militant crusading" in China, her proneness to get "worked up" into a "fighting attitude," might provoke a "third great war." Lightly regarding American vital interests in China and conscious of Russia's strategic advantages there, he must have been quite worried. He attended the first two Foreign Relations Committee hearings on December 5 and 6, when Hurley gave the bulk of his testimony on alleged Foreign Service sabotage in China. And he paid close heed to Hurley's allegations, taking notes and refreshing the general's memory on his own previous testimony at one point.[49] But, aside from that brief instance, he neither questioned witnesses nor made any statements. Rather, he stood mute as Hurley and Bridges impugned the loyalty of diplomats whose judgments of the Chinese revolution closely resembled his own; nor did he challenge the conservatives' assertions about the strength, virtue, and exclusive identity with American interests of the Nationalist regime. Neither did Thomas make any speeches on China during November and December of 1945; he apparently issued no statements or essays on East Asia, save his accustomed weekly speeches on Japanese reconstruction. In light of his intense interest in China, his normally outspoken commentaries, his prominent position, and the force of the public debate, his silence is both paradoxical and intriguing.

The basic reason for Thomas's circumspection seems to have been his strong sense of loyalty to the Democratic Party and a correspondingly intense—though not very visible— animosity toward most Republicans. Although he was capable of fruitful bipartisan cooperation, as his enduring friendship and collaboration with Senator H. Alexander Smith attest,[50] Thomas harbored a profound mistrust of most Republican bipartisan leaders, whom he regarded as arrogant, self-serving, and ruthlessly ambitious. In response to a column critical of Vandenberg's "conversion" to internationalism, sent to him the previous January by the United Automobile Workers of the C.I.O., Thomas had pleaded his heavy Senate workload in declining to comment on, or even to read, the short piece on what he termed "Senator Vandenberg's current foreign policy." In August 1945, commenting on a domestic industry-labor conference, Thomas had written Truman that "the only criticism" in the Senate "came from Bridges, who incidentally is a Republican and sits very close to Vandenberg to whom the press is giving full credit" for the project. By the summer of 1946, cognizant of the disastrous mid-term Congressional elections then in the offing, Thomas would indulge in bitter recriminations about Truman's wooing of key Republicans. He bared his soul to some old friends:

> Since the appointment of the Senators to go to San Francisco, it has been a policy of our President and State Department to try to make a show of national unity on foreign relations, and Vandenberg has made the boast that since Republicans

now run our foreign policy, it is a good policy. I have never been much of a man to believe in ever allowing a national policy to become dependent upon the good will and the actions of leaders of the opposing party, especially when those leaders feel that the lightning from heaven is about to strike them and turn them into Presidents of the United States.[51]

He added that Truman had "honored Vandenberg, [Senator Warren] Austin, Eugene Meyers and Mr. Dulles to such an extent that these people have become the beneficiaries of what has been done under American leadership for world financial and political progress. I don't believe a one of them will be worth two hoots on an election day."

Thomas continued to recognize the value of bipartisan cooperation, noting in the same letter:

If the new world organization succeeds and becomes part of the future political world, I have gotten in a word here and there. With Senators Green and Vandenberg, I helped to work out the technique that made UNRRA acceptable to Congress. But the real significance of that institution has not been realized yet.[52]

Yet, on the same day, he lamented to the State Department's legal adviser that since Byrnes's accession, he had been called to only one Foreign Relations subcommittee consultation, of which there had been so many with Secretary of State Cordell Hull during the war. Presuming it "likely [that] Connally, Vandenberg and Austin became a sufficiently large advisory group," Thomas suggested that a government in which the Constitution implicitly told "the world that the last word is here on the Hill, should be wise enough to realize that some first words should once in a while be indulged in with those who have the last word."[53]

Harking back to Republican avowals of 1920 that the election of Senator Warren G. Harding to the presidency would gain America entrance into the League of Nations— "the most dishonest political act in the history of America" —as well as to more recent backstabbing episodes involving Vandenberg, "the sorts of goings on, the world knows nothing about," Thomas wondered

> just how the Democratic candidate for Senator in the State of Michigan feels when wherever he goes he must face the picture of his President presenting his opponent with a silver plaque and calling him the greatest senator of the ninety-six. It is hard to campaign against that stuff.[54]

Bitterly recalling the lack of support given him in his own reelection campaign by Franklin Roosevelt in 1938, and with Vandenberg's current political collaboration with the president directly in mind, Thomas warned that "if Truman imagines that he is going to be renominated and reelected by playing 'ring around the roses' with the Royal Opposition, he has a surprise coming."[55]

Although the sourness of his rhetoric in 1946 was clearly heightened by the upcoming elections coinciding with Truman's quickening efforts to befriend prominent Republicans, Thomas just as clearly had basic partisan reservations in 1945. His pairing of Bridges and Vandenberg, even if on a mild domestic issue, is particularly suggestive. For if he then perceived them in sly unison against the Administration, then how much more severe must have been his anger and frustration as Vandenberg, the bipartisan "golden boy," joined Bridges in hammering at American China policy, Thomas's pet project, at the December hearings! There is no doubt that Vandenberg shared many of the assumptions about China held by Bridges and the right-wing ideologues. To the casual observer, or to the politically biased and emotionally involved—such as Thomas—Vandenberg appeared to be gracing Hurley's notions about a pro-Russian, Communist-inspired plot against Chiang's government and American interests. What Thomas failed to perceive was the relative moderation and openness with which Vandenberg addressed the problem, and his tentative search for the fundamental issues involved. Thomas certainly did not know that Vandenberg had restrained Hurley from revealing the Yalta secrets in order to keep alive hopes of a Soviet-American accommodation at the Moscow Conference. And even if he had known, he probably would have taken a jaundiced view of the personal ambition which Vandenberg naturally harbored as a foreign policy formulator.

If, as is likely, Thomas viewed the China debate as a partisan Hurley-Bridges-Vandenberg onslaught against American policy, he could only leave its defense to Tom Connally, the Administration's prime Congressional foreign policy spokesman. Senior to Thomas and chairman of the Foreign Relations Committee, Connally undertook to define the Administration's case against Hurley. While Thomas, too, was powerful, he was seriously at odds with the Administration, for the *de facto* American military support of Chiang Kai-shek pushed against what seemed to Thomas the tide of Asian revolution and threatened to provoke a confrontation with Russia. Through a combination of personal pique and party loyalty, he held his peace, rather than expose the Administration to more criticism from the left while it was under a conservative attack. No doubt he was frustrated by what he regarded as simplistic debates about how best to aid Chiang, among men like Connally and Vandenberg who belonged to an inner circle that excluded him. The last two hearings, featuring the testimony of Byrnes, Acheson, and China correspondent Theodore White, he did not even bother to attend.[56]

It is ironic that Thomas remained silent because of an attitude which included a deep mistrust of Vandenberg, for he
and Vandenberg were uniquely equipped to utilize the hearings as a constructive public forum exposing the issues which
divided the noninterventionists from Chiang's champions.
This was true because Thomas and Vandenberg, while somewhat representative of the views of liberals and conservatives, respectively, were substantially superior to most in
those groups in their intellectual grasp of international
politics, of East Asia, and of Soviet-American relations.
Vandenberg, although sharing the rightists' attachment to
Chiang, at least had always recognized—if reluctantly—
Soviet political strength and military power in the Eastern
Hemisphere. America, he knew, had to live with Soviet-
dominated regimes in eastern Europe, barring a military
confrontation and a possible world war. Vandenberg had
always advocated tough bargaining with the Russians, and
a willingness to compromise (not "appease"). Having
matured from his prewar isolationism, he was not blinded
by ideological zeal, like Bridges, but was capable of intellectual growth. On the other hand, Thomas, although not
quite able to admit the possibility of a natural adversary relationship with the Soviet Union, differed from other noninterventionists in one important respect: his willingness to see
a continuation of colonial influence in Asia. Unlike those
who demanded a prompt and complete imperial evacuation, he saw the need to maintain a colonial power balance
—presumably based, as in tradition, on mutual jealousies,
but given stability by the United Nations framework—to
give orderly form to Asia as her peoples erupted in social
and national revolution. Hence Vandenberg might have
sensitized Thomas to the notion of the conflicting interests
of Russia, which desired a harmless China on its border,
and America, which would gain from a strong and independent China counterbalancing Soviet Asiatic power. And
Thomas might have underscored the permanence and

desirability, from a Chinese viewpoint, of a communist revolution aimed at national dignity, political modernization, and economic innovation.

It is easy to construct a neat scenario in which Vandenberg prevails on the need to balance Soviet power on the Asian land mass, in which Thomas elucidates the futility of attempting to thwart revolution in China, and in which, interacting with other senators and witnesses, they help to create a consensus in favor of a continued diplomatic relationship with Chiang's regime, along with a *de facto* relationship with the Communists in North China, thereby minimizing the dependence of the CCP on Russia while scotching the threat of a military confrontation with Russia in North China and Manchuria. Of course, anything so simple, direct, and complete was in actuality most unlikely in any political debate, let alone in the chaos of a Senate hearing during a foreign policy crisis. This was particularly true in the absence of a host of crucial witnesses necessary to clarify the issues: Stilwell, Service, Davies, Atcheson, Gauss, Forrestal, Patterson, Vincent, Drumright, and others. Yet, at the very least, a dialogue involving Thomas and Vandenberg would have clarified *some* conflicting perceptions and assumptions about the Sino-Russian-American relationship —hopefully enough to compel the calling of expert witnesses who might have explored the issues in more depth. And even if this step were blocked by a reluctant Administration, open senatorial debate on the strength of the Communists, their aims and relationship with Russia, and the need for continued American influence among them, would surely have exposed in a general way some of the issues dividing the American public, Congress, and the policymakers.

It is possible that such a debate would have revealed the ultimate military problem confronting those who would support Nationalist China: the need at some point to intervene massively with American men and arms to save the regime. Such a revelation might conceivably have generated the public support necessary for a military commitment to forestall a Communist victory in China, if convincingly justified by the Administration; but it is far more likely that the revelation would have shown so clearly the public antipathy to intervention as to demonstrate the need for an accommodation with the CCP, and thus discredit pro-Nationalist demands. One thing is clear: a more searching debate would have heightened public understanding of the issues in China as they affected America and Russia, while reducing the impact of uninformed sentiment for or against intervention. It would have helped Americans to assess, as discrete but related phenomena, Soviet diplomacy and the Chinese revolution. It might possibly have defined pragmatically the United States-Chinese Communist relationship before the onset of the Cold War hysteria on both sides. But no such debate occurred. Vandenberg, probing uncertainly, found no contradicting analysis to test or alter his own assumptions, his simple perceptions. By staying silent, Thomas deprived the public of an unusually informative yardstick with which to evaluate the Chinese revolution at a very critical time in the development of Sino-American relations.

V THE GOVERNMENT DEFENSE

Connally and the Public

Among the many Americans who were wrestling with the China problem late in 1945, Tom Connally was one of the most vocal and influential. Disturbed by widespread criticism of America's military commitment in China, he pondered the wisdom of that commitment as the central issue for American policy. Angered by right-wing attacks on the Administration, he ridiculed partisan allegations of disloyalty in the State Department. Coming to define the China question in military terms, he ultimately deprecated underlying political issues, and thus drew apart from his bipartisan associate, Vandenberg. Both senators continued to cooperate in efforts to develop a bipartisan foreign policy generally. But in reacting to a crossfire of criticism, Connally began to defend with mounting righteousness the policy in China which Vandenberg was questioning, and which

Hurley and Bridges were openly attacking.

Connally recalled it all, years later. After the defeat of Japan, conflict had erupted between Chiang's forces and "northern Chinese," competing to fill the Manchurian vacuum "when the Russians . . . finished looting the area and moved out." Connally had "discussed the world-wide menace of this Chinese civil war" with Truman and had urged him to dispatch General Marshall or another "top military figure" in place of Hurley, who "was doing little in China except grumble about his aides." Apprised of Hurley's report that the "northern Chinese were not real revolutionaries in the Russian meaning of the word," but mostly poverty-stricken peasants falling into the "tightly knit Chinese Communist organization" as Chiang and the greedy landlords ignored their needs, Connally had suggested that America "try to reconcile the two groups" in order to create "a solid front" against Russia:

> "If we satisfy the simple economic wants of those fighting . . . Chiang Kai-shek, . . . perhaps they will become less restless and merge into his government. If we don't Chinese Communists may take over all those who oppose the Nationalists and then oust Chiang and his government from China.
>
> "With two Chinese armies facing each other, Marshall would make an ideal emissary because he is such an outstanding military man. If we don't send a peacemaker, we will either have to pull out of China entirely or fight a full-scale war on the side of Chiang Kai-shek's corrupt and reactionary government. This would mean sending an American expeditionary force of more than two million men."

President Truman saw clearly the Chinese dilemma.[1]

160

The Government Defense

Before the outbreak of the China debate, Connally seems to have soured on a cooperative Sino-Russian-American framework for East Asia. Ambiguous about the Chinese Communists, he minimized the depth of their political strength, yet acknowledged the need to conciliate them through negotiation. More explicitly than Vincent's speech of October 20, he envisioned the expansion of dissidents' representation in a coalition regime, and the ultimate erosion of Communist appeal through a broadly based improvement in the Chinese standard of living. Sensitive to the misery of the Chinese population, he hinted that some sort of Chinese New Deal, supported by American aid, might both reform and strengthen the Kuomintang. Although unimpressed with Chiang, he eschewed, like Byrnes and Forrestal, an independent relationship with the CCP. In the absence of a political settlement, he foresaw unpleasant choices for the United States.

Early in November 1945, Connally began to receive a growing volume of complaints about American military involvement in China. Letters and telegrams came from constituents, from other concerned citizens, and especially from G.I.'s, marines, and their relatives. On November 5, a marine sergeant from Dallas, stationed at Tsingtao on the southern coast of the strategic Shantung peninsula, asserted, "I am entitled to know why I am here." Declaring that many marines would appreciate a clarification, he noted:

> We were told when enroute to Tsingtao that we were to assist in the disarming of Japanese troops in this area. Before we arrived, the Chinese had the situation well in hand, and have since gone so far as to re-arm some Japanese units for added protection against Chinese Communist forces. Recently we have been told that the reason for our prolonged visit is to hold the area in lieu of the arrival of General Chiang Kai-shek's Nationalist

161

forces. In other words we are here to protect General Chiang's interests against possible Communist uprisings. Everything we do here points directly or indirectly toward keeping the Chinese Communists subdued.[2]

Stating that he was no communist, but "a Democrat who believes in the republican form of government," he posed three questions: Did not American policy promise liberated peoples "'the opportunity to choose their own form of government once they are liberated'?" How did America "know what form of government is best for China?" And was America "at war with the Chinese Communists?" Deeming "the highly touted point system" of amassing credits for discharge "such a joke to the men in the Pacific, it isn't even worth discussing," he cited the unrest caused by "expeditions of this nature" among servicemen who "should be at home with our families," and he warned lest they be "'used' by interests foreign to our beliefs, for reasons unknown to us or to our people at home."

In the same vein, a marine private stationed in Tientsin, between Peking and the Shantung-Jehol-Manchuria coastline, wrote that "the longer they keep us here, the more trouble," and the likelier a Chinese civil war. Suggesting that if America continued such meddling, "World War III will soon be under way," he warned:

Everybody is getting the Civil War blood in them. First Spain, Russia, Spain again, Java, and now China. If civil war does break and we are still here, what will happen? Will Russia back the Communists, or stay [neutral]? What will the U.S., Britain, France and other countries with interest here do? Can't anybody see what can happen.[3]

Expressing resentment that America was risking "a bloody

world" to protect "some money makers in China," he charged that the Administration was "wasting the best part of my life," while giving the "Stateside boys" and the army personnel all the breaks.

Anxious parents similarly confided their fears to Connally. On November 15, a woman asked: "Why are our Marines in China? Is our country deliberately trying to get us involved in China's civil war? Must more of our sons be sacrificed? If so, for what?" Her son, she stated, a veteran of the Philippine campaign and other Pacific action, was "one of the many pawns being pushed around by our so called Democracy." There was certain "to be 'an incident,'" and as his unit was "in direct line of fire . . . some of them are bound to be killed. All I want to know is *why*!" The same day, a Brooklyn man expressed his "most emphatic disapproval" of America's troop commitment. While the original justification "was most coherent," more recent policy "smacks of imperialism." Pleading with Connally to press for an American evacuation, he asked: "Why should my son's life, and those of thousands of other American boys, be placed in jeopardy, in order to force any particular form of government, down the throats of the Chinese people?"[4]

Along with the letters and wires to the State Department, communications to Connally multiplied. On November 17, an army private stationed in Kyoto, Japan, sent him a news clipping "reporting the use of American transports to move Nationalist troops into Communist held areas of North China":

If transports are available for such purposes it is an insult to our intelligence for veterans like myself with more than 3 years of service and over 20 months in the Pacific to be told that it is only the lack of shipping which delays our return home. The article also gives the lie to the "eyewash" excuse that these Nationalist troops are being

transported into these areas to affect [*sic*] the surrender and disarming of Japanese forces.[5]

The soldier knew "of no American commitment" binding
her to intervene on behalf of one Chinese faction; "from the
Atlantic Charter to Potsdam, we have pronounced our adherence to the principle of self-determination for our allies."
Along the same lines, Connally on November 19 received
from Senator McMahon copies of several telegrams protesting American intervention in China. On November 26, a
Texan noted that "the State and Navy Departments do not
realize the seriousness of the situation in North China"; citing the explanation that "the Marines were there to protect
life and property," he lamented that too many Americans
were "willing to give the lives of someone else's sons for their
companies." The next day, as Hurley was resigning, a Houston woman apprised Connally of her confusion: "We
thought the war was over and we hear that we [are] about
to become involved in a war of intervention in China." The
same day, a Tucson resident queried why America continued its risky commitment "without any public protest"
from Congress, and pointed out that there was "plenty being said from the crossroads, but nothing from high places."
His alarm echoed the sentiments of Connally's other correspondents, most of whom demanded that Congress take action, or that Connally use his influence, to change policy or
at least secure an explanation of current China policy.[6]

As criticism mounted, Connally rapidly froze into a de-
fensive pro-Administration stance. The exact nature of his
relationship with top policymakers, and the degree of influence he wielded with them, are not certain, but he loyally acted as the Administration's Congressional spokesman.
As a member of the bipartisan foreign policy system, he
could be privately candid; before the buildup of public tension, he had pressed "high authorities" to terminate military
intervention—presumably in favor of political mediation to

resolve "the Chinese dilemma." But Washington needed room to maneuver, and had to be spared the controversy which to Connally was understandably but injuriously aroused by America's Asian adventure. So in response to queries, he repeatedly issued throughout late November a lame stock reply. Citing Secretary of War Patterson's assertion that American forces "would not be used in the suppression of civil strife, but would protect American lives and property," he quoted Patterson's assurance that

> there is no danger of our troops becoming involved in civil strife in China unless they are attacked, in which event we may expect the American troops to react with vigor and success.[7]

Inwardly sympathetic with the noninterventionists, Connally responded with venom to the right-wing attack following Hurley's resignation. After Senator Wherry's reiteration of Hurley's allegations on November 28, Connally voiced amazement that Wherry had "so hurriedly swallowed" Hurley's "entire statement." He noted that Hurley's press release "bore evidences of rather mature preparation," despite Hurley's sudden change of heart after assuring Byrnes he would return to China. Alluding to Hurley's denunciation of the DeLacy attack, Connally marveled that "one little speech drives a great Ambassador from his post in China." Between Hurley's indication that he would stay on, and his resignation the next day, Connally wondered aloud, "What happened to him? To whom did he talk? What kind of a conference did he have . . . ?"[8]

Connally was deeply angered by what he regarded as the malicious intent of the Hurley-Wherry accusations. At this time, he and Vandenberg were at pains to get the Administration's ear on atomic energy control and other policies. Only the week before, Connally's cherished bipartisan liaison with the State Department had been strengthened when, at Byrnes's suggestion, Connally had named an eight-member panel from the Foreign Relations Committee to have frequent discussions with the secretary of state, in a resumption of Secretary Hull's wartime practice. With committee members craving information, the new plan was "to keep in touch with Byrnes on the whole range of postwar foreign policy issues"; and, at the first meeting on November 24, Byrnes and the senators had been enthusiastic.[9] Now, the conservative attackers were endangering the delicately engineered consultative system and exploiting a complex diplomatic problem. They were articulating goals in China which seemed totally at variance with the public will to implement them, judging by the pained outcry to bring the boys home.

Furthermore, Hurley had been grossly imprecise in his blanket accusations. Connally noted that Hurley had expressed complete agreement with the policies of Truman and Byrnes, while they had guaranteed the removal of staff members interfering with his work. Essentially, Hurley had found that "there is a clerk or two somewhere in the service who does not agree with him." Never, Connally added, had he pointed out what these "Assistant Secretaries, or clerks, or other subordinates," had done. He was, in Connally's view, "a little ungracious" to resign "in a moment of anger, or pique, and undertake to cover the foreign policy of the United States all over with obloquy and diplomatic slime." In response to Bridges's complaint that he was taking the whole issue too lightly, Connally emphasized that it was "not a frivolous matter," especially in view of the grave world situation; it was, in fact, "no time to interject into our foreign relations matters of political expediency." Assuring Wherry that the Foreign Relations Committee was "entirely competent to conduct any investigation" of the State Department, he agreed, with evident distaste, that the committee would consider Wherry's proposal to appoint a special panel for the purpose. He wanted Hurley to "take the stand, look some of us in the eye and tell us what are these terrible acts of treachery."[10]

In the week which now passed before the first hearing, Connally was subject to a continuing stream of mail condemning American intervention in China. A number of constituents expressed confusion and dissatisfaction. A Washington, D. C. resident argued that traditionally, America had aimed at "the unification of all China and . . . China's administrative and territorial integrity"; but, he concluded, "today we have swerved from that path," becoming instead "the tool of one faction against the other," and pursuing a policy which would help neither to unify nor to strengthen China. At the same time, liberal wrath increasingly transferred to Hurley and his supporters, as the right demanded a more pro-Nationalist posture. A Dallas physician commended Connally's Senate stand against Hurley, wondering aloud "if the former Secretary of War under Hoover" was not "trying to return to the folds of his old [Republican] cronies." A New Yorker warned lest Congress be used as "a springboard to get Hurley named on the GOP ticket for president," and advised Connally to let "him make a fool out of himself—you are a good enough lawyer to know how to tangle him up." A Pennsylvania physician, partially paralyzed from a stroke, agonized for an entire day in writing longhand to Connally, but summoned up the humor to dismiss Hurley as "the comic opera general— major or minor." A St. Paul man urged that the committee summon Stilwell and former Ambassador Gauss, "who probably know far more about China, than does a typical GOP politician like Hurley, who I suspect aims to embarrass our kindly President Mr. Truman." And a Wichita resident, having lived in Hurley's home town of Tulsa, revealed that "Brother Hurley speaks for the Vatican and our big industrialists only. All people who disagree with his views are 'Communists.'"[11]

At the same time, several people cited Hurley's rumored

connections with the oil industry at home and abroad. His highly successful representation of the Sinclair oil interests in Mexico during the late 1930s was well known. But a letter from Senator William Langer (Republican, North Dakota) to the State Department in June 1945, probing the relationship of Hurley's China and Middle Eastern policies to the wartime payments he continued to receive from Sinclair, merely portended the lurid accusations now crossing Connally's desk. On December 1, an old campaign aide informed Connally that Hurley's effort to undermine public confidence in the Administration presaged a drive for the Republican presidential nomination or for secretary of state, with the goal of influencing oil policy. The same day, another man hinted that Hurley and Sinclair had secured questionable oil concessions in Alaska, Iran, Iraq, and Ethiopia. Two days later, a Mississippian suggested that Hurley had been attending primarily to Sinclair's interests "while in China."[12]

Like Connally, these people perceived in Hurley's actions an opportunistic effort to deflect American diplomacy. They wanted the Administration to fight back; and they were concerned more with the impact of American intervention in China than with the convoluted motives of junior diplomats there. The crippled Pennsylvania physician wrote that "the Kuomintang which Hurley & Wedemeyer are supporting consist of a Chinese Tory element worse than . . . the British crowd." Urging that Stilwell, "kicked out of China by Chiang," be brought back to testify, he chided:

> Disarming the Japs does not constitute the use of air service to transport troops from we will say Republican Chinese to fight Democratic Chinese —or permitting the Republican Chinese a gift of 3000 planes.[13]

Along the same lines, a San Antonio woman asserted that

Hurley's "high-handedness" both with the Chinese factions and with his subordinates had "prevented the citizens of this country from receiving a clear picture of the problems in China." Asking Connally to investigate and publicize Hurley's record, she pressed for a cutoff "of military personnel, supplies and advisors" to all Chinese factions. Another critic urged that "the vast differences of opinion" within "the upper strata of the State Department" be explored, especially "the reasoning behind those differences."[14]

Even as anti-Hurley opinion waxed strong, Connally began to receive, for the first time, a groundswell of communications endorsing Hurley's cause. Bridges, Wherry, Dondero, and other ideologues had struck a responsive chord in the American mind; as Connally had feared, the conservative assault on China policy was gathering momentum. On November 29, a Houston man explained that "[t]he 'explosion' has met with universal approval," and commended to Connally an editorial citing Hurley's action as "a great service to the country." Two days later, a Galveston businessman warned that "[t]o side step charges made by a representative of our government occupying the position that General Hurley did and to ridicule the charges makes the public all the more suspicious." On November 29, a Marylander termed Connally's reaction "cheap" and "contemptible," declaring that his direction of "any inquiry into General Hurley's charges, would be a farce, since you are so obviously biased." The same day, a Kansan ex-marine urged that "some of you professional politicians . . . break away from the bondage of public opinion."[15]

Linked to these criticisms of Connally was a warm response to Hurley, in contrast to the cynical, exploitative image of the general reflected in noninterventionist letters. A Michigander praised Hurley as "an *honest* American." Someone else explained:

When a man like Gen. Hurley becomes fed up

with run-arounds, buck passing, Etc. far into the night, and pent up emotion becomes too great, nature has provided him with a soft plug to blow out, just as a boiler is provided with the same thing for the same purpose. Perhaps if you had been a soldier before politics took hold of you, you'd better understand his natural reactions.[16]

A self-styled "Kentuckian-Texan" lauded Hurley's "truly magnificent service to America, China, and the whole allied cause—much greater than we may know until the future of China is secured." On November 30, the *Tulsa Tribune* ran an editorial—which duly found its way to Connally—boosting Hurley for president, as the man who had "given the State Department a sock in the jaw it needs," doing "more in the last half dozen days to bring our government back to American principles and practices than has been done by any man since Franklin Roosevelt went into the White House a dozen years ago." Soon thereafter, Hugh Grant, the former diplomat cited by Bridges at the ensuing hearings, sent Connally his article corroborating Hurley's charges on the basis of his own experience in Thailand, and terming the accusations "a distinct public service in revealing the obstructionist tactics of American Foreign Service 'career' officers in the Far East and State Department."[17]

The other Hurley backers all seemed to agree with Grant's dim view of the Foreign Service. "Doubtless," one wrote to Connally, "there is something radically wrong in the State Department." Another termed the continued employment "of this pack of communist-minded officials" by the Department "positively dangerous," and asserted that "[t]hese traitorous officials . . . are causing trouble in China, Korea, England, and in other countries." The *Tulsa Tribune* announced that Hurley had abandoned high office so "that the public might know who the little un-American, foreign-minded members of our Congress and the State

Department are," and might understand "the subtle intrigues and the timidities of our State Department [which] are laying the fagots for a third world conflagration."[18]

Nor were the fears of the Hurley sponsors confined to foreign affairs. A Michigander sought "to establish the *truth* that America is filling up with dirty Communists"—in the C.I.O., in white collar jobs, and in Washington—and he pressed for legislation to bar Communists from government employment. The Kentuckian-Texan raged against union racketeers, "the communist press," infiltrators into radio and government, and other "double-crossing skunks." Fearing that "poison propaganda" was "polluting our system of government, our schools and free enterprise," he warned Connally:

> American citizens are, as you well know, getting very, very tired of being pushed around by Communist agitators who are fomenting strikes in every part of our country and promoting "jurisdictional" strikes, C.I.O., F.E.P.C., street car strikes, elevator strike, telephone strike, "Teamsters under Tobin" strikes, bus strikes, auto workers' strikes, steamship strikes, milk delivery strikes, and what have you?[sic][19]

A newspaper charged that for the previous twelve years,

> the men who made the wheels of industry go round have been looked upon with suspicion by a business incompetent in the White House. Gullible citizens have been taught by the small-minded New Deal politicians that anyone is a foe of society who labors [through business enterprise] to pave the pathway of progress.[20]

Another critic, generalizing from Connally's behavior to the

171

overall domestic political climate, wrote that there existed "entirely too much selfish interest shown by many of our officials," and not enough emphasis on "fair representation without personal prejudice."[21]

Commenting to Connally on China, these anticommunists displayed a profound mistrust of Russian activities. One man, lamenting reports "of Russian officers ordering American officers out of occupied sections of China at gunpoint," while the Soviet Union "stripped Manchuria" and other regions, insisted that America firmly tell Russia "exactly what we expect of her." Another critic asserted that "Communist agitators" had taken advantage of the misery of the Sino-Japanese war to foment "dissension among the millions of Chinese citizens," who ultimately were "absorbed" into the CCP:

> The pattern they use is that displayed by Russia in her war against Finland, Poland, Roumania, and her present course now in China, where she applies a little variation in the approach—but the result to the conquered peoples is the same—their liberty is lost, their country occupied and pillaged, many of them put in prison, starved in concentration camps or murdered by wholesale —all too horrible for the free American citizen to contemplate.[22]

And as an Oklahoma merchant simply put it, America ought "to do what we can to stop the Communists in China and to let Russia know we are getting tired of their tactics."[23]

In tension with mounting noninterventionist and liberal criticism of American China policy, Connally's correspondence in the immediate aftermath of Hurley's resignation reflected a simultaneous and deeply troubled reaction among conservatives to American policies, foreign and domestic. Events at home and abroad were repugnant to the values of individual enterprise, capitalist economy, and political freedom as they understood them, values which they associated with a probusiness environment at home and with an unwavering support of pro-Western regimes around the world. The conservative reaction to the China crisis thus involved a virtual transference of long-standing domestic grievances to foreign policy issues, for the people whose words reached Connally seemed genuinely to sense a merging of dangers to America. Resentments seething since the apparent leftward drift of American politics in the 1930s were generalized, as America emerged from the greatest armed victory in her history only, it seemed, to permit communism and socialism unprecedented global opportunities. Conservatives felt that the fabric of their society was being destroyed by pervasive influences. It was easy for them to believe that an allegedly "soft" China policy stemmed from Communist infiltration of the State Department.

For the whole world—and now, especially for China—conservative observers urged upon Connally a much stronger American policy against communist revolution as an arm of Russian expansion. Assuming that China was a stake in a larger, Soviet-American struggle, they ascribed to the support of Chiang a symbolic significance transcending Chinese affairs and decisively affecting world politics. Differing with Hurley's assessment of Soviet good faith, but in line with most leading conservative politicians, they mistrusted Russia's intentions and they wanted her called every step of the way; yet they glossed over Hurley's great aberration from conservative orthodoxy regarding Russia, while echoing his attack upon subversion, which strongly reinforced their own ideological zeal and aggressive nationalism. Since they viewed the world in an ideological context, Hurley's trust of Stalin seemed less important than his abhorrence of communism.

In one important respect, however, both liberals and conservatives were alike: all were avowedly puzzled by recent

events, and all craved more information about China and
an explanation of American policy there. The demand from
all sides for a clarification was legitimate; for there was considerable confusion regarding Administration attitudes
toward China, Russia, and world communism. The public
perception of American interests was very hazy. Thus
Hurley's supporters echoed his detractors in calling upon
Connally to conduct a "full, fair examination" and to "have
it out in the open."[24]

Connally was surely alert to the need for a clarification of
American interests in China, in line with American will
power and military strength. A veteran of interwar neutrality debates and of wartime efforts to legitimize the United
Nations concept in the minds of Americans, he was sensitive
to the need for public support and understanding in the
making of successful bipartisan foreign policy. The confusion and emotionalism of his mail undoubtedly troubled
him. And, fearing the implications of a massive military
commitment in China, he naturally reacted hotly to conservative leaders' demands that America more stoutly cham-
pion Chiang's cause. But the reasons for his terse stock reply
to those seeking an American withdrawal from China were
more complex. They lay in the continuing development of
Administration perceptions and policies regarding China,
and in the difficult role which Connally was beginning to
play as Administration spokesman in the Senate against attacks on China policy both from the left and from the right.

The Discrediting of Hurley

Until Hurley quit, the State Department orchestrated its
policy defenses exclusively to counter noninterventionist complaints. It clarified the general tenets delineated in its *Policy
Manual* statement on China circulated internally in mid-
November, and publicized in Vincent's speech of October

20. In a letter prepared under Drumright's direction on November 23, initialed by Vincent, and sent out under Byrnes's signature a week later, the department responded to a Congressional inquiry about China. For the most part, the letter reproduced almost verbatim the *Policy Manual's* call for Chinese unity, democracy, and economic development within a Far Eastern framework of great power collaboration. But more firmly than the manual, it insisted that "China solve her internal problems . . . largely through her own efforts." Written at the height of Administration uncertainty and internal debate, the letter was an obvious effort to reaffirm the traditional goals expressed both in the *Policy Manual* and in the Vincent speech, while allaying fears of American intervention in China. Yet in an atmosphere of growing national anxiety, a more explicit justification seemed necessary. So at the same time, a different answer was composed to another Congressional query. Approved by Drumright, Vincent and Byrnes, this letter contained the germ of the Administration's argument in forthcoming statements: that since the Japanese surrender, American marines and G.I.'s had been in China primarily to aid in disarming and repatriating more than one million Japanese armed forces in China, in accordance with the Potsdam Agreement of August 1945, and for the related, incidental purposes of assisting American and allied war prisoners and civilians, protecting American property, and aiding the Chinese to restore "transportation, the public utilities and other essential public services in a number of Chinese cities, such as Shanghai, Tientsin and Peiping." The letter echoed Wedemeyer's claim that all American forces "not needed for the reoccupation program or for closing out of installations" were being repatriated as quickly as possible, including more than sixteen thousand in September alone; it added that the marines would "be withdrawn from north China, where there are in excess of 300,000 Japanese soldiers, when Chinese forces have been deployed

to that area to relieve our men"; and it disavowed any "intention . . . to become involved in the internal affairs of China." Enclosed with this and with subsequent letters in defense of China policy was a copy of the Vincent speech.[25]

Hurley's bombshell sent shock waves through a State Department already besieged about American intervention in China. The Chungking embassy was "in an uproar," with suppressed animosities erupting amidst widespread confusion over events in Washington. From Tokyo, Service and Atcheson sent Byrnes angry refutations of charges that they were procommunist, in league with the imperialist bloc, or ever had connived with the CCP to wreck Hurley's policy. At the top of the Administration, the response to Hurley was rapid and effective. To be sure, the news of his attack, coming during a weekly Cabinet luncheon on November 27, caught everybody by surprise, for Truman and Byrnes had found him ready to return to his post in conversations only hours earlier. But in the ensuing deliberations, all enthusiastically agreed to the suggestion by Secretary of Agriculture Clinton Anderson that the prestigious General Marshall be tapped, to "take the headlines away from" Hurley; and the consensus developed that Marshall "would make an able ambassador." After Marshall had agreed to go to China and his forthcoming mission had been announced, the State Department took heart that the new appointment "has gone over very well." Indeed, an aide suggested that at his next press conference, Byrnes might "comment in the light vein" about Hurley's "contradictory statements" that the Foreign Service was supporting imperialism and communism in the Far East at the same time.[26] But, like the noninterventionist criticism, the Hurley furor could not be calmed by reassurance or ridicule. Demands for an investigation of his claims by men like Bridges and Wherry made Hurley a formidable political force. The Truman Administration relied on Connally to plead its case in the Senate forum.

To Connally, the demand by the right to be heard was an

intrusion. He was absorbed with atomic energy control, the prospective British loan, the Palestine issue, and the consultations preparatory to the Moscow Conference. But the nation was buzzing with the China issue. Connally read editorials criticizing as long overdue the recent disclosure by Byrnes that the United States had been secretly committed to help in the repatriation of the large Japanese armies still in China, and not merely to facilitate the Japanese surrender, as the State Department had maintained for months. "Our policy in China," claimed the *Washington Post*, "would be as plain as the Constitution if all the relevant facts and circumstances had been forthcoming." Similarly, Connally kept a running tab on speeches and resolutions in Congress pertaining to China and the Hurley charges during the week following November 26.[27] Before long, in response to the national furor and the widespread resentment against governmental secrecy, Connally scheduled public sessions to gather testimony from Hurley and others. He did so undoubtedly with much resentment. Reflecting the Administration's viewpoint, he regarded the craving for open hearings as partly misguided, partly cynical. To debate publicly the fragile coalition program which Washington was trying to implement in China would embarrass the Administration and undermine its credibility with the Kuomintang, the CCP, and Russia. To pressure, cajole, and threaten the Chinese factions into a unified regime, Marshall would need confidentiality and faithful public support—an acquiescence in secrecy and military manipulation which no longer seemed forthcoming.

Having no choice now but to face the China issue, Connally studied the comments of informed analysts whose judgments fortified his belief in the righteousness of America's policy. In Walter Lippmann's column, he read that "the horrid dilemma" in China was explicable "only in light of the military facts." With some 59,000 marines still in North China, Lippmann reasoned that America faced three alternatives: to help Chiang occupy and defend the region in an outright and open-ended intervention against the Communists; to undertake the repatriation of the 325,000 Japanese troops there, thus leaving "strategic centers" open to Communist occupation, and setting the stage "for a protracted and indecisive civil war" inimical to Chinese independence and territorial integrity; or, as Roosevelt, Hurley, the China hands, and all others "who understood the Chinese problem" had agreed all along, "to mediate a peace between Chiang and his Chinese opponents." The tactical debate which had raged on the means to this common end, Lippmann dismissed as "academic," in light of the military problem now occasioned by the continued Japanese presence in China. On the other hand, Connally read an article by Mark Gayn—one of the six *Amerasia* suspects—emphasizing the profound differences between Hurley, supporting the Chiang "clique," and the brilliant China hands who had endured risk and hardship in gathering valuable information "far afield," before Hurley discarded them for criticizing the Kuomintang. Similarly, Eric Sevareid, whose commentary on the controversy Connally kept, cited the prescience of the China hands in predicting civil war, in contrast with Hurley's obtuseness in denouncing their reports "as Communist propaganda." According to Sevareid, these men had argued from no basic belief in Marxism, but from the conviction that the CCP "was far too strong to be ignored or liquidated except after years of tragic civil war"; and he pointed out that they "were in thorough agreement with Stilwell," who, although admiring the Communists, never had suggested that the CCP be "given top control" in a coalition, as Hurley accused the China hands of advocating.[28]

If not to Lippmann, then to Gayn and Sevareid, the Hurley-career service rift was of the gravest importance. Hurley's tactics, they felt, tended to divide the Chinese, embolden Chiang, foment war, and either involve the United States militarily or defeat America's objective of a strong, united China. In contrast to Vandenberg, they regarded Hurley's deference to Chiang, and not the China hands' proposed concessions to the CCP, with alarm. It remained to be seen how Connally would utilize their insights. But for the time being, he kept in close touch with Byrnes, who was to join with him in a coordinated defense of the State Department and China policy at the forthcoming hearings. He wrote to Byrnes on December 5, submitting a list of materials desired from the department by Hurley for use before the Foreign Relations Committee, and asking Byrnes's advice "as to what documents can properly be released and which should be not so treated." The two men very likely plotted their strategy, either in person or by telephone, and it was decided to have Byrnes testify in answer to Hurley's charges. In the interim, Connally closely followed Byrnes's current comments, as reported in the press and in a preliminary copy of Byrnes's remarks at the hearings. In these comments, Byrnes contradicted Hurley's accusations against the Administration and the Foreign Service; defended the diplomat's right (indeed duty) to express dissent "within proper channels"; reaffirmed America's stated goal of a united China and a cooperative great power relationship in the Far East; declared that the solution of China's problems depended "primarily on . . . the Chinese leaders themselves"; and asserted that America clearly supported the Nationalist regime, yet intended no military intervention in Chinese domestic politics.[29]

It is clear that Byrnes continued to place his hopes in a Communist-Kuomintang accommodation, and especially in a joint Soviet-American policy to facilitate such an accommodation. Looking to the forthcoming meeting of the American, British, and Soviet foreign ministers at Moscow, he confided to Harriman on December 1 that he hoped to discuss, among other things, the operation in Japan of the Far Eastern Commission which so troubled Stalin, the establishment of an independent Korean government, the "[d]isarming and evacuating [of] the Japanese from northern China," and the "[t]ransfer of control of Manchuria to [the] Chinese National Government." Trying to overcome the reluctance of the British to discuss items of interest to China and France in the absence of those countries' representatives, Byrnes argued on December 4 that "China's greatest hope lies in the possibility of agreement between the U.S., Great Britain and the Soviet Union, and therefore China would not offer complaint." Perhaps, as he and Forrestal had envisioned on November 27, the Americans could "lay their cards on the table," explaining the need for temporary military operations in North China to sustain Chiang's occupation, and enlisting Soviet aid in securing a Nationalist occupation of Manchuria, as suggested by the Soviet treaty pledge to support Chiang's government.[30] In anticipation of an international settlement in China, Byrnes therefore walked a tightrope at home, reacting to the conflicting winds of public opinion and striving to justify the balance between intervention in a civil war and utter abandonment of the Chinese Nationalists.

In a similar fashion, Connally sought to damp the controversy which seemed to threaten the settlement sought by the Administration. On December 5, he assured numerous marines, soldiers, and their families that "I am doing all I can toward the speedy return of our boys from overseas." The same day, he wrote to others that American forces apparently "have been withdrawn from the battle area," and would not intervene in the raging factional struggle. If these messages were terse and somewhat dated in comparison with contemporaneous State Department explanations, it is not surprising; for Connally was simultaneously emerging as the primary Administration spokesman against those who demanded still more aid for Chiang, and was preparing for his upcoming confrontation with Hurley.[31]

At the public sessions of his committee, Connally was mean and unrelenting in cross-examining Hurley,

browbeating him for facts and hounding him for inconsistencies. Time and again, tempers flared and egos clashed
in an atmosphere of undisguised hostility. Connally spat
sarcasm, and Hurley bellowed against his humiliating
bullying. By pressing Hurley to the limit and by eliciting
clarifications from Byrnes and others through friendly inter-
rogation, Connally publicly discredited Hurley's poorly
thought out charges against the State Department and
American China policy.

In a series of leading questions, Connally forced Hurley to
acknowledge the strong record of American aid to China.
"You say, 'Give help to Chiang Kai-shek,'" Connally
chided; "did we not send over the Hump a constant stream
of arms and ammunition, with aviators flying 19,000 or
20,000 feet, to aid the Chinese armies, carrying supplies to
them?" Hurley had to agree. "Did we not have General
Chennault out there in the Air Corps," Connally continued,
and "General Stilwell aiding the Chinese by organizing
their armies"? Hurley concurred that both soldiers had done
"brilliant work"; and he was quick to emphasize that it was
the middle-level career diplomats, rather than the top policymakers who favored a Nationalist downfall. In fact,
Connally was well aware of Hurley's repeated expressions of
agreement with the broad outlines of the Truman-Byrnes
foreign policy. Hurley's point was that American policy
around the world was being subverted by disloyal career
diplomats in Washington and in the field; his quarrel with
the Administration lay in its alleged failure to enunciate its
China policy publicly, to support him against disloyal subordinates, and to eliminate those subordinates from influential posts in the Far Eastern policy field.[32] So Connally spent
most of his energy in trying to refute these allegations.

Connally doggedly sought to demonstrate the fundamen-
tal unity of objectives among American policymakers and
China hands over the preceding year. At the first session,
Hurley reaffirmed that his directive from Roosevelt to

prevent a Nationalist collapse, sustain the Chinese war effort against Japan, and restore Sino-American harmony had been undermined by career men who had "continuously advised" the CCP, "recommended in my absence" that the Communists be armed, and "charged me with making my own policy in China." Quickly establishing that this had taken place during the war, Connally got Hurley to admit that his instructions had included the creation of a joint Communist-Kuomintang effort against Japan. Connally then suggested that the provision to Mao of lend-lease equipment had been envisioned as bait for Communist support of Chiang's regime. When Hurley adduced the Atcheson report of the previous February as evidence that "the entire embassy" had opposed his policy, Connally had him confirm that Atcheson had used "all of my arguments for unification"—even though the real aim of "everybody" on the staff had been to "destroy" the Nationalists all along. When Connally later asked him point-blank whether the career men "were working for the *purpose* of fighting Chiang Kai-shek and destroying his government," Hurley termed such an interpretation "a little strained," and preferred to hedge that "the *effect*" of arming the CCP would have been a Nationalist collapse. Having won his point, Connally still later commented to Byrnes that there was no apparent difference between Hurley's and Atcheson's objectives—the uniting of Chinese forces to fight Japan—but merely a difference in the method of implementing their common goal. When Byrnes agreed, but cautioned that the difference in method was "serious," Connally ignored the distinction. Capitalizing on the offer of numerous China correspondents to have one of their number testify in defense of the China hands, he had Theodore White come down from New York. Connally asked White whether the policy of Hurley, the president, the secretary of state, "and of everybody" had been to secure a factional union to fight Japan; whether such a policy made it "quite appropriate" to supply the Communists with lend-lease for the war effort; and whether "all of our representatives out there, supposedly, including General Hurley, and the State Department, here," had explicitly favored such a policy. White emphatically agreed.[33]

In focusing like Walter Lippmann on the military circumstances defining a common American policy objective in China, Connally looked back to the wartime weakness of Chiang's armies and the universally accepted necessity of utilizing Chinese Communist power against Japan. Notwithstanding the comments of Eric Sevareid, Mark Gayn, Hurley, and even Byrnes, he downplayed the serious differences in tactics favored by Hurley and the China hands within the larger consensus on wartime objectives. Along the same lines—and contrary to the views of Bridges and Vandenberg—Connally tried to demonstrate the strength of support given Hurley in executing American policy by the Roosevelt and Truman Administrations. Asked whether he had not, while ambassador, received information "outlining the policy in China," and whether he had understood the State Department's position, Hurley complained that there had been no public statement to counteract his subordinates' subversion; but under Connally's questioning, he admitted that he had no differences with Truman's China policy and that, in conference with Byrnes on November 27, he had agreed to return to Chungking. Later, Connally suggested to Byrnes the danger of issuing periodic public "statements with regard to all the different governments of the earth"; and Byrnes agreed that it was "utterly impractical and unwise to do it."[34]

Connally sought also to refute Hurley's accusations of sabotage against the Foreign Service, and hence to shatter his credibility. He got Hurley to concur that "these subordinates in the State Department, with all their endeavors," had failed to destroy his policy. He repeatedly challenged Hurley to substantiate the assertion that the China hands

had "continuously advised the Communists" against interpreting his policy as the American policy; and Hurley
responded only with citations of leaked information and
anti-Nationalist reporting. When Hurley mentioned John
Service's report of October 30, 1944, "a general statement of
how to let the government that I was sent over there to sustain fall," Connally drew from him the admission that Service had not been in his charge at the time, but had been on
General Wedemeyer's staff. Connally similarly had Byrnes
confirm that the dissenting Atcheson telegram had properly
suggested that Hurley and Wedemeyer, then in Washington, be consulted about its recommendations. When Vandenberg criticized Atcheson's action, Connally argued that
in Hurley's absence, Atcheson had been acting ambassador;
that things in China "were moving pretty rapidly . . . in
February"; and that it had not been inappropriate for Atcheson to suggest "a modification not of the objectives but of
the methods" used to secure crucial Chinese Communist
assistance.[35] Finally, Connally gave Theodore White a
forum for a ringing defense of the Foreign Service. Speaking
for a number of China correspondents, White told of his in-
timate relationship with the China hands under hardship
conditions. Declaring that these men had "zealously
fought" to achieve the common American goal of a united,
democratic China, he termed it impossible "for any member
of the press in Chungking to be unaware of any conspiracy
or of any attempt to sabotage Ambassador Hurley." Never,
he added, had they conveyed the impression that they,
rather than Hurley, were right about China policy:

> We were never all there at any one time, but all of
> us know the people who are under attack, and we
> wanted a chance to proclaim in public our faith in
> their loyalty and in their honesty and in their good
> service for our government. That is, we feel that
> these men who underwent hardship, were really

ordered into danger by our Government, should
not be hauled up in public and so attacked without somebody speaking in their defence. They did
work for our Government, which I believe was
finer intelligence work than the organization of
any other foreign country. It was magnificent
work.[36]

In yet another line of attack, Connally sought to show
that Hurley had diverged from the highly respected Stilwell
on wartime policy. "Did you not," he inquired, "have a
break with General Stilwell over the policies with regard to
the Communist army?" He asked if "the division of opinion"
had been "rather sharp," enough so "to get General Stilwell
out of China"; and he wondered whether Stilwell "had
aided in sabotaging" Hurley by advocating a factional unification in fighting against Japan. Hurley denied any such
rupture, and warned Connally not to "get me in any conflict with General Stilwell." He insisted that, with Chinese
armies in retreat, and the ally on the verge of collapse, he
had been sent to China to stem the tide and that, "in order
to bring about harmony whereby we could cooperate with
the Chinese Government, a fine officer who was incompati-
ble [temperamentally with Chiang] was relieved." There
was, Hurley continued, no disagreement regarding the
Communist armies, for in two and one-half years in China
controlling lend-lease, Stilwell had not given the CCP any
supplies. Furthermore, Stilwell had advocated a united
front against Japan, just as Hurley had; he could not have
sabotaged Hurley, as "[m]y policy was not well under way"
while Stilwell had been in China. "[W]e have never had a
controversial word between us," Hurley concluded.[37]
So, while Connally effectively interrogated Hurley and
others to shed doubt on Hurley's charges against the Foreign
Service, he failed to establish any rift between Hurley and
his predecessor and temporary colleague in China, Stilwell.

Indeed, this latter line of questioning was totally at odds with the larger thrust of Connally's probing—that the entire State Department had been encouraging a factional coalition under Chiang, first to defeat Japan and later to unify China in peacetime; and that differences in tactics had been incidental until blown all out of proportion by Hurley. Nothing better exemplifies the muddled thinking and partisan dissimulation surrounding American China policy than the paradox of Connally denying the existence of any serious governmental dissension on China, yet probing Hurley on a very serious difference with Stilwell about the CCP; while Hurley, who had based his whole indictment on the fundamental governmental rifts on China, denied the existence of any divergence between himself and the popular, outspoken Stilwell, who long had held Chiang in contempt.

By this time, certainly, Connally was not being very honest with the public, and perhaps with himself. In order to parry the conservative attack on the Administration, he probed Hurley's inconsistencies, in part by minimizing State Department disagreement over China, even though his questions about Hurley and Stilwell, his reading of Sevareid and Gayn, and his own letters and memoirs indicate his perception of dilemmas and policy rifts regarding American relations with the Chinese factions. He surely understood that total support for a Kuomintang suppression of the CCP, as advocated by some, differed critically from formulas for the radical reorganization or eclipse of the Kuomintang as espoused by others. Yet, unlike Vandenberg, he tried to paper over these issues in an effort to allow American policy to unfold within the prudent, semiprivate framework of bipartisan consultations. A continued public debate on China, it seemed, would only encourage further damaging partisan attacks. So, instead of hearing expert testimony from Gauss, Stilwell, Atcheson, and others in order to explicate the dilemmas dividing American policymakers, he came down to the level of Bridges and Wherry, indulging in the personal discrediting of Hurley and the further clouding of the major issues in China. It is ironic, and perhaps inevitable, that, acting from devotion to the painstakingly constructed bipartisan foreign policy system and responding to the corrosive right-wing attack piled on top of rumbling noninterventionist discontent, he helped to smother the constructive public debate which was the hallmark of bipartisanship's vitality and success.

Yet Connally was merely reacting to the pressure created by the partisan attack of ultraconservative Republicans. Hurley and his supporters had a long jump on Connally in muddling the pertinent issues. In smearing those who emphasized the need to deal with the Chinese Communists, they precluded a reasoned evaluation of the relative merits and strengths of the Chinese factions, of Soviet aims in the Far East, and of the alternatives for American policy. When they impugned the integrity and loyalty of Chiang's detractors, the chance for a healthy debate was lost in an emotional uproar, a red herring.

Through Connally the Administration exposed to ridicule Hurley's indiscriminate and ill-informed charges. To be sure, the national concern over China persisted during the course of the hearings (December 5 through 10); and Hurley's supporters continued to defend him against Connally's taunts, while vocalizing their suspicions about America's diplomats. But the tide was running against the anticommunist ideologues. December 6 was the date that the State Department analyzed its incoming mail for a cross-section of opinion, finding a widespread and practically unanimous protest against American intervention in China. And, while pro-Hurley letters to the highly visible Connally during the hearings numbered less than ten, dozens of people conveyed to him their support against Hurley and their continued insistence that America extricate herself from China. It appeared that Hurley had aroused as much hostility toward himself as toward the State

Department, while generating as much backlash support as negative criticism of Connally and the Administration. He drew much of the wrath of noninterventionist critics who earlier had focused more generally on the Administration.[38]

Yet the mails indicated, if anything, an upsurge in curiosity about events in China. Those who resented Connally's browbeating of Hurley demanded a complete, unbiased investigation of Hurley's charges; and those who were skeptical of the charges urged that acknowledged experts and the accused diplomats be permitted to rebut Hurley publicly. An uneasy confusion persisted.[39] But, with the single exception of Theodore White, who refuted claims of Foreign Service disloyalty, Connally called on no one with special knowledge of China to testify. With the debate limited to Hurley's assertions and the Connally-Byrnes refutations, discussion remained on a vague and personal level.

Connally was relieved by the outcome of the hearings, confident in the public discreditation of Hurley, and insensitive to the frustration of the public's demand for a more searching probe than he had provided. On December 17, he explained to an editor who had urged the summoning of Stilwell that Hurley's allegations "were so exploded that it was unnecessary to pursue the inquiry further." The same day, he gloated to an old friend: "Pat's fiasco did not confer any credit upon him. All we had to do was let him rave." Indeed, it did seem, to Connally's mind, that the hearings and publicity had thoroughly fulfilled their purpose. With Hurley refuted and the esteemed George Marshall about to undertake a mission to unify China, it appeared that the debate and the change in command had achieved a catharsis of sorts. If not satisfied, the American people were at least talked out, and tension over China seemed to ease. The flood of letters to Connally dropped off to a small trickle after the hearings had ended. From December 11 through New Year's came dying echoes of noninterventionist thunder.[40]

The Government Defense

Similarly, the tide of noninterventionist complaints to the State Department had virtually spent itself by the end of the hearings. Organized pressure, it is true, did not completely abate. On December 17, the Committee for a Democratic Far Eastern Policy sent to Truman a petition signed by three thousand people, deploring America's military presence in disputed areas of China as "military intervention . . . in the internal affairs of a friendly power," and warning that a continued presence might cause further American casualties. The petition urged that the United States "immediately withdraw" from China, "stop abetting one side against the other in the Chinese civil war," and "stop the use of American Lend-Lease or other equipment to kill any Chinese." And on December 23, a committee member wrote to Acheson in response to Administration claims that the Chiang regime afforded the "best basis for developing democracy in China." He warned that "democracy has not arrived," that "Chiang and some of his unsocially minded colleagues" would avoid "real concessions" unless prodded, and that "our influence must be clear, practical, and effective, to get those concessions without which a democratic China is impossible." But other communications were sparse. Even more suddenly than the public furor over China had arisen a month earlier, it died down in December.[41]

Basis of the Marshall Mission

Throughout December 1945, as the nation's interest in China rose, peaked, and ebbed, the Truman Administration laid the foundations of the new mission which had been only vaguely defined at the time Hurley resigned. In two hectic weeks following his acceptance of the assignment on November 27, Marshall joined with Byrnes, Truman, aides from the State and War Departments, and officers from the Army and Navy General Staff to hammer out a public letter from Truman to Marshall, a public statement, a private directive to Marshall, a memorandum to the War Department, and an oral understanding, together comprising the announced and confidential methods and objectives defining Marshall's forthcoming effort. Even now, China did not monopolize the Administration's attention, for other issues continued to make demands. Byrnes, imminently to depart for the Moscow Conference, and Truman faced leading senators from the Foreign Relations and Atomic Energy Committees (Connally among them) who were upset by alleged plans for sharing atomic energy information with Russia prior to the establishment of effective international safeguards, while Marshall consumed valuable days in testifying before yet another Congressional committee, which was investigating the Pearl Harbor attack.[42] But meetings and draftings proceeded apace, as disagreements were resolved and a new China policy formulated.

Conferring with Byrnes on November 28 and 29, Marshall received a memorandum prepared by Vincent, following the main lines indicated by Byrnes and Acheson at the State-War-Navy meeting of November 27. The memorandum emphasized America's willingness to assist the Nationalists in transporting troops to ports in Manchuria and in effecting a rapid demobilization and repatriation of Japanese troops in North China, with the direct aid of the marines stationed there. But it rejected any American intervention in Chinese politics, and called for a factional truce, "accompanied by the immediate convocation of a national conference to seek and find a peaceful solution of China's present internal strife." Asserting that America was committed to Chinese unity, stability, and democracy, it called for a broadening of the Nationalist Government to include "other political elements," a dissolution of autonomous armies like that of the Communists, and the integration of Communist forces into the Nationalist army upon the institution of representative government. Washington, it concluded, would request London and Moscow to reaffirm their commitment to such a policy, and would give advisory and financial aid toward Chinese economic and military rehabilitation.[43]

Finding the Vincent memorandum "susceptible of serious misunderstanding," Marshall on November 30 rewrote and tightened it, with the aid of the Army General Staff. In further criticisms, the State Department proposed that Nationalist troops not be transported to North China when such movements "would prejudice the objectives of the military truce and the political negotiations." The army in turn warned that in light of America's diminishing ability to assist in troop transportation, the Communists would have an interest in delaying a truce or settlement if America imposed such limits on its sea and air lift; that the transportation program was essential to Japanese repatriation; that the Manchurian situation might not "await the outcome of Chinese internal negotiations"; and that if the repatriation plan was to materialize, "then operational arrangements must go forward now." The army also counseled that the disbandment of autonomous armies must precede or coincide with (not follow) the establishment of representative government "in a country which has never had an election."[44]

In the end, these issues were left to Marshall's discretion, pending his arrival in China. But more fundamental was the debate on policy options in the event Marshall failed to secure "a conference by Chinese leaders and a cessation of hostilities." On December 9, Vincent suggested to Byrnes that if the failure were "clearly due to" Communist noncooperation, "we should proceed to assist the Chinese in transporting troops to North China," notwithstanding the risk of civil war; and that if failure resulted from Chiang's "stubbornness," American troops should rapidly evacuate the Japanese from that region, making necessary "arrangements with the Chinese Communist troops," and permitting a Communist occupation of recently evacuated communication lines.

The next day, asked by Marshall what to do if the Communists made reasonable concessions while the Nationalists stood rigid, Byrnes replied that economic and military aid to Chiang would cease, and that "we would be forced to deal directly with the Communists" in evacuating the Japanese from North China. Unsatisfied, Marshall raised the point with Truman and Byrnes on December 11, noting that if America abandoned Chiang, "there would follow the tragic consequences of a divided China and of a probable Russian reassumption of power in Manchuria, the combined effect of this resulting in the defeat or loss of the major purpose of our war in the Pacific." And he secured their concurrence that, in case of Nationalist obduracy, America would have to "assist . . . in the movement of troops into North China," although Washington "would have to swallow its pride and much of its policy in doing so."[45] But the whole purpose of Marshall's mission remained to avoid such an eventuality and to maintain an even-handed facade.

Sent off to China, Marshall was given two weapons: threat and promise. Although the army and navy were authorized to arrange for the evacuation of Japanese forces from North China, and for the transportation of Nationalist troops both to that region and to Manchurian ports, this was held secret in order to increase Marshall's leverage with both factions in maneuvering to secure a compromise truce. And in order to shroud Marshall's tactics and objectives, parts of his confidential directive were not publicized: specifically, that the United States would continue to transport Nationalist troops to "liberated areas of China, including Manchuria," but would refrain from such activity when it jeopardized progress toward a truce and political negotiations. With the extent of American military aid to the Nationalists uncertain, Chiang, unaware of America's ultimate commitment to him, presumably would fear a complete cutoff; and Mao would dread a massive American commitment enabling Chiang to conquer all of China. Truman's public letter to Marshall, released on December 15, gave point to the pressures Marshall could exert:

> In your conversations with Chiang Kai-shek and other Chinese leaders you are authorized to speak with the utmost frankness. Particularly, you may state, in connection with the Chinese desire for credits, technical assistance in the economic field, and military assistance (I have in mind the proposed U.S. military advisory group which I have approved in principle), that a China disunited and torn by civil strife could not be considered realistically as a proper place for American assistance along the lines enumerated.[46]

This warning, plus Truman's simultaneously publicized offer of extensive loans and technical assistance "[a]s China moves toward peace and unity," were efforts to stimulate a conciliatory spirit among the Chinese.[47]

To the American people the announcements carried a familiar message. "Secretary Byrnes and I are both anxious that the unification of China by peaceful, democratic methods be achieved as soon as possible," Truman wrote. The marines were in China, he emphasized, to aid in Japanese disarmament and evacuation, "[i]n continuation of the constant and close collaboration" between America and China in time of war. The Pacific peace might "be jeopardized, if not frustrated, unless Japanese influence in China is wholly removed and unless China takes her place as a unified, democratic and peaceful nation." In accordance with "its often expressed views regarding self-determination," America felt that "the detailed steps" toward political unity "must be worked out by the Chinese themselves"; United States support would not include "military intervention to influence the course of any Chinese internal strife."[48] All of this was basically in line with the Vincent speech of the previous October, the State Department *Policy Manual* of November, and recent letters to noninterventionists defending American policy. Such letters continued in the same vein as the Marshall mission came to life. Byrnes wrote to a congressman on December 10:

> Having fought side by side with our Chinese allies to effect the defeat of Japan and the destruction of Japanese imperialism, we feel that our mission will not have been completed unless all the Japanese armed forces in China and elsewhere in the Far East have been returned to the Japanese homeland.[49]

With the effort under way to gain public acceptance for the mission, and to signal to the Chinese factions America's intention to use its influence ruthlessly to secure a coalition, the Administration sought to implement the third, the most sensitive, and perhaps the most revealing element in its tripartite program: to secure Soviet goodwill, perhaps even support, for Marshall's efforts. Indeed, the cultivation of Russia in this matter seemed crucial to American chances for success. To American policymakers it seemed only natural that, given a weak Nationalist China and a power vacuum in North China and Manchuria, Soviet power would inevitably flow into and control those regions. The *Peabody Report* of July 1945 had forewarned of this eventuality, as had Drumright, Forrestal and Patterson in November, and Marshall in his appeal for a contingency plan to back Chiang. So the need to contain Soviet Asiatic expansion was basic to Administration thinking. Referring on November 20 to the possibility of Soviet expansion into the Manchurian vacuum, Forrestal had presented his colleagues with a sobering analysis:

[I]n any future war between a combination of Russia and the Asiatic powers [and an enemy] the manpower available to such a combination would be so tremendous and the indifference to the loss of life so striking that it would present a very serious problem to this country.[50]

And on December 9, Byrnes predicted to Acheson and Marshall that if the Chinese factions did not form a unified government, "we could expect Russia to ultimately take control of Manchuria and maintain a dominant influence in North China . . . . [T]here was no other step the Russians could be expected to take if China could not, itself, control Manchuria." A strong, unified China, he concluded, was "essential" to American interests.[51]

In the climate of the irresistible public clamor for the repatriation of American troops, the consequent dizzying demobilization of America's formidable wartime forces, and the refusal of American leaders to court domestic political disaster or risk a military confrontation with Russia by containing Soviet power through a military entrenchment in China, the only way to secure American interests was to convince Russian leaders that Soviet and American interests in China could be reconciled. Tensions in Asia might be eased through the implementation of Vincent's conception of China as a "buffer," or preferably, as a "bridge" between Russia and America—a strong and independent China, open to commerce, free of foreign military power, and menacing neither to Russia nor to the United States. Byrnes and Forrestal assumed that the Russians would be agreeable to such an accommodation; for it seemed as much in the Soviet interest as in the American that a confrontation there be avoided. Less formal than the *Peabody Report*'s suggestion of a joint military occupation of Manchuria, or than Wedemeyer's later suggestion of a United Nations trusteeship over that region,[52] the idea grew

out of the Patterson-Forrestal proposal for a political understanding with Russia, or a concert of powers, respecting and
upholding the unity and independence of China. Hence the
need, as Byrnes and Forrestal had envisioned, to talk the
matter over with the Russians.

The need for such discussion seemed all the more urgent
in light of growing Soviet alarm about the continued
American military presence in North China. On November
30, the Moscow embassy reported a Soviet dispatch on
DeLacy's resolution for a withdrawal from China; on
December 11 came word of a Soviet story about DeLacy's
speech demanding a cessation of American intervention and
declaring that "'you cannot preach unity abroad while
creating anti-Communist bases in China.'" Before Marshall's efforts got into gear, it was vital to reassure the Russians. At Moscow, Byrnes sought, in Feis's words, "to fit our
policy into the Allied pattern of peace-making." At the
least, he hoped to preclude Soviet encouragement of
Chinese Communist obstinacy, or an indefinite Soviet occupation of Manchuria; at best, he might secure active
Soviet cooperation "to bring about a truce and facilitate the
entry of the Chinese government administration in Manchuria." Thus, on December 8, Byrnes informed the Soviet
foreign minister, Molotov, that notwithstanding China's
absence from the forthcoming conference, he would be
pleased to discuss informally America's military activities
there. "We simply want," he advised Harriman two days
later, "to advise Molotov of the status of affairs and of the
reasons why we have not been able to remove our troops."[53]

But at Moscow, between December 16 and 23, the Russians proved very suspicious. Byrnes explained to Molotov
that with the paucity of available shipping and with
400,000 Chinese Communist troops in North China blocking the way of 100,000 Nationalist troops, the American
marines were remaining in place, pending a truce which
would allow them to go inland, disarm and evacuate

325,000 Japanese troops without becoming embroiled in a civil war. Hopefully, he added, a truce would enable Marshall to secure Chiang's agreement to Communist representation in the Chinese regime; but without such a truce, America would be forced either to evacuate the Japanese and leave China teetering on the brink of civil war, or to transport Nationalist troops to occupy evacuated areas. In response, Molotov termed it "very abnormal that four months after the surrender there were still fully armed Japanese troops" in China, and claimed that the Nationalists exaggerated Communist strength in Manchuria and North China in order to avoid fighting and "have others do it for them." Adding that "eight years of war should have been long enough for Chiang Kai-shek to learn how to handle Japanese, particularly after the latter had capitulated," Molotov expressed doubt whether Chiang really wanted "to settle his internal problems." This was followed by a Soviet memorandum which noted that the continued existence of armed Japanese troops in China was a violation of surrender terms, that the Japanese were being used in North China by the Nationalists against the CCP, and that no date of Japanese evacuation and American withdrawal had been indicated. Contrasting this to the rigid adherence of Russia to withdrawal dates in Manchuria until requested by the Nationalists to stay on temporarily, the memorandum charged that foreign military interference in Chinese internal affairs was aggravating China's domestic struggle. Arguing that Japanese disarmament should be done by the Nationalist Government and not by foreign troops, the memorandum suggested that the United States and Russia undertake to evacuate simultaneously from China by the middle of January 1946.[54]

Following a frustrating meeting in which he repeatedly insisted to Molotov that the complications of Japanese repatriation did not allow for any imminent or precise withdrawal schedule, Byrnes encountered a more conciliatory

Stalin. Explaining the situation in North China, and outlining Marshall's embryonic attempt to secure a truce without American intervention, Byrnes heard Stalin reply:

> [I]f the Chinese people became convinced that Chiang Kai-shek was depending on foreign troops, he would lose his influence. Chiang Kai-shek apparently does not understand this, but the three Governments should understand it for him. It would be much better for Chiang Kai-shek to rely on his own forces, but if we desired to help Chiang Kai-shek we should not give him help in such a manner as to destroy his authority with the Chinese people.[55]

Displaying interest in Byrnes's depiction of the size and juxtaposition of the Communist and Japanese forces in northern China, Stalin joked with Byrnes that all Chinese—Mao and Chiang among them—were boasters, exaggerating the sizes of their forces and those of their enemies. He paid tribute to Marshall, claiming that he, if anyone, could "settle the situation." He reaffirmed Soviet support of the Nationalist regime along with American policy, eschewed any action which would increase Nationalist difficulties, and expressed hope for China's unification.[56]

After this talk, the Soviet negotiators softened their demand for a scheduled American withdrawal. A public agreement was reached on "the need for a unified and democratic China under the Nationalist Government, for broad participation by democratic elements in all branches of the National Government, and for a cessation of civil strife." The three powers—Foreign Minister Bevin representing Britain—also agreed on the "desirability of withdrawal of Soviet and American forces from China at the earliest practicable moment consistent with the discharge of their obligations and responsibilities." On December 24, Byrnes wired Truman that, among other things, the three nations were "in general accord as to Far Eastern issues. The situation is encouraging." Leaving Moscow convinced that Stalin intended to respect his treaty with China, and would not intentionally sabotage the new mission, he wired Marshall the optimistic news.[57] There was hope that, with the third leg of support—Soviet cooperation—emplaced, the mission might stand the test of time.

But, as American leaders knew, the structure of their endeavor was fragile. It seemed necessary to pacify widespread domestic jitters by denying any interventionist intent and by explaining the general purposes of the Marshall mission, as State Department letters and the comments of Truman and Byrnes effectively did. And the temptation to discredit soundly the hysterics of Hurley—a task too indelicate to be handled personally by the president or the secretary of state, but performed with skill and élan by Tom Connally in his Senate forum—was irresistible.

Given the requirements of the program upon which the Administration was embarking, it would clearly have courted failure by inviting the kind of debate which the release of controversial State Department reports and the public testimony of Stilwell, Gauss, knowledgeable reporters, and the China hands would have generated. For such a debate would have explored not only America's methods in China, but also her objectives there. John Service has observed that "the attempt to differentiate between short-term and long-term policy is usually illusory. . . . [What] is done today cannot help but affect the future: short-term actions thus come to determine long-range policy."[58] This is just as true of the attempt to isolate ends from means, particularly where the differences in proposed methods are as great as they were with respect to revolutionary China. Lying just below the surface of universal American homage to the goal of a Chinese coalition were differences so profound as to imply drastically divergent

courses of Chinese political development and foreign orientation—an insight constructively expressed by few senators
other than Vandenberg, but surely grasped by Administration spokesmen who successfully muted those differences.

The military cooperation advocated by Davies, Service,
and Atcheson in wartime, and the postwar coalition envisioned by these men, implied a degree of conciliation by
Chiang Kai-shek that would have given the Communists
military and political power commensurate with their numbers and popular appeal, power that would have shaken
Chiang's predominance, which rested on his military pyr-
amid buttressed by American aid. Had Chiang resisted such
a conciliation, their proposals for aiding and recognizing the
CCP would have guaranteed the revolutionaries virtual control of at least the bulk of North China and Manchuria. On
the other hand, the coalition favored by Hurley, Drumright,
and Forrestal—and ultimately sanctioned in Marshall's confidential instructions should Chiang prove obdurate—
amounted to a military subordination of Communist power
to the Nationalist regime. In effect, the internal debate
focused—as it had throughout 1945—on the comparative
vitality and legitimacy of the two factions, and on how
American influence could best be preserved in China
through one or both of them. The Administration could not
afford to let these issues come into the open. The reports and
testimony of the China hands would have aired them mer-
cilessly, as would extensive testimony from China correspondents, who already were writing books citing the
Communist movement as the source of regeneration in
China.[59]

In this connection, Connally's failure to summon Stilwell,
as so many people were urging, is significant. In some
respects, he would have made an ideal witness: tough,
bright, articulate, widely known and admired, he would
have discredited, as nobody else could have, the attacks on
Davies, Service, and others who had served him loyally and

effectively in the field. Hurley had good reason to fear him. But so, too, did the Administration; for he was brutally frank, and would have spelled out China's troubles as he saw them. He was, after all, the general who, after the Burma campaign three years earlier, had stunned and charmed the nation with his terse evaluation: "I claim we got a hell of a beating." He had openly scorned Chiang—his military commander and an allied head of state—as the "Peanut." He had deprecated the military prowess of the Kuomintang, while admiring the fighting spirit of the Chinese Communists, advocating pressure on Chiang to make him fight the Japanese instead of sealing off the Communists, and ultimately sanctioning the arming of the Communists over Chiang's objections, before his expulsion from China in October 1944. Connally, in discussing "the situation in China" with Stilwell during the Hurley hearings, could only have found that the outspoken general would raise the very issues that the Administration was at pains to smother. Indeed, asked by Marshall for confidential advice on the upcoming mission, Stilwell declared that it would fail: "Once Chiang Kai-shek had sensed the situation he would merely become more intransigent." And when the mission developed problems the next spring, with the spread of fighting to Manchuria, he wrote in disgust: "But what did they expect? George Marshall can't walk on water. It makes me itch to throw down my shovel and get over there and shoulder a rifle with Chu Teh," the Chinese Communist general.[60]

In contrast to Stilwell, the Administration obfuscated. In claiming that its China policy had been clear, consistent, and unified all along, it ignored a continuing rift of enormous proportions regarding the treatment of the Chinese Communists. In fact, it brushed aside the one legitimate aspect of Hurley's charges, even if distorted by Hurley's characterization: that Washington had not given sufficient policy guidance in China in late 1944 and early 1945, and was therefore responsible for the uncertainty which had hampered effective policy implementation at that time. Espousing unity, strength, and democracy in postwar China in cooperation with other great powers, it continued its commitment to its internationalist goals in East Asia. Herein lay the deeper reason for the Administration's need to muffle dissension about American policy; just as to liberals and conservatives, China had become to the Truman Administration a test case and symbol of American diplomacy in the making of a postwar order. If the conservative yearning for a united, anticommunist China, strongly receptive to American influence, and the leftist dream of Soviet-American accommodation in a progressive, unified China each was an improbable myth, then the Administration's vision was infinitely more so, for it combined both in its pursuit of traditional and wartime internationalist goals. In the disorder and strain of the postwar world, the Marshall mission was the last hope of accomplishing this grandiose task.

Hence, in smothering the national debate, the Administration was not so much fooling the public as it was deceiving itself. It misread or ignored the intentions of the Kremlin, predicted by Foreign Service officers and confirmed by Russia's cautious efforts to build her influence in North China and Manchuria through the CCP. It paid little heed to its China specialists when they warned of the Kuomintang's decadence or of the necessity to settle at best for a loose coalition in which Chiang would control the south of China and the Communists the north. Top policymakers continued to believe both in a Chinese coalition and in Soviet cooperation in making America's Chinese dream come true. With the Russians controlling eastern Europe, Germany in dispute, Europe generally in disorder, and the world still chaotic from the war, it seemed particularly important to achieve a satisfactory settlement in China—the world's most populous country, America's hope for the stabilization of Asia, and the ally for whose rights, in large part, America had become directly involved in the war in the first place. It was thus for psychological reasons, as well as for the practical purposes of the Marshall mission, that the Administration could not hear the dissenting notes of pessimism about China. A weak China, a Communist take-over, a Soviet confrontation—these were distressing thoughts to men who had directed a war for contrary purposes. In the absence of the manpower or the will power to fight for their interests in China, they took refuge in their idealistic rhetoric and their unreasonable ambitions, long after their internationalism had become wishful thinking.

Of course, the depth of America's problems in China was not fully appreciated in 1945. In fact, with Marshall's arrival in Chungking, there was some reason for optimism. Russia had, after all, given her blessing to the enterprise; and Marshall went about at the end of December, telling Nationalists and Communists alike about the American public's limited tolerance for United States involvement in China, except so as to achieve a lasting unity and peace. All sides seemed to listen with respect, and early in January 1946, a truce was arranged. Similarly, American opinion seemed responsive. A moratorium on Congressional debate ensued, partly because people were hopeful for Soviet-American cooperation in East Asia, and partly because Congress wished to avoid any interference with Marshall's efforts. Even the pro-Nationalist Walter Judd expressed pleasure with the Moscow communiqué, citing its goal of a united, democratic China under Chiang as his own. As Fetzer has noted:

> For the time being, the members of Congress who had expressed interest in the question of China seemed content to await the developments that would flow from Marshall's endeavors. They waited to see if the promises contained in Truman's statement [of December 15] would be

fulfilled. Several months would pass before this mood would be broken.[61]

It thus appeared that the three legs of American policy—the Chinese factions, the Soviet leaders, and the American public—would support a coalition. As became apparent later in 1946, this was not to be. During that year, assumptions about Soviet cooperation and Chinese responsiveness to American pressure became untenable. But in the long run, the assumption about the American public may have been the most significant. By neutralizing both pro-Chiang and noninterventionist criticism, Connally and the Administration had preserved the immediate functioning of bipartisan foreign policy, while buying time for Marshall to contrive the desired order in China. But they had achieved these successes at great cost and grave risk.

The cost was an opportunity to capitalize on deep-rooted public concern to create an informed new consensus on the goals and methods needed to secure America's interests in China henceforth. In the final analysis, the noninterventionists—from Thomas in the Senate to the marines and their relatives who yearned for their return home—paralleled the State Department experts who advocated an extrication from constraining ties to the Kuomintang. Had a more open debate occurred, a consensus *might* have emerged—consistent with America's reluctance to use military force and her traditional attachment to China—calling for a program of support for Chiang in the south, and a *de facto* relationship with the Communists in the north, pending a Nationalist occupation of the north or other eventualities. Or, if the Administration had argued its case persuasively, it might have secured support for a program of military aid to help Chiang reoccupy all of China, in line with America's historic interests in the country and her Pacific war aims. Or a public debate might well have resulted in some such mission as the one undertaken, with the public more enlightened as to its possibilities and limitations, and with the Chinese well aware of the public's support for Administration policy. Then, Americans might have been readier in case the mission failed, and perhaps better prepared for the correct governmental decision to extricate the United States from China thereafter. In the event, the opportunity was lost.

The risk entailed was directly related to the cost of missing the opportunity for enlightenment. For, already, the depth—if not as yet the wide scope—of ill feeling about Russia, Chinese communism, and internal subversion, had been articulated by sincere conservatives and exploited by demagogues of the right. In the context of the developing Cold War, this ill feeling spread rapidly, and was etched deeply into America's consciousness. In skirting the opportunity for a debate on the relationship of America to Chinese communism in 1945, the Administration delayed that debate until it could no longer be separated from overriding fear of Russia. When the full-fledged outbreak of civil war in 1947 was followed by the ascendancy of the Chinese Communists in 1949, evoking a neurotic and convulsive reaction to China along with a vicious partisan backlash at home, the Truman Administration could not be absolved of responsibility for the ignorance and superstitious dread underlying this response.

The Senate did not forget China. Yet, as quickly as the military crisis and the Hurley resignation had thrust it to center stage, just as rapidly did it recede:

> The Foreign Relations Committee voted to discontinue hearings and dispense with a report. Even Senator Bridges, who had led the GOP attackers, agreed the time was not yet ripe for a fuller investigation of the State Department.[62]

Hurley complained that with "a hostile Chairman and a largely hostile Committee," the hearings "succeeded to some extent in confusing the public mind." Denied the use of incriminating documents and unwilling to release these secret materials on his own, he "took a terrific beating not only in the public press but from my friends who believed that I had made charges against the Department of State and the career diplomats which I had not upheld."[63] As Marshall attempted to carry out the best hopes of the American people for bringing peace to China, Asia faded again into the larger scheme of world politics and Soviet-American relations.

Other issues flared up and were debated at the close of 1945. Connally and Vandenberg fretted about the Truman-Byrnes proposals for atomic energy control, badgered the Administration for more effective safeguards, and prepared to serve as delegates at the first General Assembly meeting to organize the United Nations at London in January 1946, as the bipartisan foreign policy system chugged hopefully along. Vandenberg and Dulles, now close collaborators, exchanged thoughts on the projected billion-dollar loan to Britain, with Vandenberg reflecting on the unpopularity of the idea, the arrogance of the British, and the possibility of killing the loan to avoid arousing the Russians. Elbert Thomas made his weekly broadcasts to Japan, concentrating on democratic Japanese reforms and referring neither to China nor to Far Eastern international politics. Styles Bridges, too, fell silent on China, but he continued into 1946 to keep a wary eye out for spy rings, Communist threats, and Russian obstructionism.[64]

And so, as 1946 began, the China issue was deceptively quiescent. Hurley, it is true, continued to insist that the questions he had raised must be faced; while Mike Mansfield again queried the State Department about the status of American troops in China.[65] But with the country rooting expectantly for Marshall, nobody really perceived that the recent controversy had been a side squall of a distant but violent approaching storm.

VI   A PRELUDE TO COLD WAR

America's response to China in 1945 clearly reflected, even as it helped to shape, a nationwide anxiety. As Americans at all levels—from the Foreign Service and policy making elites to ordinary people with selfish or idealistic motives—sought to cope with chaos and revolution in Europe and Asia at the end of World War II, they found such conditions typified, even embodied, by China. In their effort to comprehend China, Americans sought to apply the definitions and values which had been their common creed in wartime; they found that universal democracy, national self-determination, great power harmony, and a strong, united China were pitifully inadequate concepts in reference to the poverty, partisan animosity, and military impotence which characterized China after decades of foreign war and domestic turmoil. In trying to reconcile a disintegrating China with their wartime ideals, or at least with their particular political predilections, Americans became engaged in a spirited debate about China's political development and her relationship to American and Soviet aims in postwar Asia.

The issues raised in 1945 were central to America's problem of adjustment to the postwar world. Yet, after all was said and done, how much had the intense China debate influenced preexisting American notions about China? And how closely did these notions conform to reality in China, in America, and in world politics? Both questions hinge on four phenomena, central to American diplomacy, which were exemplified and reinforced by the China debate of 1945: (1) dissension and confusion about the implications of Soviet power and Chinese instability for the United States; (2) difficulties in the national assimilation of insights developed by perceptive American diplomats abroad; (3) the limitations of a bipartisan political system in its self-conscious efforts to educate and unify the country in its foreign policy ventures; and (4) an imprecise correspondence between ideals and power considerations in the formulation and discussion of American foreign policy. To evaluate the significance of these four interrelated phenomena is to clarify the meaning of the American reaction to China in 1945.

Senate dissension over China flowed from a spectrum of domestic political allegiances and from a variety of perceptions of great power relationships. For extreme political conservatives like Styles Bridges, individualism and free enterprise at home and strong nationalism in foreign relations were basic values. To them, liberalism was misguided, and communism or revolution was anathema. To deal with the Soviets was a distasteful necessity during the war, and the alliance inspired neither trust nor any disposition to hope for a friendly Soviet-American relationship thereafter. Conservatives assumed a basic antagonism between free, capitalist values and collective, authoritarian communism. With this assumption seemingly confirmed in 1945 by Soviet military and political control of eastern Europe, the

American right assumed that in China, too, communism was a part of the Soviet-led anti-Western movement, to be crushed through American support of the pro-Western, conservative Nationalist regime. More moderate Republicans, like Arthur Vandenberg, were just as committed to the Nationalists and just as wary of Russia and the Chinese Communists; yet, in advocating hard bargaining with Russia in China and elsewhere, they exhibited more awareness of world power relationships, and they tended less to blur liberalism or internationalism at home with Communist expansionism in other countries.

In contrast, internationalist Democrats like Tom Connally took the wartime ideal of international cooperation and Soviet-American harmony very seriously. While conscious of a potential Chinese Communist menace to American interests in Asia, such Administration supporters found their greatest hope in a Soviet-American concert in the Far East, with a parallel Communist-Kuomintang accommodation in China. They hoped America might maintain a favorable balance of power in Asia through a regime which menaced neither Russian nor American interests; a strong, viable China seemed a common interest of the two powers. And to the left—liberal Elbert Thomas and others more radical than he—America had no business competing with Russia on the Asian mainland. To this group, Soviet ambitions on her Asiatic periphery were understandable, a parallel to United States interest in Latin America. They felt it crucial to preserve Soviet-American friendship—the very heart of a peaceful postwar system—through accommodation of vital Soviet interests. And they deemed it only natural that degraded, poverty-stricken China should follow Russia a generation later on the revolutionary path toward economic prosperity and human dignity.

It thus appears that in 1945 there was considerable confusion about Sino-Russian-American relations. Certainly, the right overestimated the connection between the Chinese

Communists and the Russians, just as it distorted the commonality of Kuomintang and American interests. Obsessed with the implications of ideology for world politics, arch-conservatives overlooked the Communists' indigenous strength, their nationalistic appeal, their long history of troubled relations with Russia, and their recent feelers toward the United States. The right also confused the aim of the Kuomintang, which was to stay in power at all costs, with the interest of the United States, which was different: to maintain her influence in China, to help that country grow strong, and to limit Soviet penetration of China and her periphery. Cooperative internationalists and liberals, on the other hand, more fully understood the social and historical sources of Chinese communism as a movement growing out of long-lived misery, misgovernment, and foreign incursion; they understood that an ideological affinity to Moscow might not translate into a political alliance, unless Washington made it happen with a self-fulfilling prophecy of enmity. Yet the left, in its postwar hopes, was blind to an elementary condition which was grasped, if distorted, by conservatives: that there indeed was a basic conflict of Soviet and American interests in postwar China. The left did not see that Soviet-American political competition in China was in any event likely, since each power would seek to expand its influence in that key country, while viewing with alarm the other power's efforts at penetration.

Closely related to the persistent confusion about Russia and China was the second basic phenomenon of the 1945 debate: the failure of the Truman Administration to make effective use of its own China experts. The full complexity of the Asian situation was best perceived by American field diplomats like John Paton Davies, who recognized the national strength of the Communists, and who proposed to treat with them—as well as with the Kuomintang, as long as it survived—in order to further American influence in a future China and to help a nationalistic Chinese regime resist "the possessive Russian embrace." Ideology, the China hands knew, is just as easily modified as confirmed by geopolitical realities, particularly in a self-directed regime in a large country. But their absence from policy debates and from public discussions prevented them from bringing their views to bear on the China debate which followed their expulsion from China and the defeat of Japan.

The failure of the China experts to be taken into account was related to the nation's traditional attitude toward the Foreign Service, and to the Administration's conception of the postwar Asiatic order. For one thing, Franklin Roosevelt generally had relied on trusted envoys like Patrick Hurley for counsel on foreign policy matters; he had been prejudiced against the Foreign Service, a reflection, as Tuchman notes, of "the deep-seated American distrust that still prevailed of diplomacy and diplomats."[1] And when these experts, silenced by Hurley, attempted to make their views known in Washington, the ambassador had them drummed out of China. But just as significant was the Administration's failure to accede to the public clamor for their testimony during the crisis of November-December 1945, or even to take their counsel in its private deliberations. The simple fact was that the China experts stood for policies which directly contradicted the Administration's persistent wish to implement in full its wartime program in China: to bolster a strong, unified regime under Chiang Kai-shek in cooperation with the Soviet Union. Since the experts denied both the possibility of Chinese unity and the likelihood of Soviet support for such an objective, they were ignored. As the Administration fumbled with China throughout November, frantically searching for a solution for the spreading civil war, it knew at least what it did *not* want to hear; and the coalition program embodied in the new Marshall mission was directly contrary to all the prescriptions of the China hands. Stilwell even informed Marshall privately that it would not work; Chiang would sense America's continuing support, and would remain firm. Yet, unwilling to accept the fact of a divided China or of Soviet-American competition there, Washington went through with the mission. Patterson and Forrestal even urged Byrnes to secure Soviet collaboration in pursuit of America's aims; and the secretary of state in December explained everything personally to Stalin and secured the dictator's goodwill, or thought he did. Thus the diplomats, who contradicted everything the Administration wanted to believe and achieve, became irrelevant. Shrewd political intelligence clashed with set governmental objectives, and was quashed.

Insofar as the *public* debate was concerned, the diplomats were not only irrelevant, in the Administration's view; they were positively dangerous. This fact stemmed from the third basic phenomenon of the China debate: the limited effectiveness of a democratic bipartisan foreign policy system when confronted with critical controversial issues. At a time when public sentiment was strongly against intervention and demanded an authoritative explanation, and when the Republican right was attacking American China policy as procommunist, the last thing the Administration wanted was a public airing of the China hands' pessimistic views. They would only stimulate more demands for an American withdrawal, while provoking a yet more shrill conservative cry of treason. It seemed clear that such an eventuality would undercut American prestige with the Russians and with both Chinese factions, thus crippling the Marshall mission from the outset. Hence Connally's reluctance to put Stilwell, Gauss, and Davies on the stand, although they might effectively have destroyed Hurley.

Ironically, the government, in defending itself against a partisan attack from the right, contributed mightily to the stifling of public demand for enlightenment. Caught in a classic democratic foreign policy bind, criticized from both right and left, it sought to walk a delicate line in China between military intervention and outright abandonment.

Understandably enough, it also sought to discredit the red-baiting of Hurley and Bridges. But, unhappily, in the process the Administration, through Connally, stooped to the level of its attackers, muddled the already confused issues before the public, and forfeited the opportunity for a badly needed reevaluation of American policy. Novel problems posed by the Chinese revolution, Russian expansion, the evaporation of Japanese power, and America's unprecedented military capability in East Asia went unexplored.

Connally's was a tragically narrow interpretation of bipartisanship for the China issue. He tried, with short-term success, to make bipartisanship a mask for Administration decisions rather than, as in theory, a conduit to educate the public and to mobilize mass support behind a plausible foreign policy grounded in the national interest and in public comprehension. Successful diplomacy for a democratic government is a fragile undertaking. The Administration artificially dampened public criticism and Senate debate, at its own future risk, and at the nation's peril. The failure of American leadership to confront the issues squarely left Americans unprepared for the disappointment of American hopes in China, symbolized by the Communist triumph of 1949.

To be sure, publicization of the experts' opinions would have jeopardized the Marshall mission. But it would also have encouraged foreign policy and public opinion to come into phase. It might conceivably have solidified public opposition to American military intervention in China and, by demonstrating the awful military commitment necessary to save Chiang, it could possibly have discredited pro-Nationalist criticism. At the least, it would have aired the China hands' suggestion that a political competition with Russia in China was preferable to a provocative military entrenchment, a complete abdication of American interests, or an ill-fated American attempt to mediate a coalition while secretly committed to support Chiang in a pinch. At most, it might have helped to define a pragmatic American relationship with the Chinese Communists at the prelude, and not at the climax, of the Cold War, and thus have been a step toward the maintenance of significant leverage in China for the foreseeable future, with which to discourage undue extensions of Soviet Asiatic power.[2]

In the event, America's bipartisan institutions failed her. The key members of the investigating Senate Foreign Relations Committee were, at best, impotent, and at worst, maliciously partisan. And the Administration, clinging desperately to its grandiose wartime aims in China, slighted the debate. The failure of political leadership to untangle China policy left popular opinion to drift along in what Almond has described as a "mood"—that is, an undifferentiated reaction to foreign policy, "formless and plastic," undergoing "frequent alteration in response to changes in events," a "superficial and fluctuating response."[3] By discouraging debate, the Administration had aggravated the problem, posed by the extremely limited number of experts on Far Eastern affairs, to any competitive policy discussion about China and had left public opinion to react with impulses—withdrawal and intervention, optimism and pessimism, idealism and cynicism, tolerance and intolerance, superiority and inferiority—which characterized ordinary people's reactions to the little-understood country of China.[4] Americans continued to view Chiang, the Communists, and the prospect of American intervention according to the prejudicial lights of domestic political conservatism, liberalism, radicalism, nationalism, internationalism, and isolationism. Such preconceptions continued to obscure the crude realities of Chinese poverty, illiteracy, custom, military weakness, xenophobia, and the Confucian reaction and Maoist revolution which they had spawned. Kuomintang and Communist remained convenient but deceptive symbols for those things which Americans thought they loved, hated, welcomed, or dreaded in China's current and potential development.

The fourth basic phenomenon exemplified by the China debate—America's ambiguity in relating her ideals to international power considerations—had a direct bearing on the problems of confused dissension, Foreign Service alienation, and bipartisan dysfunction just discussed. Having idealized World War II as a struggle for liberty, democracy, self-determination, and collective security from aggression, the United States Government similarly held up an ideal of China—a strong, pro-American, democratic pillar of East Asian peace and stability in the postwar period. Successfully stimulating national morale, international wartime cooperation, and a unified American mobilization for the war effort, such idealizations had a strong impact on Americans' consciousness, often obscuring power considerations which were irrelevant or even contradictory to the ideals stressed. People with disparate political predilections applied the same ideals quite differently to developing policy problems; and when such ideals were frustrated at the end of the war—whether in Poland, in Greece, in Iran, or in China—Americans reacted with the dissonance and confusion which characterized the debate on China.

In this context, it is not hard to see why the Administration shunned the views of diplomats whose predictions of Chinese disunity and revolution contradicted the wartime hopes instilled in the American people. Nor is it strange that the bipartisan system, already under attack by disillusioned pro-Chiang conservatives, responded poorly to the challenge of China; for in admitting publicly to harsh Chinese realities, the Administration would have tarnished the image on which it continued to rely to stimulate confident and unified public support for its postwar policies. In a circular fashion, persistently mouthed ideals reinforced a distorted image of China, which in turn increased public pressure on the Administration to implement varying interpretations of

215

the ideals which seemed to be losing meaning in the context of Chinese weakness and civil war. The consequent strain and disillusionment in American thinking were merely covered up, not relieved, by Administration tactics. And the persistent effects of the four phenomena would be visible in the years ahead, as they had in the past.

There were many and varied precedents in American foreign policy for the type of reaction to China which occurred in 1945. Certainly, a cold reception at home was nothing new to America's diplomats. The public and Congress traditionally held them to be snobbish, European-oriented "cookie-pushers," and resented their effete manners and dress. Brilliant diplomats, such as Lewis Einstein, who before World War I presciently forecasted the dangers implicit in a general European war, lived in quiet obscurity. In the Manchurian crisis of 1931-32, Stanley Hornbeck of the State Department's Far East desk vainly argued for a strong policy against Japanese encroachment in China while President Hoover and Secretary of State Stimson argued over who should get credit for a "nonrecognition" policy which did practically nothing. During World War II, Ambassador to China Clarence Gauss, an informed and perceptive man, grew used to being ignored, while Roosevelt sent envoy after envoy to deal directly with Chiang Kai-shek; he finally resigned after Hurley appeared in 1944. Indeed, under Roosevelt, the status of the professional diplomats reached a new low, as the Administration used civilian and military troubleshooters; and the State Department, under the aging Cordell Hull, went frequently uninformed, not to mention impotent. It is easy to see why, with such a weak base of support, the China experts were effectively ignored.

Neither confusion nor dissension was novel to American foreign policy in 1945. In 1898-1900, a massive public debate had centered on the acquisition of a Far Eastern empire (the Philippines, captured in the Spanish-American

War); and such diverse men as Social Darwinist William G. Sumner and egalitarian William Jennings Bryan had both rationalized their opposition to empire for diametrically opposed racial reasons. In 1919-20, an emotional controversy raged about the decision at the Versailles Conference to let Japan retain the Shantung Peninsula, captured from the Germans in World War I but in actuality belonging to China. In 1939-41, the nation debated how best to stay out of World War II—by avoiding partisanship for any belligerent, or by aiding the Allies to fight Hitler, thereby scotching the Nazi menace to America. Similarly, problems of partisanship had surfaced frequently in American diplomacy. Federalists and Anti-Federalists had advocated pro-British and pro-French postures, respectively, in the age of Washington and Adams. In 1898, President McKinley, a Republican, had based an uncompromising stand toward Spain's problems in its chaotic Cuban colony partly on a fear that the Democratic platform of 1900 might ring "Free Silver, Free Cuba!" Woodrow Wilson had faced his final and decisive test in the Versailles Treaty controversy of 1919-20, when his own uncompromising partisanship had enabled Republican Henry Cabot Lodge, his enemy, to maneuver enough Senate votes to reject Wilson's prized League of Nations along with the treaty. The costly lessons of partisanship, especially Wilson's case, bred in the Roosevelt Administration an extreme sensitivity to this problem; and during World War II, the government succeeded in creating a broad-based bipartisan front, both through the appointment of numerous Republicans to the Cabinet and lesser posts and through cooperation with Republican Congressional leaders in the development of postwar international programs. In 1945, the achievements, rather than the limitations, of bipartisanship stood out.

One of the most effective methods traditionally used by presidents to overcome disunity and partisanship was the idealization of foreign policy. An apathetic and particularistic public was galvanized into wartime action by Wilson's impassioned rhetoric of making the world safe for democracy; so too did Franklin Roosevelt talk of self-determination, democracy, and the Four Freedoms as wartime goals. America was fertile soil for such ideals, for she had traditionally nursed a sense of righteousness and moral superiority to the class-bound and warring Old World states. But in World War II, as in World War I, such ideals, in the absence of clearly defined political goals and strategic orientations, were sure to bring with them disillusionment, confusion, dissent, and partisanship. So it was with China in 1945; and the abortive debate of that year was to have profound consequences for American foreign policy in the years thereafter.

From 1945 to 1950, confusion about China grew apace; in its wake came increasing dissension, and ultimately, a vicious partisan battle. When the furor over China temporarily died down, other problems confronting American leaders in the immediate postwar years came to have a great bearing on China policy. During 1946-48 in particular, policymakers sought to reconcile the need to support western, central and southeastern Europe against internal disorder and Soviet pressure with public reluctance to make financial sacrifices and accept military risks for these purposes. The recurrence of the selfish withdrawal impulse after 1945 flowed partly from the same interests and emotions which had spurred Americans to demand an end to the military adventure in China. This danger to the Truman Administration's planned initiatives caused Washington to overreact, to engage in the "crisis diplomacy" which Vandenberg so resented, in drumming up support for the Truman Doctrine, Interim Aid for Europe, and the Marshall Plan, in 1947-48.[5] Following the discredited lead of the arch-conservatives, it portrayed American programs as a response to a worldwide ideological-military challenge posed by the Soviet Union, and it pledged full support to independent governments anywhere threatened with attack or subversion. It thus distorted beyond recognition the actual, limited economic and military nature of the crisis in parts of Europe. In so doing, it secured arch-conservative support for Administration programs and stirred up a wave of moral enthusiasm to replace the public's indifference.

As with China in 1945, the American elite had failed to confront the complexity of the problem, but had so oversimplified and overstated it—idealized it, in fact—as to insure subsequent misunderstanding and recrimination. And, not surprisingly, the major subject of the ultimate controversy was China. Time and again, as programs for European or Middle Eastern aid came before Congress in 1947-48, legislators pressed the State Department: Why was China left out? In the global Truman Doctrine commitment, what was so special about tiny Greece, which got so much aid, while large, friendly China got almost nothing? Why had military aid to China been suspended, they wondered? Why was there no comprehensive program for economic aid to China? The answer was simple and obvious, if unstated: after the failure of the Marshall mission (1946) and the spread of China's civil war, the United States had abandoned an active China policy and was prepared to cut its losses by detaching itself from Chiang's failing regime—as its China experts had urged years earlier. But neither the China debate of 1945 nor the bipartisan consultations of 1947-48 had done anything to alert the Senate or the public to these changed conditions and policies. Indeed, the special China problem had been blurred beyond recognition by the Administration's imprecision and guile in promulgating the Truman Doctrine.[6]

Congress therefore began its long campaign on China's behalf. The China Lobby, embryonic in the Bridges-Hurley crusade of 1945, rapidly matured and exerted its political muscle. To Interim Aid for Austria, Italy, and France for the winter of 1947-48, the House of Representatives appended an appropriation for China, embarrassing the Senate and the Administration into a new pro-Chiang initiative. Faced with continued legislative pressure, the State Department reluctantly presented a new program of economic and military aid for China, and the China Aid Act was passed on April 3, 1948—the same day as the European Recovery Plan. Congressional pressure increased, especially from Republicans, as Chiang lost ground to the Communists through 1948. With Truman's upset election victory of November 1948, following a comparatively bipartisan foreign policy campaign by the heavily favored Republican candidate, Thomas E. Dewey, dissension was transformed into partisanship. Truman came under mounting Republican attack in 1949. When the Administration published its own defense, *The China White Paper*, in August 1949, Republicans raised a shrill cry of whitewash. After October 1949, when the Chinese Communists established their government over the entire Chinese mainland, pro-Chiang efforts centered on the protection of the Kuomintang regime on Taiwan. With the onset of Senator Joseph McCarthy's smear campaign and the Korean War, in 1950, the "Who lost China?" debate was in full swing, as the China Lobby and pro-Chiang Republicans accused the Administration of harboring procommunists who had "sold Chiang down the river"—just as Patrick Hurley had claimed five years earlier. Confusion about China, an idealized crusade against communism, and partisan animosity had ushered in one of the most damaging foreign policy imbroglios in the nation's history, poisoning national political life and haunting American diplomacy decades into the future.

Among the most blameless victims of the confusion and partisanship were the China experts who had challenged the government's policies five years earlier. Caught up in the Cold War hysterics, they were hounded by an angry Congress for having accurately foreseen the success of the Chinese revolution and for having recommended the means of coping with it. Subjected to repeated loyalty investigations, Davies, Service, and Vincent were ultimately driven from the Foreign Service by a cowed government during the McCarthy era.[7] In the Cold War tension of the 1950s, American policy was firmly tied to the Kuomintang on Taiwan and officially oblivious to the Chinese Communist regime, which was temporarily allied with the Soviet Union against a hostile United States. The legacy of the 1945 debate was complete. Especially after the Sino-American military engagement in Korea, China was, to America, both a pariah nation and an untouchable issue.

In the momentous events of 1946-50, the senators prominent in the abortive China debate continued to play leading roles. Powerful men, they remained absorbed in foreign affairs, and each took an active hand in formulating a legislative response to the Chinese revolution. As the Cold War matured, they continued to exemplify the range of opinion, the frustrated idealism, and the bitter partisanship which colored postwar American China policy.[8]

Styles Bridges maintained throughout the period his fiercely anticommunist stand. He asserted in 1946 that communism was a "world challenge," attacking "the very foundations of Christian civilization," and he argued that the two systems and ideologies could not coexist. Closely following right-wing exposés of such alleged "pro-Communists" as Service and Vincent, Bridges in 1947 joined with Alfred Kohlberg, Walter Judd, Albert Wedemeyer, and Hurley in an effort to block Vincent's promotion to career minister. He used the Senate Appropriations Committee, which he chaired in 1947-48, as a forum for exponents of American aid to China. In 1948, he accepted a thousand-dollar campaign contribution from a grateful Kohlberg, the self-professed "China Lobby man." In 1949, Bridges and three other senators rebutted the *China White Paper*; they denied that China had given up her fight, urged continued succor to Chiang's "free areas," and deplored the Administration's use of Chiang as a scapegoat for its own previous blunders and betrayals. Later that year, he counseled against recognizing "Moscow as the governing authority in China" even if the Kuomintang were exiled, lest America abet the "Soviet scheme" for conquering all of Asia and the Pacific. In 1950, he charged that the "Democratic foreign policy" had "turned over" China to Stalin and communism. And, as Joseph McCarthy cut his demagogic path, his ally Bridges watched with satisfaction as offending China experts were purged from government service.

Less decisively committed to the Nationalist cause was Arthur Vandenberg. As the Republicans' foreign policy leader and the main link in the bipartisan system which secured massive European aid programs in 1947-50, Vandenberg was highly ambivalent about China. To be sure, he continued to equate American interests with the Kuomintang's survival. Repeatedly asserting that the hitherto secret Yalta provisions had virtually "sold China down the river," he maintained that the Truman-Marshall effort to pressure the Kuomintang into a coalition with the CCP had been a blunder, given the Communists' thirst for total power. Frequently expressing admiration for Chiang, he warned lest China, or all of Asia, fall under Soviet domination. Prodded by Bridges, Vandenberg in 1947 blocked in the Foreign Relations Committee (which he then chaired) the Vincent promotion at the Far East desk. He claimed partial credit in 1948 for China's inclusion in American foreign aid. Early in 1949, he warned Truman lest an abrupt termination of China aid saddle America with responsibility for the imminent Kuomintang collapse. Yet he was, throughout, sensitive to America's limited capabilities in China. In 1947, he disclaimed any "illusions" about "China's future"; responding to pressure from Senator Knowland for more China aid, he wrote in 1948 that there were "limits to our resources and boundaries to our miracles"; by 1949, he admonished that after two billion dollars in American postwar aid, Nationalist forces were surrendering by the division, "without firing a shot." And he warned against shouldering a military responsibility in China which would unjustifiably "jeopardize our own international security."

After the *China White Paper* and the Nationalist expulsion, Vandenberg had his hands full in restraining the more vitriolic Republican attacks on the Administration, while barely muting his own anger about the lack of bipartisan consultations. In January 1950, he opposed recognition of the Communist regime "at this immediate moment," but left future options completely open. But by early 1951, in the hardening of the Cold War, he cited Chinese aggression in Korea in opposing any recognition, direct or implied (in the United Nations), of the People's Republic. During 1949-51, as China became an adversary and as Vandenberg's health deteriorated, the bipartisanship for which he had stood came crashing down. He died in April 1951, the same month that Truman fired General MacArthur for publicly criticizing American restraint in fighting the Chinese in Korea.

In contrast to developing Republican criticism was the view of Tom Connally, who steadfastly supported the Administration's China policy. In 1946, Connally still thought that the Marshall mission might conjure a Chinese coalition; he continued to emphasize that America's military presence in China was temporary. But with the Truman Doctrine (1947), Connally's rhetoric altered. Following the Administration line, he urged resistance against expansionist Soviet ideology, particularly in Europe, a center of democracy and world trade, and the key to Soviet plans for eventual world domination. In contrast, he shied away from a debilitating commitment to Asia, denying that America had any "business trying to run the whole world." By 1948, facing a groundswell of demands in China's behalf, he reminded constituents of the three billion dollars in American aid to China during and since the war. Strongly opposing any hint of

American military involvement in China, he castigated Chiang for inept military leadership; and he fought against the effort of 1949 to secure more China aid, forcing such "Chiang-lovers" as Senators Smith and Knowland to accept a diluted compromise. After the Korean outbreak, he castigated Communist China's "aggression," while opposing her seating in the UN; but he insisted that America not be "tricked into a shooting war on the Chinese mainland," even to save Taiwan. For such a war would simply "bleed us white," while freeing Russia, "the *real* danger to the United States and to world peace," to "subjugate mankind." Hence Connally's scorn for MacArthur and for those Republicans who pressed for an expansion of the Korean War into China.

More skeptical still of the Kuomintang than Connally, and more doubtful about an aggressive American posture in East Asia, was Elbert Thomas. Philosophically opposed to the American conservatives, Thomas customarily "paired" with Bridges, in the Senate tradition, when both were absent from important roll calls. Although he supported plans for an American military mission to China in connection with Marshall's effort to secure a factional military integration, he expressed doubt whether Chinese armies could be subjected to superior political authority. He also continued to warn against American efforts to channel the destinies of Europe and Asia, particularly if that meant a war with Russia. With the promulgation of the Truman Doctrine, Thomas first expressed disquiet at the unforseeable and grave consequences of a program aimed at forcefully countering ideological and political movements abroad; yet, citing the paramount need for American unity, he went along with the rest of the Foreign Relations Committee in supporting the aid package. At the same time, he was coming to the conclusion that he must acquiesce in a China policy whose wisdom he questioned. Having decided for certain by 1947 that the Nationalists had little conception of China's movement—that they had lost the "mandate of

Heaven"—he was not surprised when the Communists wrested power from them. Although convinced of America's inability to stop the revolutionary tide, he thereafter supported all Foreign Relations Committee decisions, feeling "very much a minority in my basic thinking about things."

But in the heightening Cold War tensions, he lost his wartime enthusiasm for Asian revolutions and began to laud America's efforts "to halt the spread of communist influences abroad." By mid-1949, he lamented the shameful necessity of helplessly watching the Communists "take over" China; he expressed empathy with Chinese, Japanese, and Korean fears of Russia; and he noted the strategic importance of Taiwan to the United States. Still, he deplored America's arrogant approach to worldwide problems, and he noted in January 1950 that the Chinese Communists must ultimately be recognized, if not approved, by the United States. He followed the Administration policy of noninterference in Taiwan, and then supported the Administration's switch to a neutralization of the Taiwan Strait after the Korean outbreak. Throughout the balance of 1950—his last year in office—Thomas supported America's "firm stand against continued Communist aggression," lest such aggression later assume more serious proportions in Indochina, Taiwan, or beyond. Thus had the cooperative internationalist of 1945 been converted to the more aggressive, anticommunist internationalism of the Asian Cold War.

It is unfortunate, but not surprising, that the communization of the Chinese mainland found the American and Chinese Communist leaderships bitterly estranged. American aid to the Nationalists in 1947-49—granted under duress by the Administration, and quite modest by standards of European aid—nonetheless earned the United States the lasting hatred of the Communists, whose civil war and bloodshed it had prolonged. And in their turn, the American people were so stunned by the outcome in China as to provide a receptive audience for the demagoguery of the

McCarthy period. Lamentably, the American response to the Chinese revolution became the model for America's reaction to other Third World revolutions after 1949. That reaction was characterized by hatred, fear, and frantic efforts to push back the revolutionary tide. The anticommunist reaction to the Chinese Communists in the Cold War's prelude came to define America's attitude toward revolution in general during the Cold War era. There was no attempt to assess indigenous support, nationalistic tendencies, or potential foreign orientations—only a reflexive assumption that revolutionary or communist successes were identical with an extension of Soviet Communist power in antipathy to American ideological and strategic interests. This syndrome reached its truly ironic and tragic climax in the Vietnam War, which escalated even as the United States moved toward détente with Russia and a reevaluation of China, the two sources of American misgivings with respect to any revolution in the world. Thus had ideology distorted reality.

Notes

PREFACE

1. See Barbara W. Tuchman, "If Mao Had Come to Washington: An Essay in Alternatives," *Foreign Affairs* 51 (October, 1972): 44-64.

2. See H. Bradford Westerfield, *Foreign Policy and Party Politics: Pearl Harbor to Korea* (New Haven: Yale University Press, 1955), chap. 12; Tang Tsou, *America's Failure in China, 1941-50* (Chicago: University of Chicago Press, 1963), pp. 447-51; Athan Theoharis, *Seeds of Repression: Harry S. Truman and the Origins of McCarthyism* (Chicago: Quadrangle Books, 1971), p. 76; Richard M. Freeland, *The Truman Doctrine and the Origins of McCarthyism: Foreign Policy, Domestic Politics, and Internal Security, 1946-1948* (New York: Alfred A. Knopf, 1972), pp. 109-14.

3. Akira Iriye, "1922-1931," in Ernest R. May and James C. Thomson, Jr., eds., *American-East Asian Relations: A Survey*, Harvard Studies in American-East Asian Relations, no. 1 (Cambridge, Mass.: Harvard University Press, 1972), p. 242.

AMERICAN IDEALS AND WORLD POLITICS

1. Vandenberg speech in U.S., *Congressional Record*, 79th Cong., 1st Sess., 1945, 91, pt. 1: 164-68. Cited hereafter as *Cong. Rec.* See also "Scrapbook. 1945," in Arthur H. Vandenberg Papers (William L. Clements Library, University of Michigan, Ann Arbor, Michigan). Cited hereafter as Vandenberg Papers.

2. For Vandenberg's early relationship with Dulles, see Arthur H. Vandenberg, Jr., and Joe Alex Morris, eds., *The Private Papers of Senator Vandenberg* (Boston: Houghton Mifflin, 1952), pp. 55-62.

3. Letter of John Foster Dulles to Styles Bridges, January 8, 1945, in John Foster Dulles Papers (Princeton University Library, Princeton, New Jersey), Box 140. Cited hereafter as Dulles Papers. See also Ray Tucker, "The News Behind the News," January 1945, "Scrapbook. 1945," Vandenberg Papers. This article reported that internationalist Chan Gurney, of South Dakota, was passed over, although senior to Wiley.

4. See letter from Dulles to Henry R. Luce, January 29, 1945, Dulles Papers, Box 140.

5. "Notice of meeting," n.d., in Tom Connally Papers (Library of Congress, Washington, D.C.), Box 116. Cited hereafter as Connally Papers.

6. Richard Cope, "Bridges of New Hampshire: A Cagey Senator," *The Reporter* (April 1, 1952), pp. 6-10, in Styles Bridges Papers (New England College Library, Henniker, New Hampshire), File 29. Cited hereafter as Bridges Papers. See also "Current Biography" (March 1948), pp. 3-5, Bridges Papers, File 94; and "Preparedness and Styles Bridges," Bridges Papers, File 25.

7. *"America's Position in the International Crisis,"* n.d., Bridges Papers, File 25.

8. "Current Biography" (March 1948), p. 4, Bridges Papers, File 94.

9. Bridges speech, *Cong. Rec.*, 91, pt. 6: 8165.

10. Resolution of the Polish-American Congress, New Hampshire Division, April 4, 1945, in *Cong. Rec.*, 91, pt. 3: 3393-94; Joseph J. Betley to Styles Bridges, April 4, 1945, and Bridges to Betley, April 16, 1945, Bridges Papers, File 94.

11. Betley to Bridges, May 11, 1945; Bridges to Betley, May 14, 1945, Bridges Papers, File 94.

12. See news clippings, Bridges Papers, File 27; also Bridges's comments, *Cong. Rec.*, 91, pt. 11: A1659-60.

13. *Cong. Rec.*, 91, pt. 3: 4110-11.

14. Ibid., pt. 4: 5316.

15. Ibid., pt. 5: 5845.

16. Ibid., pt. 10: A534.

17. C. David Tompkins, *Senator Arthur H. Vandenberg: The Evolution of a Modern Republican, 1884-1945* (East Lansing, Mich.: Michigan State University Press, 1970), p. 176.

Notes

18. Ibid., p. 238; Vandenberg and Morris, eds., *Private Papers*, p. 130.

19. Vandenberg and Morris, eds., *Private Papers*, p. 148.

20. Ibid., pp. 150-51.

21. Ibid., p. 154.

22. Ibid., pp. 159-60.

23. Ibid., p. 196.

24. Ibid., p. 161.

25. Ibid., p. 173.

26. Ibid., pp. 155-56.

27. *Cong. Rec.*, 91, pt. 5: 6983.

28. Vandenberg speech, February 5, 1945, reprinted ibid., pt. 10: A534.

29. Tom Connally and Alfred Steinberg, *My Name Is Tom Connally* (New York: Thomas Y. Crowell, 1954), pp. 98, 100, 200, 254, 256, 257; and chaps. 10-11, 32-33, *passim*.

30. Connally speech, "At the Dinner for the Presidential Electors," January 19,1945, Connally Papers, Box 562.

31. Connally press statements, February 12 and 14, 1945, Connally Papers, Box 562.

32. Connally speech, "At the Dinner for the Presidential Electors," January 19, 1945, and Connally press statement, February 7, 1945, Connally Papers, Box 562; *Cong. Rec.*, 91, pt. 1: 168.

33. Connally and Steinberg, *My Name Is Tom Connally*, pp. 271-72.

34. Ibid., p. 271.

35. Ibid., pp. 281, 283.

36. *Cong. Rec.*, 91, pt. 11: A2341-42.

37. Ibid., pt. 6: 8017. Emphasis added.

38. Ibid., pt. 11: A2341.

39. Ibid., p. A2342.

40. "Biographical Sketch of Senator Elbert D. Thomas," in Elbert D. Thomas Papers (Franklin D. Roosevelt Library, Hyde Park, New York), Box 127. Cited hereafter as Thomas Papers. See also Elbert D. Thomas to Betty Brunson, March 15, 1945, Thomas Papers, Box 109.

41. Robert A. Divine, *The Illusion of Neutrality: Franklin D. Roosevelt and the Struggle over the Arms Embargo* (Chicago: Quadrangle Books, 1962), pp. 153, 239, 312-13; Connally and Steinberg, *My Name Is Tom Connally*, p. 229.

42. "Biographical Sketch of Senator Elbert D. Thomas," Thomas Papers, Box 127.

43. Elbert D. Thomas, *The Four Fears* (Chicago: Ziff-Davis, 1944), pp. 11-27, 28-44, *passim*.

44. Ibid., pp. 47-55, 58-63.

45. Ibid., pp. 59-60, 63-69.

46. Ibid., pp. 3-10.

47. Ibid., pp. 70, 74-77, 81.

48. Ibid., pp. 81-87.

49. Ibid., pp. 97-102, 111-33, 143, 147-55.

50. William Allan Neilson, "Release From Hampering Fear," *New York Herald Tribune*, October 15, 1944, Thomas Papers, Box 132. See also Elbert Thomas to Elvon Orme, March 21, 1945, and Elvon Orme to Thomas, n.d., Thomas Papers, Box 109.

51. Elbert D. Thomas, "The World Wants More Democracy," *Free World* (June 1945), reprinted in *Cong. Rec.*, 91, pt. 12: A3039.

52. Ibid., and pt. 1: 330; pt. 2: 1994-95, 2075; pt. 5: 6206-14; pt. 6: 7906-8; Thomas to Edward R. Stettinius, May 22, 1945, Thomas Papers, Box 117.

WISHFUL THINKING ABOUT CHINA

1. See Wesley R. Fishel, *The End of Extraterritoriality in China* (Berkeley: University of California Press, 1952), chap. 11.

2. See Fred W. Riggs, *Pressures on Congress: A Study of the Repeal of Chinese Exclusion* (New York: King's Crown Press, 1950).

3. Ibid., pp. 155, 157; p. 240, n. 3; p. 241, n. 13; and John L. Snell, *Illusion and Necessity: The Diplomacy of Global War, 1939-1945* (Boston: Houghton Mifflin, 1963), pp. 193-94.

4. For this discussion of wartime Sino-American relations, I am indebted to Barbara W. Tuchman, *Stilwell and the American Experience in China, 1911-45* (New York: Macmillan, 1970), chaps. 10-19; Tsou, *America's Failure in China*, chaps. 2-8; and Herbert Feis, *The China Tangle: The American Effort in China from Pearl Harbor to the Marshall Mission* (Princeton: Princeton University Press, 1953).

5. For the negotiation of the Yalta Far Eastern agreement, see William Hardy McNeill, *America, Britain, and Russia: Their Co-operation and Conflict, 1941-1946, Survey of International Affairs, 1939-1946*, ed. Arnold Toynbee (London: Oxford University Press, 1953), pp. 543-47; Feis,

Notes

China Tangle, chap. 23; Diane Shaver Clemens, *Yalta* (New York: Oxford University Press, 1970), pp. 244-55; and Michael Schaller, *The U.S. Crusade in China, 1938-1945* (New York: Columbia University Press, 1979), pp. 209-12.

6. Tuchman, *Stilwell*, p. 250; Wesley R. Fishel, "The Abolition of Extraterritoriality in China" (Ph. D. dissertation, University of Chicago, 1948), p. 362, n. 12; Riggs, *Pressures on Congress*, pp. 170ff.

7. Tuchman, *Stilwell*, pp. 372, 387.

8. Excerpt from Dulles address before the Cleveland Council on World Affairs, January 17, 1945, enclosed with letter from Dulles to Henry R. Luce, January 29, 1945, Dulles Papers, Box 140.

9. Dulles to Luce, January 29, 1945, and other correspondence in Dulles Papers, Box 140.

10. Tompkins, *Senator Arthur H. Vandenberg*, pp. 15, 16, 162-63, 189, 233-34; Vandenberg and Morris, eds., *Private Papers*, pp. 17-18, 22, 45, 51-53, 77-89; James Alan Fetzer, "Congress and China, 1941-1950" (Ph. D. dissertation, Michigan State University, 1969), pp. 15, 17; William Manchester, *American Caesar: Douglas MacArthur, 1880-1964* (London: Hutchinson & Co., 1979), pp. 356-63.

11. Vandenberg and Morris, eds., *Private Papers*, pp. 91-92, 95-96, 103-4; Tompkins, *Senator Arthur H. Vandenberg*, pp. 225, 228-29.

12. *Cong. Rec.*, 91, pt. 1: 165-67. Vandenberg and Morris, eds., *Private Papers*, pp. 136-38, and Tompkins, *Senator Arthur H. Vandenberg*, p. 239, give the background and impact of the speech.

13. Arthur H. Vandenberg, "Diary," April 27, 1945, p. 20, Vandenberg Papers. Italics in original.

14. Ibid., March 23, and June 2, 7, 8, and 14, 1945, pp. 3, 42, 49, 50, 53. See also Jay G. Hayden, "Battle Between Vandenberg and Molotov Nears Climax," *Detroit News*, n.d., "Scrapbook. 1945," Vandenberg Papers.

15. Connally and Steinberg, *My Name Is Tom Connally*, pp. 179-80, 232, 246-47, 252, 255, 259; Fetzer, "Congress and China, 1941-1950," p. 15.

16. Connally and Steinberg, *My Name Is Tom Connally*, pp. 259-60.

17. Connally speech, "At the Dinner for the Presidential Electors," January 19, 1945, Connally Papers, Box 562.

18. Tsao Shu-ming to Tom Connally, April 27, 1945; Connally to Shu-Ming Tsao [sic], May 1, 1945; Tsao to Connally, May 2, 1945; Victor Chi-tsai Hoo to Connally, May 8, 1945, Connally Papers, Box 562.

19. *Cong. Rec.*, 91, pt. 5: 6875.

20. See Connally press statements, February 7, 12, and 14, 1945; Connally "OWI Broadcast," April 5, 1945, Connally Papers, Box 562.

21. Elbert D. Thomas to Betty Brunson, March 15, 1945, Thomas Papers, Box 109; see also "Biographical Sketch of Senator Elbert D. Thomas," Thomas Papers, Box 127.

22. The books included a Japanese translation of Mormon scripture (1911); *Chinese Political Thought: A Study Based upon the Theories of the Principal Thinkers of the Chou Period* (New York: Prentice-Hall, 1927); *Thomas Jefferson, World Citizen* (New York: Modern Age Books, 1942); and *The Four Fears*.

23. Fetzer, "Congress and China, 1941-1950," pp. 34, 49; Fishel, "The Abolition of Extraterritoriality in China," p. 362; Fishel, *The End of Extraterritoriality in China*, p. 210; p. 294, n. 12; and preface by Elbert D. Thomas, p. vi; Riggs, *Pressures on Congress*, p. 187.

24. Thomas, *The Four Fears*, pp. 84, 85; and Elbert D. Thomas, *Extraterritoriality in China*, Senate Doc. 102, 78th Cong., 1st Sess., October 6, 1943, inserted as appendix to Thomas, *The Four Fears*.

25. Thomas, *The Four Fears*, pp. 102-3. See also Vandenberg and Morris, eds., *Private Papers*, pp. 51-52, which relates that at a Senate subcommittee meeting in June 1943, Thomas had pressed T. V. Soong "whether his government would consent to some possible 'territorial re-arrangements' if found necessary in the ultimate peace"; according to Vandenberg, Soong "certainly gave no ground" on the issue.

26. Thomas, *The Four Fears*, pp. 64-69.

27. Elbert D. Thomas, *"Asia after the War* (Tentative Title)," n.d., Thomas Papers, Box 99; "Senator Thomas on China's Youth," April 19, 1945, Thomas Papers, Box 96; *Cong. Rec.*, 91, pt. 6: 7275; NBC University of the Air, "Our Far Eastern Policy," July 14, 1945, p. 14, Thomas Papers, Box 98.

28. Tsao Shu-ming to Thomas, June 8, 1945; Elbert D. Thomas, "Article in Commemoration of the 8th Anniversary of Chinese Resistance Against Japan," July 7, 1945, enclosed with letter from Thomas to Tsao Shu-ming, June 27, 1945; NBC University of the Air, "Our Far Eastern Policy," July 14, 1945, p. 14, Thomas Papers, Box 98. See also *Cong. Rec.*, 91, pt. 6: 7275.

29. See correspondence between Thomas and Wirt W. Hallam, M. Allen Banks, and Maurice William, during March-July 1945, Thomas Papers, Boxes 107, 108.

30. Laurence E. Salisbury, "Our China Policy," *Far Eastern Survey* 14 (April 25, 1945), 89-92; and Salisbury to Thomas, April 20, 1945, Thomas

Papers, Box 108.

31. For Thomas's communications and materials received from the IPR, see Thomas Papers, Boxes 83, 108.

32. Gloria Draper for Elbert D. Thomas to Laurence E. Salisbury, April 25, 1945, Thomas Papers, Box 108.

33. *Cong. Rec.*, 91, pt. 5: 6414.

34. NBC University of the Air, "Our Far Eastern Policy," July 14, 1945, p. 16, Thomas Papers, Box 98. At this time, Thomas sidestepped the pressing issue of local autonomy as opposed to outright independence for Asian colonies. Asked whether he would find acceptable "self-government [for dependencies] within the British or French or Dutch Community of Nations," he replied, "Yes. If they have real self-government, . . . they can take independence any time they want it."

35. Elbert D. Thomas, "What We Are Up Against in Asia," *Washington Star*, July 29, 1945, reprinted in *Cong. Rec.*, 91, pt. 12: A3884-85. See also speech draft, Thomas Papers, Box 98.

36. Elbert D. Thomas, "The Way to the Next Great War," August 2, 1945, p. 6, Thomas Papers, Box 99.

37. Ibid., p. 5.

38. Snell, *Illusion and Necessity*, p. 202.

39. Connally press statement, August 8, 1945, Connally Papers, Box 562.

40. Connally press statement, August 9, 1945, Connally Papers, Box 562.

41. Connally press statement, "For Release upon Announcement by the President that the War is Over," Connally Papers, Box 562.

42. Elbert D. Thomas, "Regular weekly message to the people of Japan," OWI, August 9, 1945, pp. 2-3, Thomas Papers, Box 99. An advocate of psychological warfare, Thomas had made monthly wartime broadcasts (increased in frequency to weekly in 1945) in Japanese. See Thomas Papers, Boxes 96, 99; *Cong. Rec.*, 91, pt. 12: A3482, A3697-3701, A3773.

43. Elbert D. Thomas, "Regular weekly commentary on the Far East," OWI, August 17, 1945, p. 2; NBC University of the Air, "Japan After Surrender," August 18, 1945, pp. 11-12, Thomas Papers, Box 99.

44. NBC University of the Air, "Japan After Surrender," August 18, 1945, p. 7; Elbert D. Thomas, "Regular weekly commentary on the Far East," OWI, August 30, 1945, p. 2, Thomas Papers, Box 99.

45. NBC University of the Air, "Japan After Surrender," August 18, 1945, p. 2, Thomas Papers, Box 99.

46. Elbert D. Thomas, "Statement to the United Press for release to

Indian newspapers," enclosed with letter from Thomas to Charles Cord-dry, September 17, 1945, Thomas Papers, Box 107.

47. Kien-wen Tang to Thomas, August 31, 1945, Thomas Papers, Box 107.

48. Elaine F. Hatch for Elbert D. Thomas to Kien-wen Tang, October 31, 1945, Thomas Papers, Box 107.

49. Alfred E. Driscoll to H. Alexander Smith, August 13, 1945, Decimal files, Department of State, National Archives, Washington, D.C., 761.93/8–1845. Cited hereafter as DS Decimal files.

50. H. Alexander Smith to Dean Acheson, August 18, 1945; Acheson to Smith, August 30, 1945, DS Decimal files, 761.93/8–1845.

51. *Cong. Rec.*, 91, pt. 7: 8883–911.

52. Dulles to Dean Acheson, August 17, 1945; Dulles to Mrs. William F. Knowland, August 24, 1945, Dulles Papers, Box 140.

THE CONSERVATIVE CRITIQUE

1. Reprinted in U.S. Senate, Committee on Foreign Relations, *Hearings, Investigation of Far Eastern Policy*, 79th Cong., 1st sess., 1945, pp. 19–20. Unpublished transcript in Committee Papers, Senate Committee on Foreign Relations, 79th Cong., Record Group 46, File No. SEN 79A–F10, Tray 142, National Archives, Washington, D.C. (Mimeographed.) Cited hereafter as *IFEP Hearings*.

2. Ibid., p. 19.

3. Ibid., pp. 21–25.

4. Russell D. Buhite, *Patrick J. Hurley and American Foreign Policy* (Ithaca, N.Y.: Cornell University Press, 1973), p. 166.

5. Ibid., p. 201; Feis, *China Tangle*, p. 222.

6. Tsou, *America's Failure in China*, pp. 201–8; Buhite, *Patrick J. Hurley*, pp. 199–202; John Paton Davies, Jr., *Dragon by the Tail: American, British, Japanese, and Russian Encounters with China and One Another* (New York: W.W. Norton, 1972), p. 362; Lewis McCarroll Purifoy, *Harry Truman's China Policy: McCarthyism and the Diplomacy of Hysteria, 1947–1951* (New York: New Viewpoints, 1976), pp. 19–21.

7. Davies, *Dragon by the Tail*, pp. 362, 371.

8. Ibid., p. 363.

9. John S. Service, *The Amerasia Papers: Some Problems in the History of US-China Relations* (Berkeley: Center for Chinese Studies, University of California, 1971), pp. 161–62, 166, 183, and chap. 7, *passim*.

Notes

10. Buhite, *Patrick J. Hurley*, pp. 200–201; Tsou, *America's Failure in China*, pp. 209–18.

11. See Davies, *Dragon by the Tail*, p. 428. Recent works on the promise of Chinese Communist-United States relations at the end of World War II include Tuchman, "If Mao Had Come to Washington"; Schaller, *U.S. Crusade in China*, chaps. 9–10; Kenneth E. Shewmaker, *Americans and Chinese Communists, 1927–1945: A Persuading Encounter* (Ithaca, N.Y.: Cornell University Press, 1971); Jim Peck, "America and the Chinese Revolution, 1942–1946: An Interpretation," in Ernest R. May and James C. Thomson, Jr., eds., *American-East Asian Relations: A Survey* (Cambridge, Mass.: Harvard University Press, 1972), pp. 319–55; John Gittings, *The World and China, 1922–1972* (London: Eyre Methuen, 1974), pp. 96–115; Joseph W. Esherick, ed., *Lost Chance in China: The World War II Despatches of John S. Service* (New York: Random House, 1974); and Robert G. Sutter, *China-Watch: Toward Sino-American Reconciliation* (Baltimore: The Johns Hopkins University Press, 1978), pp. 12–26. For criticism of the China hands' prescriptions for remolding China, see Walter LaFeber, "New Perspectives on American-East Asian Relations," *Journal of Asian Studies* 32 (August, 1973): 679–82.

12. Davies, *Dragon by the Tail*, pp. 352, 371.

13. Ibid., chap. 35; Buhite, *Patrick J. Hurley*, pp. 190–92.

14. See Tuchman, "If Mao Had Come to Washington"; and Schaller, *U.S. Crusade in China*, pp. 204–6.

15. U.S., Department of State, *Foreign Relations of the United States: Diplomatic Papers, 1945*, Vol. 7: *The Far East: China* (Washington, D.C.: U.S. Government Printing Office, 1969), pp. 244–46. Cited hereafter as *FRUS, 1945: China*. See also Davies, *Dragon by the Tail*, pp. 393–94; Service, *Amerasia Papers*, pp. 186–88.

16. Service, *Amerasia Papers*, p. 189.

17. Davies, *Dragon by the Tail*, p. 394.

18. Ibid., pp. 386, 388; Service, *Amerasia Papers*, pp. 124–26; Buhite, *Patrick J. Hurley*, pp. 221–22. In April 1945, the American chargé in Moscow, George F. Kennan, predicted that Russian policy would persist as "in the recent past: a fluid, resilient policy directed at the achievement of maximum power with minimum responsibility on portions of the Asiatic continent lying beyond the Soviet border." *FRUS, 1945: China*, pp. 342–44. But for the view of American specialists on the Soviet Union and world communism that the China hands were underestimating the Chinese Communists' affinity for Moscow, see Service, *Amerasia Papers*, p. 166, n. 47; Tsou, *America's Failure in China*, p. 204, n. 95; p. 215, n. 135.

19. For a more detailed discussion of Sino-Russian-American relations late in 1945, see below, chaps. 4, 5.

20. Buhite, *Patrick J. Hurley*, pp. 240–41, 243, 261–62, and chap. 10, *passim*. See also letter from Patrick J. Hurley to secretary of state, January 31, 1945; memorandum of conversation, April 7, 1945; Hurley to secretary of state and to American Embassy, Paris, August 13, 1945, all in Patrick J. Hurley Papers (Western History Collections, Bizzell Memorial Library, University of Oklahoma, Norman, Oklahoma), Boxes 87, 88. Cited hereafter as Hurley Papers.

21. Buhite, *Patrick J. Hurley*, pp. 259–68; Everett F. Drumright to Hurley, n.d., enclosing *New York Herald Tribune* editorial, Hurley Papers, Box 93. For communications critical both of Hurley and of Chiang, and for some letters favorable to Hurley during September-November 1945, see Hurley Papers, Boxes 93, 94.

22. Walter Millis, ed., *The Forrestal Diaries* (New York: Viking Press, 1951), p. 113. See also James F. Byrnes, *All in One Lifetime* (New York: Harper & Brothers, 1958), pp. 328–29; below, chap. 5.

23. "Preparedness and Styles Bridges," Bridges Papers, File 25; James Alan Fetzer, "Congress and China, 1941–1950" (Ph.D. dissertation, Michigan State University, 1969), p. 17.

24. Bridges Papers, File 27; Service, *Amerasia Papers*.

25. Bridges Papers, File 27. For Service's arrest and vindication, as well as the development of the *Amerasia* case as a political issue, see E. J. Kahn, Jr., *The China Hands: America's Foreign Service Officers and What Befell Them* (New York: Viking Press, 1975), pp. 161–72, 179–81.

26. Communist Party resolution, July 28, 1945, enclosed with letter, John A. Danaher to senators, September 25, 1945, Bridges Papers, File 27.

27. *Cong. Rec.*, 91, pt. 7: 8910–11.

28. Speech by George Dondero, October 10, 1945 (mimeographed copy), Bridges Papers, File 27.

29. Alfred Kohlberg to trustees, American Council, Institute of Pacific Relations, August 31, 1945, copy in DS Decimal files, 811.43 Institute of Pacific Relations/8–3145. On Kohlberg, see Charles Wertenbaker, "The World of Alfred Kohlberg," *The Reporter* 6 (April 29, 1952): 19–22; Joseph Keeley, *The China Lobby Man: The Story of Alfred Kohlberg* (New Rochelle, N.Y.: Arlington House, 1969).

30. William Loeb to Dean Acheson, October 6, 1945, DS Decimal files, 123 Service, John.

31. Service, *Amerasia Papers*, pp. 41–45.

32. Raymond Dennett to IPR trustees, April 4, 1945, Thomas Papers, Box

Notes

108. The IPR claimed that its membership and publications expressed a variety of viewpoints.

33. General P. E. Peabody, "*Secret*: Chinese Communist Movement," July 1945, pp. 1, 6, 7, mimeographed copy in Bridges Papers, File 27. Cited hereafter as *Peabody Report*. General Peabody's analysis was based on the in-depth study, U.S. Department of War, Military Intelligence Division, "Secret: The Chinese Communist Movement," July 5, 1945, mimeographed copy in Bridges Papers, File 26. Both the in-depth study (some four hundred typed pages) and the Peabody précis were declassified in 1949, and may be found in Lyman P. Van Slyke, ed., *The Chinese Communist Movement: A Report of the United States War Department, July 1945* (Stanford, Calif.: Stanford University Press, 1968).

34. *Peabody Report*, pp. 1–2.

35. Ibid., pp. 2–4.

36. Ibid., pp. 1, 4–6.

37. Memorandum accompanying letter, Albert LaVarre to Patrick J. Hurley, n.d., Bridges Papers, File 27.

38. "Hurley Collection Office Diaries," November 27, 1945, Hurley Papers; Hurley to Mrs. Constantine Brown, August 1, 1955, Hurley Papers, Box 104; letter draft, Hurley to Hiram Bingham, n.d., Hurley Papers, Box 101; anonymous Hurley assistant to Dr. John C. Clark, November 29, 1945, Hurley Papers.

39. Many such favorable comments may be found in Hurley Papers, Boxes 93, 94.

40. Buhite, *Patrick J. Hurley*, p. 272.

41. Bridges foreign policy statement, Bridges Papers, File 27. According to Bridges, senators who had pleaded in vain "for a clarification of American position in international affairs and for effective action" included Joseph Ball (R-Minn.), J. William Fulbright (D-Ark.), Carl Hatch (D-N.M.), and Burton Wheeler (D-Mont.).

42. *Cong. Rec.*, 91, pt. 8: 11110–12.

43. Ibid., pp. 11114, 11117.

44. Bridges Papers, File 27.

45. Bridges Papers, File 26.

46. *IFEP Hearings*, pp. 12, 73.

47. Ibid., pp. 132–33, 141.

48. Ibid., pp. 141–42.

49. Ibid., pp. 251–52. For additional evidence of conservative attachment

to Nationalist China, see Paul A. Varg, *The Closing of the Door: Sino-American Relations, 1936–1946* (East Lansing, Mich.: Michigan State University Press, 1973), pp. 226, 233.

50. *IFEP Hearings*, pp. 123–24, 231.

51. Ibid., p. 232.

52. Ibid., pp. 232–33.

53. Ibid., pp. 128–29, 248–49.

54. Working draft of Bridges address to Concord Chamber of Commerce, October 1, 1945, pp. 3–4, Bridges Papers, File 69.

55. *IFEP Hearings*, pp. 86–89, 120–25, 129–30, 142.

56. Ibid., pp. 124, 236, 239–41, 243, 244. Defending Service, Byrnes cited the diplomat's exoneration by the grand jury, the Justice Department's opinion that he should be reinstated, and General Wedemeyer's tribute to his work. Ibid., pp. 237–39.

57. Ibid., pp. 107, 109ff, 142.

58. Ibid., pp. 142–49; article, "Hurley Renders Service to U.S., Hugh Grant Says," Bridges Papers, File 27.

59. *IFEP Hearings*, pp. 252–53; letter, anonymous to President Truman, September 28, 1945, copy in Bridges Papers, File 27; memorandum accompanying letter from Albert LaVarre to Patrick J. Hurley, n.d., Bridges Papers, File 27.

60. Vandenberg and Morris, eds., *Private Papers*, chap. 12; "Scrapbook. 1945," Vandenberg Papers.

61. *Cong. Rec.*, 91, pt. 8: 10696–97; Vandenberg and Morris, eds., *Private Papers*, pp. 226–36; George Curry, *James F. Byrnes* (New York: Cooper Square Publishers, 1965), pp. 167–68, 355.

62. *Cong. Rec.*, 91, pt. 8: 10696; "Scrapbook. 1945," Vandenberg Papers; Vandenberg and Morris, eds., *Private Papers*, p. 227.

63. Hurley to Mrs. Constantine Brown, August 1, 1955, Hurley Papers, Box 104; letter draft, Hurley to Hiram Bingham, n.d., and Hurley to Mrs. George A. Fitch, June 14, 1952, Hurley Papers, Box 101. For the view that Vandenberg cynically allowed Hurley to be discredited in order to preserve bipartisanship and his own influence, see Don Lohbeck, *Patrick J. Hurley* (Chicago: Henry Regnery, 1956), pp. 427, 439–40, 446, 462, 472–73.

64. *Cong. Rec.*, 91, pt. 9: 11313.

65. Ibid., pp. 11313–14.

66. *IFEP Hearings*, pp. 40M, 41–43, 64–65, 213–14, 218, 222.

Notes

67. Ibid., pp. 220, 221, 228, 320. Remarks of DeLacy and Luce appeared in *Cong. Rec.*, 91, pt. 8: 10993–95; pt. 9: 11480–82.

68. *IFEP Hearings*, pp. 310, 311, 315, 318.

69. Below, chap. 4.

70. *IFEP Hearings*, p. 159.

71. Ibid., pp. 72–73.

72. Ibid., pp. 167–69.

THE LIBERAL CRITIQUE

1. Feis, *China Tangle*, pp. 388–89.

2. Ibid., pp. 362–66; Tsou, *America's Failure in China*, p. 308; Lyman P. Van Slyke, ed., *The China White Paper: August 1949* (Stanford, Calif.: Stanford University Press, 1967), pp. 311–12; *FRUS, 1945: China*, pp. 527–721, *passim*.

3. *FRUS, 1945: China*, pp. 527–28, 532, 611–13, 653–56, 662–65; Feis, *China Tangle*, chaps. 31, 32, and p. 401; Tsou, *America's Failure in China*, pp. 341–42.

4. *FRUS, 1945: China*, pp. 615, 617, 629–34; Feis, *China Tangle*, p. 397, n. 3.

5. Feis, *China Tangle*, pp. 390–94; Curry, *James F. Byrnes*, pp. 148–49, 152–53, 158.

6. Curry, *James F. Byrnes*, pp. 158–59; Feis, *China Tangle*, p. 394; Millis, ed., *Forrestal Diaries*, pp. 102, 106–7, 110.

7. *FRUS, 1945: China*, pp. 606–7, 646–47, 685.

8. Ibid., pp. 670–78.

9. Ibid., p. 607.

10. Ibid., pp. 590–91, 619–21, 644–45.

11. Ibid., pp. 606–7, 664, 674–76.

12. Davies, *Dragon by the Tail*, p. 415.

13. Ibid., pp. 428–29. See also Service, *Amerasia Papers*, pp. 188–92, for a speculative scenario envisioning the adoption of a flexible policy including the arming of the CCP early in 1945.

14. Feis, *China Tangle*, p. 398.

15. *FRUS, 1945: China*, pp. 639–43, 686.

16. Ibid., p. 685.

17. U.S., Department of State, *Bulletin* 13 (October 21, 1945): 644–48.

18. U.S., Department of State, *Bulletin* 13 (October 21, 1945): 647–48.

19. Lt. Charles E. Carroll to G. W. Carroll, September 16, 1945; G. W. Carroll to Sen. Theodore F. Green, October 11, 1945; Theodore Francis Green to James F. Byrnes, October 17, 1945; Walston Chubb to Dean Acheson, October 17, 1945, DS Decimal files, 711.93/10-1745.

20. *FRUS, 1945: China*, pp. 2–26, 577–78, 580–81; *Cong. Rec.*, 91, pt. 10: A1121.

21. Ilona Ralf Sues to Elbert D. Thomas, November 2, 1945, Thomas Papers, Box 108; Leland Stowe *et al.*, to Harry S. Truman, November 4, 1945, DS Decimal files, 711.93/11-445; Ilona Ralf Sues, *Shark's Fins and Millet* (Boston: Little, Brown, 1944), especially chaps. 1, 11, 12. Field, Stewart, Pope, and Stein had written extensively on China and international relations.

22. Committee for a Democratic Policy toward China, "*U.S. Policy In China as Carried on by Ambassador Hurley Responsible for Civil War Outbreaks*," p. 2, Thomas Papers, Box 108.

23. Ibid.; Sues to Thomas, November 2, 1945; Elsie Fairfax-Cholmeley to Thomas, November 3, 1945, Thomas Papers, Box 108.

24. See Thomas's weekly commentary on the Far East, September-December 1945, Thomas Papers, Box 96; Elbert D. Thomas, "Can America and Russia Stay Friends?" *Pageant* (November 1945), cited in *Cong. Rec.*, 91, pt. 13: A4997; Nora Hallgren to Thomas, November 7, 1945, Thomas Papers, Box 107.

25. Gloria Draper for Elbert D. Thomas to Elsie Fairfax-Cholmeley, November 7, 1945; E. F. Hatch for Thomas to Kien-wen Tang, October 31, 1945; Thomas to Harry S. Truman, November 30, 1945; press release on Thomas's attendance at International Labor Organization Conference, n.d., Thomas Papers, Boxes 107, 108, 117.

26. Stowe *et. al.* to Truman, November 4, 1945, DS Decimal files, 711.93/11-445; Harry Bridges to Robert Patterson, November 10, 1945, DS Decimal files, 711.93/11-2645; Communist Party, New York State, to James F. Byrnes, November 13, 1945, DS Decimal files, 711.93/11-1345.

27. Department of State, Moscow (unsigned) to secretary of state, November 2, 1945, DS Decimal files, 711.93/11-245; Rev. Richard Morford to James F. Byrnes, November 10, 1945, DS Decimal files, 711.93/11-1045; Pastor F. Clyde Helms to Byrnes, November 23, 1945, DS Decimal files, 711.93/11-2345.

28. *Cong. Rec.*, 91, pt. 13: A4734-35; Rep. Ellis E. Patterson to James F. Byrnes, November 14, 1945, DS Decimal files, 711.93/11-1445.

Notes

29. Quotation from *Cong. Rec.*, 91, pt. 8: 10995. See also ibid., pp. 10993, 11007, 11156; John M. Coffee *et al.* to Edward R. Stettinius, May 31, 1945, DS Decimal files, 711.00/5-3145. The six representatives were DeLacy, Ellis E. Patterson, John M. Coffee (D-Wash.), Helen Gahagan Douglas (D-Calif.), Ned R. Healy (D-Calif.), and Charles Savage (D-Wash.). On November 28, Rep. Adam Clayton Powell (D-N.Y.) introduced a similar resolution.

30. *Cong. Rec.*, 91, pt. 9: 11480–81; Dondero speech, October 10, 1945, Bridges Papers, File 27; above, chap. 3.

31. *IFEP Hearings*, pp. 127–28.

32. Hon. R. A. Parker to Byrnes, November 8, 1945; Hon. H. M. Carr to Harry S. Truman, November 10, 1945; Rep. Lindley Beckworth (to Department of State), November 17, 1945; Byrnes to Beckworth, December 10, 1945; Sen. Ernest McFarland to Byrnes, November 17, 1945; R. M. Riddell to McFarland, November 16, 1945; Rep. John R. Murdock to Byrnes, November 17, 1945; Rep. Richard F. Harless to Byrnes, November 20, 1945; Byrnes to Rep. Jack Z. Anderson, November 30, 1945; Rep. William R. Thom to Byrnes, November 23, 1945; Rep. Louis Ludlow to Byrnes, November 23, 1945; Sen. Hugh B. Mitchell to Byrnes, November 27, 1945, DS Decimal files, 711.93 and 711.00, November 1945.

33. See DS Decimal files, 711.93 and 711.00, November and December 1945.

34. Lewis R. Whitehead to Sen. Brien McMahon, November 16, 1945, DS Decimal files, 711.93/11-3045.

35. Mrs. Quinn Calhoun to Rep. Jed Johnson, November 25, 1945, DS Decimal files, 711.93/11-3045.

36. Rep. Jed Johnson to James F. Byrnes, November 30, 1945, DS Decimal files, 711.93/11-3045.

37. Joseph Dauber to Rep. William A. Rowan, November 17, 1945, DS Decimal files, 711.93/11-2345; F. A. Norman to Harry S. Truman, December 5, 1945, DS Decimal files, 711.00/12-545; Ruth Weinblatt to John Carter Vincent, December 2, 1945, DS Decimal files, 711.00/12-245; Whitehead to McMahon, November 16, 1945, DS Decimal files, 711.93/11-3045; Roy McCorkel to James F. Byrnes, November 28, 1945, DS Decimal files, 711.00/11-2845; Mrs. N. B. Honeycutt to Tom Connally, November 21, 1945, Connally Papers, Box 103. For the shift from wartime to postwar American perceptions of China, see Harold R. Isaacs, *Scratches on Our Minds: American Images of China and India* (New York: John Day, 1958), pp. 176–209.

38. DS Decimal files, 711.93 and 711.00, November-December 1945.

39. Paul V. Bacon to John Carter Vincent, November 28, 1945, DS Decimal files, 711.93/11-2845.

40. Rep. John H. Folger to James F. Byrnes, November 29, 1945, DS Decimal files, 711.93/11-2945; Dr. Samuel J. Prigal to Dean Acheson, November 30, 1945, DS Decimal files, 711.93/11-3045; Philip Kaplan to Sen. Brien McMahon, December 5, 1945; McMahon to Department of State, December 13, 1945; Acheson to McMahon, December 28, 1945, DS Decimal files, 711.93/12-1345.

41. *FRUS, 1945: China*, pp. 581–82, 1035; Department of State, Moscow (unsigned), to secretary of state, November 2, 1945, DS Decimal files, 711.93/11-245.

42. *FRUS, 1945: China*, pp. 577–80, 635, 637, 655, 658, 664, 683; Feis, *China Tangle*, pp. 365–66.

43. S. Shepard Jones to James K. Penfield, December 14, 1945, enclosing report, "Organization Opinion on U.S. Policy Toward China as Reflected in State Department Mail," December 13, 1945, DS Decimal files, 711.93/12-1445.

44. Department of State, *Policy Manual*, p. 89, DS Decimal files, 1945, no file number.

45. Ibid., pp. 88, 89.

46. *FRUS, 1945: China*, p. 600.

47. Ibid., p. 688.

48. Thomas to Truman, November 30, 1945; Thomas to Matthew J. Connelly, November 30, 1945, Thomas Papers, Box 117.

49. *IFEP Hearings*, pp. 1, 70, 97. Under questioning by Senator Green, Hurley did not recall earlier mentioning John K. Emmerson, a diplomat. Thomas interjected, "You mentioned Em[m]erson. I wrote it down as you mentioned it." This was Thomas's only comment at the entire series of public sessions.

50. Thomas and Smith (R-N.J.), a strong internationalist, enjoyed a fruitful relationship, serving together on the Education and Labor Committee, the Military Affairs Committee (1946), and, after 1946, the Foreign Relations Committee. For their common religious interests, see H. Alexander Smith to Elbert Thomas, December 9, 1947; Thomas to Smith, December 16, 1947; and Thomas to Smith, December 18, 1947, Thomas Papers, Box 176. Smith was an active lay Presbyterian and Thomas an elder in the Mormon Church—and they enthusiastically exchanged Biblical stories and parables.

Notes

51. Elbert D. Thomas to Dr. Willis W. Ritter *et al.*, August 15, 1946, Thomas Papers, Box 204. See also Thomas to Irving Richter, January 30, 1945, Thomas Papers, Box 110; Thomas to Harry S. Truman, August 25, 1945, Thomas Papers, Box 117.

52. Thomas to Ritter *et al.*, August 15, 1946, Thomas Papers, Box 204.

53. Elbert D. Thomas to Charles Fahy, August 15, 1946, Thomas Papers, Box 141.

54. Ibid.; Thomas to Ritter *et al.*, August 15, 1946, Thomas Papers, Box 204.

55. Thomas to Ritter *et al.*, August 15, 1946, Thomas Papers, Box 204.

56. *IFEP Hearings*, pp. 186, 263.

THE GOVERNMENT DEFENSE

1. Connally and Steinberg, *My Name Is Tom Connally*, p. 313. Cf. Truman's recollections in *Memoirs: Years of Trial and Hope* (Garden City, N.Y.: Doubleday, 1956), p. 63.

2. Sam Chester McKay, Jr., to Connally, November 5, 1945, Connally Papers, Box 103.

3. Albert R. Burke to Connally, November 7, 1945, Connally Papers, Box 103.

4. Mrs. Sam C. McKay, Sr., to Connally, and Herman Horowitz to Connally, November 15, 1945, Connally Papers, Box 103.

5. George Schwartz to Connally, November 17, 1945, Connally Papers, Box 103.

6. Sen. Brien McMahon to Connally, n.d.; Katherine Houghton Hepburn to McMahon, n.d. (copy); Marion Potter to McMahon, n.d. (copy); L. E. Winder to Connally, November 26, 1945; Mrs. E. L. Cooper to Connally, November 27, 1945; J. H. Burns to Connally, November 27, 1945; W. R. Boswell to Connally, November 4, 1945; G. R. Williams to Connally, November 6, 1945, Connally Papers, Box 103.

7. Tom Connally to G. R. Williams, November 9, 1945; Connally to Mrs. W. R. Boswell, November 15, 1945; Connally to H. W. Meyers, November 29, 1945, Connally Papers, Box 103.

8. *Cong. Rec.*, 91, pt. 8: 11112–13.

9. "Senate Link With Byrnes Agreed Upon," *Washington Post*, November 18, 1945; James F. Byrnes to Tom Connally, November 5, 1945; "Secretary Meets with Senate Committee," November 24, 1945, in Committee Papers, Senate Committee on Foreign Relations, 79th Cong.,

Record Group 46, File No. SEN 79A-F10, Tray 142, National Archives, Washington, D. C. Cited hereafter as SCFR Papers. The eight senators were Connally, Thomas, Vandenberg, Austin, Walter George (D-Ga.), Alben Barkley (D-Ky.), Robert LaFollette, Jr. (Ind-Wisc.), and Wallace White (R-Me.).

10. *Cong. Rec.*, 91, pt. 8: 11112–15, 11117.

11. Cpl. B. V. Callum, Jr., to Connally, November 29, 1945; Mrs. O. F. McLendon to Connally, December 5, 1945; George F. Friauf *et al.* to Connally, November 29, 1945; Valin R. Woodward to Connally, November 29, 1945, Connally Papers, Box 103; Abe Pollin to Connally, December 1, 1945; J. K. Roach to Connally, December 1, 1945; Samuel P. Radin to Connally, November 29, 1945; Wolfram Hill to Connally, November 30, 1945; Frank E. Goodwin to Connally, December 1, 1945, SCFR Papers, Tray 142.

12. Sen. William Langer to Joseph C. Grew, June 13, 1945, DS Decimal files, 123 Hurley, Patrick J. (Amb.); H. L. Yates to Connally, December 1, 1945; Charles Smith to Connally, December 1, 1945; Carey Spence to Connally, December 3, 1945, SCFR Papers, Tray 142. See Buhite, *Patrick J. Hurley*, chap. 4, on Hurley's work for Sinclair.

13. Samuel P. Radin to Connally, November 29, 1945, SCFR Papers, Tray 142.

14. Mrs. Dorothy C. Krugman to Connally, November 29, 1945; Abe Pollin to Connally, December 1, 1945, SCFR Papers, Tray 142.

15. E. C. Barkley to Connally, November 29, 1945, enclosing "Gen. Hurley's Charges," *The Houston Press*, November 28, 1945; W. A. Wansley to Connally, November 30, 1945; O. E. Lancaster to Connally, November 29, 1945; James B. Robinson to Connally, November 29, 1945; A. V. Kempe to Connally, November 30, 1945, SCFR Papers, Tray 142.

16. N. Desmond Crosby to Connally, n.d.; James B. Robinson to Connally, November 29, 1945, SCFR Papers, Tray 142.

17. Garnett Underwood to Connally, December 1, 1945; "Pat Hurley for President," *Tulsa Tribune*, November 30, 1945; Hugh G. Grant to Connally, December 4 and 5, 1945; "Hurley Renders Service to U.S., Hugh Grant Says," *Atlanta Journal*, November 28, 1945, SCFR Papers, Tray 142.

18. W. A. Wansley to Connally, November 30, 1945; Garnett Underwood to Connally, December 1, 1945; editorial, *Tulsa Tribune*, November 30, 1945, SCFR Papers, Tray 142.

19. Underwood to Connally, December 1, 1945; Crosby to Connally, n.d., SCFR Papers, Tray 142.

Notes

20. Editorial, *Tulsa Tribune*, November 30, 1945, SCFR Papers, Tray 142.

21. Wansley to Connally, November 30, 1945, SCFR Papers, Tray 142.

22. Underwood to Connally, December 1, 1945; A. V. Kempe to Connally, November 30, 1945, SCFR Papers, Tray 142.

23. J. W. Densford to Connally, November 29, 1945, SCFR Papers, Tray 142.

24. Editorial, *Houston Post*, November 30, 1945; H. C. McFadden to Patrick J. Hurley (copy to Connally), December 1, 1945, SCFR Papers, Tray 142.

25. James F. Byrnes to Rep. Jack Z. Anderson, November 30, 1945, DS Decimal files, 711.93/11-1745; Byrnes to Rep. Ellis Patterson, November 28, 1945, DS Decimal files, 711.93/11-1445. Cf. Byrnes to Rep. William R. Thom, December 4, 1945, and Byrnes to Rep. Louis Ludlow, December 7, 1945, DS Decimal files, 711.93/11-2345; Department of State, *Policy Manual*, p. 88, DS Decimal files, 1945, no file number.

26. John F. Melby, *The Mandate of Heaven: Record of a Civil War. China, 1945-49* (Toronto: University of Toronto Press, 1968), pp. 38–39; *FRUS, 1945: China*, pp. 726–38; Truman, *Memoirs: Years of Trial and Hope*, pp. 65–66; James F. Byrnes, *All in One Lifetime* (New York: Harper & Brothers, 1958), pp. 328–29; Millis, ed., *Forrestal Diaries*, p. 113; Feis, *China Tangle*, p. 412; Buhite, *Patrick J. Hurley*, pp. 271–72; memorandum, Walter Brown to secretary [of state], November 27, 1945, DS Decimal files, 711.93/11-2745. Truman's recollection is disputed in Lohbeck, *Patrick J. Hurley*, pp. 427–28.

27. Department of State, "Radio Bulletin," November 27, 1945, p. 6; memorandum, "*China—Ambassador Hurley's Charges*," SCFR Papers, Tray 143. For Connally's involvement in other issues, see SCFR Papers, Tray 143; Connally to Joseph E. Horowitz, November 29, 1945, Connally Papers, Box 110; Byrnes, *All in One Lifetime*, pp. 327, 331; Vandenberg and Morris, eds., *Private Papers*, pp. 226–27; Connally and Steinberg, *My Name Is Tom Connally*, pp. 288–90.

28. [Robert V.] Shirley [to Connally], "*The Dilemma in China*: Military aspects"; Walter Lippmann, "The Dilemma in China," *Washington Post*, December 4, 1945; Mark Gayn, "How Hurley Wrecked U.S. Embassy Staff," *PM*, December 5, 1945; Eric Sevareid, news analysis, November 28, 1945, Columbia Broadcasting System, typed copy, SCFR Papers, Tray 142.

29. Tom Connally to James F. Byrnes, December 5, 1945; Department of State, "Radio Bulletin," November 28, 1945, pp. 4–6; "Statement of the

Secretary of State Before the Senate Committee on Foreign Relations,"
confidential copy, SCFR Papers, Tray 143; also, "Chinese Unity is U.S.
Policy, Byrnes Says," *Washington Post*, December 5, 1945, SCFR Papers,
Tray 142.

30. *FRUS, 1945: China*, pp. 829–31; Davies, *Dragon by the Tail*, pp.
421–22; Byrnes, *All in One Lifetime*, pp. 331–32.

31. Tom Connally to S. C. McKay, Jr., December 5, 1945; Connally to
George Schwartz, December 7, 1945; and similar letters, Connally
Papers, Box 103. See also undated list of statements and questions designed to elicit "more specific information concerning" Hurley's "various
charges." SCFR Papers, Tray 142.

32. *IFEP Hearings*, pp. 183–84. See also "Hurley Investigation—December 5, 1945," SCFR Papers, Tray 142.

33. *IFEP Hearings*, pp. 38, 38a, 39, 40, 40-J, 41–43, 184–85, 223–24.
Emphases added. See also Theodore H. White, Richard J. Watts, Jr., Eric
Sevareid, Annalee Jacoby, and Jack Belden to Tom Connally, December
2, 1945, reprinted in *IFEP Hearings*, pp. 310–12.

34. *IFEP Hearings*, pp. 8–9, 74–75, 261.

35. Ibid., pp. 15–17, 82–84, 179–81, 223, 226, 256–61. For the Connally-
Byrnes probe of Bridges's sinister hints of State Department disloyalty, see
ibid., pp. 234, 240, 253–55.

36. *IFEP Hearings*, p. 325. See also ibid., pp. 316–26, *passim*.

37. Ibid., pp. 44–47, 89–90.

38. For the predominantly anti-Hurley tone of Connally's mail during the
hearings, see SCFR Papers, Trays 142, 143; Connally Papers, Box 103.

39. See Connally Papers, Box 103; SCFR Papers, Tray 142.

40. Tom Connally to Lewis M. Herrmann, December 17, 1945; Connally
to Harry B. Hawes, December 17, 1945; and a few letters from noninterventionists to Connally between December 11 and the end of the year,
Connally Papers, Box 103.

41. Harold A. Fletcher, Jr., to Harry Truman, December 17, 1945,
enclosing petition, DS Decimal files, 711.93/12-1745; Arthur Upham
Pope to Dean Acheson, December 23, 1945, DS Decimal files,
711.93/12-2345.

42. Vandenberg and Morris, eds., *Private Papers*, pp. 227–30; Feis,
China Tangle, p. 413; Dean Acheson, *Present at the Creation: My Years
in the State Department* (New York: W. W. Norton, 1969), p. 142;
Tuchman, *Stilwell*, p. 527.

43. Feis, *China Tangle*, p. 413; *FRUS, 1945: China*, pp. 745–47.

Notes

44. *FRUS, 1945: China*, pp. 747–51, 756, 758, 759; Feis, *China Tangle*, pp. 414–15.

45. Feis, *China Tangle*, p. 415; *FRUS, 1945: China*, pp. 759–60, 762, 768.

46. Van Slyke, ed., *China White Paper*, p. 606. See also *FRUS, 1945: China*, pp. 760–61, 767–68. Cf. Truman's confidential directive to Marshall, ibid., pp. 770–73, with Truman's public statement of the same date, in Van Slyke, ed., *China White Paper*, pp. 607–9.

47. Van Slyke, ed., *China White Paper*, p. 609.

48. Ibid., pp. 605, 608.

49. James F. Byrnes to Rep. Jed Johnson, December 10, 1945, DS Decimal files, 711.93/11-3045.

50. Millis, ed., *Forrestal Diaries*, p. 108.

51. *FRUS, 1945: China*, p. 762.

52. Ibid., p. 660.

53. Department of State, Moscow, to secretary of state, November 30, 1945, DS Decimal files, 711.93/11-3045; Department of State, Moscow, to secretary of state, December 11, 1945, DS Decimal files, 711.00/12-1145; Feis, *China Tangle*, p. 424; *FRUS, 1945: China*, pp. 833–35.

54. *FRUS, 1945: China*, pp. 835–45.

55. Ibid., p. 849.

56. Ibid., pp. 849–50.

57. Feis, *China Tangle*, p. 427; James F. Byrnes, *Speaking Frankly* (New York: Harper & Brothers, 1947), p. 228; Byrnes, *All in One Lifetime*, p. 336.

58. Service, *Amerasia Papers*, p. 128.

59. The first and most influential of these books was Theodore H. White and Annalee Jacoby, *Thunder out of China* (New York: William Sloane Associates, 1946).

60. Davies, *Dragon by the Tail*, pp. 253, 262–63, 301, 312–13; Tuchman, *Stilwell*, pp. 153–54, 197, 283, 300, 371, 511, 527, and *passim*; Connally to Lewis M. Herrmann, December 17, 1945, Connally Papers, Box 103.

61. Fetzer, "Congress and China, 1941–1950," pp. 67–70; *FRUS, 1945: China*, pp. 786, 795–96, 800–4, 817, 825; Tsou, *America's Failure in China*, pp. 401–12.

62. Westerfield, *Foreign Policy and Party Politics*, p. 254.

63. Patrick J. Hurley to Herbert Heath, December 26, 1945; "Release for

A.M. Newspapers," December 12, 1945, Hurley Papers, Box 93; Hurley to Hon. Wirt Franklin, December 27, 1945; Hurley to Samuel Crowther, December 18, 1945; Hurley to James C. Brown, December 21, 1945, Hurley Papers, Box 94; notes on Averell Harriman, p. 16, Hurley Papers, Box 104.

64. Connally and Steinberg, *My Name Is Tom Connally*, pp. 288–91; Vandenberg and Morris, eds., *Private Papers*, pp. 227–36; John Foster Dulles to Arthur Vandenberg, December 17, 1945, Dulles Papers, Supplementary Box 5; Thomas Papers, Box 96; Bridges Papers, Files 25, 27, 69.

65. Patrick J. Hurley to Maj. Gen. Albert L. Cox, December 27, 1945, Hurley Papers, Box 218; Rep. Mike Mansfield to James F. Byrnes, December 31, 1945, DS Decimal files, 711.93/12-3145.

A PRELUDE TO COLD WAR

1. Tuchman, "If Mao Had Come to Washington," p. 60.

2. For a stimulating discussion of United States-Chinese Communist relations during this period, see Peck, "America and the Chinese Revolution, 1942–1946," *passim*.

3. Gabriel A. Almond, *The American People and Foreign Policy* (New York: Frederick A. Praeger, 1960), p. 53.

4. Ibid., pp. 145–46.

5. See Richard M. Freeland, *The Truman Doctrine and the Origins of McCarthyism: Foreign Policy, Domestic Politics, and Internal Security, 1946–1948* (New York: Alfred A. Knopf, 1972); Vandenberg and Morris, eds., *Private Papers*, pp. 230, 339–43, 391.

6. See U.S. Congress, House of Representatives, Committee on Foreign Affairs, *Hearings, Assistance to Greece and Turkey*, 80th Cong., 1st sess., 1947, pp. 16–18, 27–28, 47–50, 360–61; Freeland, *Truman Doctrine*, pp. 198–99; Theoharis, *Seeds of Repression*.

7. For the fate of the China hands, see Kahn, *China Hands, passim*; Service, *Amerasia Papers*, Foreword, and chaps. 1–2; David Halberstam, *The Best and the Brightest* (New York: Random House, 1972), pp. 138–50, 462–78; and Gary May, "The 'New China Hands' and the Rape of the China Service," *Reviews in American History* 4 (March 1976): 120–21, 126.

8. The following brief discussion of the roles of Bridges, Vandenberg, Connally, and Thomas during 1946–50 is based on the following sources: Bridges Papers; Vandenberg Papers; Connally Papers; Thomas Papers; Hurley Papers; SCFR Papers. Also useful are James Alan Fetzer,

Notes

"Congress and China, 1947: The Congressional Effort to Aid Chiang Kai-shek" (paper read before symposium on the United States and China, n.d.); Fetzer, "Congress and China, 1941–1950"; Ross Y. Koen, *The China Lobby in American Politics* (New York: Harper & Row, 1974); Tsou, *America's Failure in China*; Vandenberg and Morris, eds., *Private Papers*; U.S. Senate, Committee on Appropriations, *Hearings, Third Supplemental Appropriation Bill for 1948*, 80th Cong., 1st sess., 1947; and U.S. Senate, Subcommittee of the Committee on Foreign Relations, *Hearings, Military Cooperation of the American States and Military Advice and Assistance to China*, 79th Cong., 2nd sess., 1946. Unpublished transcript in SCFR Papers, Bill File "S. 2337, China, 79th Cong." (Mimeographed.)

Bibliography

Archives and Manuscript Collections

Bridges, Styles. Papers. New England College Library, Henniker, New Hampshire.

Connally, Tom. Papers. Division of Manuscripts, Library of Congress, Washington, D. C.

Dulles, John Foster. Papers. Princeton University Library, Princeton, New Jersey.

Hurley, Patrick J. Papers. Western History Collections, University of Oklahoma Library, Norman, Oklahoma.

Smith, H. Alexander. Papers. Princeton University Library, Princeton, New Jersey.

Thomas, Elbert D. Papers. Franklin D. Roosevelt Library, Hyde Park, New York.

U.S. Department of State. Decimal files, 1945. Record Group 59, National Archives, Washington, D. C.

U.S. Senate, Committee on Foreign Relations. Committee

Papers, 1945–1950. Record Group 46, National Archives, Washington, D. C.

Vandenberg, Arthur H. Papers. William L. Clements Library, University of Michigan, Ann Arbor, Michigan.

Government Documents

Peabody, P. E. Chief, Military Intelligence Service, U.S. Department of War. "*Secret*: Chinese Communist Movement." July 1945. Copy in Styles Bridges Papers, File 27. (Mimeographed.)

U.S. *Congressional Record*. Volume 91 (1945).

U.S. Department of State. *Bulletin*. Vols. 12–13 (1945).

U.S. Department of State. *Foreign Relations of the United States: Diplomatic Papers, 1944*. Volume 6: *China*. Washington, D.C.: U.S. Government Printing Office, 1967.

U.S. Department of State. *Foreign Relations of the United States: Diplomatic Papers, 1945*. Volume 7: *The Far East: China*. Washington, D.C.: U.S. Government Printing Office, 1969.

U.S. Department of War. Military Intelligence Division. "Secret: The Chinese Communist Movement." 5 July 1945. Copy in Styles Bridges Papers, File 26. (Mimeographed.)

U.S. House of Representatives. Committee on Foreign Affairs. *Hearings, Assistance to Greece and Turkey*. 80th Cong., 1st sess., 1947.

U.S. Senate. Committee on Appropriations. *Hearings, Third Supplemental Appropriation Bill for 1948*. 80th Cong., 1st sess., 1947.

U.S. Senate. Committee on Foreign Relations. *Hearings, Assistance to Greece and Turkey*. 80th Cong., 1st sess., 1947.

———. *Hearings, Investigation of Far Eastern Policy*. 79th Cong., 1st sess., 1945. Unpublished transcript in U.S.

Bibliography

Senate, Committee on Foreign Relations. Committee Papers, 79th Cong. Record Group 46, File No. SEN 79A-F10, Tray 142. (Mimeographed.)

U.S. Senate. Committee on Foreign Relations and Committee on Armed Services. *Joint Hearings, Military Situation in the Far East.* 82nd Cong., 1st sess., 1951.

U.S. Senate. Subcommittee of the Committee on Foreign Relations. *Hearings, Military Cooperation of the American States and Military Advice and Assistance to China.* 79th Cong., 2nd sess., 1946. Unpublished transcript in U.S. Senate, Committee on Foreign Relations. Committee Papers, 79th Cong. Record Group 46, Bill File "S. 2337, China, 79th Cong." (Mimeographed.)

———. *Hearings, Treaty of Friendship, Commerce, and Navigation between the United States of America and the Republic of China.* 80th Cong., 2nd sess., 1948.

Van Slyke, Lyman P., ed. *The China White Paper: August 1949.* Stanford, Calif.: Stanford University Press, 1967.

———, ed. *The Chinese Communist Movement: A Report of the United States War Department, July 1945.* Stanford, Calif.: Stanford University Press, 1968.

Memoirs, Autobiographies, Published Papers

Acheson, Dean G. *The Pattern of Responsibility.* Edited by McGeorge Bundy. Boston: Houghton Mifflin, 1951.

———. *Present at the Creation: My Years in the State Department.* New York: W. W. Norton, 1969.

———. *Sketches from Life of Men I Have Known.* New York: Harper & Brothers, 1960.

Barrett, David D. *Dixie Mission: The United States Army Observer Group in Yenan, 1944.* China Research Monographs, No. 6. Berkeley, Calif.: Center for Chinese Studies, University of California, 1970.

Bloom, Sol. *The Autobiography of Sol Bloom.* New York: G. P. Putnam's Sons, 1948.

Byrnes, James F. *All in One Lifetime.* New York: Harper & Brothers, 1958.

⸻. *Speaking Frankly.* New York: Harper & Brothers, 1947.

Connally, Tom, and Steinberg, Alfred. *My Name Is Tom Connally.* New York: Thomas Y. Crowell, 1954.

Davies, John Paton, Jr. *Dragon by the Tail: American, British, Japanese, and Russian Encounters with China and One Another.* New York: W. W. Norton, 1972.

Drury, Allen. *A Senate Journal: 1943–1945.* New York: McGraw-Hill, 1963.

Esherick, Joseph W., ed. *Lost Chance in China: The World War II Despatches of John S. Service.* New York: Random House, 1974.

Gayn, Mark J. *Journey from the East: An Autobiography.* New York: Alfred A. Knopf, 1944.

Grew, Joseph C. *Turbulent Era: A Diplomatic Record of Forty Years, 1904–1945.* Edited by Walter Johnson. Boston: Houghton Mifflin, 1952.

Jones, Joseph M. *The Fifteen Weeks (February 21-June 5, 1947).* New York: Harcourt, Brace & World, 1955.

Kennan, George F. *Memoirs (1925–1950).* Boston: Little, Brown, 1967.

Melby, John F. *The Mandate of Heaven: Record of a Civil War. China, 1945–49.* Toronto: University of Toronto Press, 1968.

Millis, Walter, ed. *The Forrestal Diaries.* New York: Viking Press, 1951.

Service, John S. *The Amerasia Papers: Some Problems in the History of US-China Relations.* China Research Monographs, No. 7. Berkeley, Calif.: Center for Chinese Studies, University of California, 1971.

Snow, Edgar. *Red Star over China.* New York: Random House, 1938.

Bibliography

Stilwell, Joseph W. *The Stilwell Papers*. Edited by Theodore H. White. New York: William Sloane Associates, 1948.

Sues, Ilona Ralf. *Shark's Fins and Millet*. Boston: Little, Brown, 1944.

Truman, Harry S. *Memoirs: Year of Decisions*. Vol. 1. Garden City, N.Y.: Doubleday, 1955.

———. *Memoirs: Years of Trial and Hope*. Vol. 2. Garden City, N.Y.: Doubleday, 1956.

Tuchman, Barbara W. *Notes from China*. New York: Collier Books, 1972.

Vandenberg, Arthur H., Jr., and Morris, Joe Alex, eds. *The Private Papers of Senator Vandenberg*. Boston: Houghton Mifflin, 1952.

Wallace, Henry A. *The Century of the Common Man: Selected from Recent Public Papers*. Edited by Russell Lord. New York: Reynal and Hitchcock, 1943.

Wedemeyer, Albert C. *Wedemeyer Reports!* New York: Henry Holt, 1958.

Other Books

Adler, Selig. *The Isolationist Impulse: Its Twentieth Century Reaction*. New York: Free Press, 1957.

Agar, Herbert. *The Price of Power: America since 1945*. Chicago: University of Chicago Press, 1957.

Almond, Gabriel A. *The American People and Foreign Policy*. New York: Frederick A. Praeger, 1960.

Alperovitz, Gar. *Atomic Diplomacy: Hiroshima and Potsdam. The Use of the Atomic Bomb and the American Confrontation with Soviet Power*. New York: Vintage Books, 1965.

Barnds, William J., ed. *China and America: The Search for a New Relationship*. New York: New York University Press, 1977.

255

Beal, John Robinson. *John Foster Dulles: A Biography*. New York: Harper & Brothers, 1957.

———. *Marshall in China*. New York: Doubleday, 1970.

Belden, Jack. *China Shakes the World*. New York: Harper & Brothers, 1949.

Beloff, Max. *Soviet Policy in the Far East, 1944–1951*. London: Oxford University Press, 1953.

Bernstein, Barton J., ed. *Politics and Policies of the Truman Administration*. Chicago: Quadrangle Books, 1970.

Blum, Robert. *The United States and China in World Affairs*. Edited by A. Doak Barnett. New York: McGraw-Hill, 1966.

Buhite, Russell D. *Patrick J. Hurley and American Foreign Policy*. Ithaca, N.Y.: Cornell University Press, 1973.

Carr, Albert Z. *Truman, Stalin and Peace*. Garden City, N.Y.: Doubleday, 1950.

Chen, Lung-chu, and Lasswell, Harold D. *Formosa, China and the United Nations: Formosa in the World Community*. New York: St. Martin's Press, 1967.

Clemens, Diane Shaver. *Yalta*. New York: Oxford University Press, 1970.

Clubb, O. Edmund. *China and Russia: The "Great Game."* New York: Columbia University Press, 1971.

———. *Twentieth Century China*. New York: Columbia University Press, 1964.

Cohen, Warren I. *America's Response to China: An Interpretive History of Sino-American Relations*. New York: John Wiley & Sons, 1971.

———. *The Chinese Connection: Roger S. Greene, Thomas W. Lamont, George E. Sokolsky and American-East Asian Relations*. New York: Columbia University Press, 1978.

Congressional Quarterly Service. *China and U.S. Far East Policy, 1945–1966*. Washington, D.C.: Congressional Quarterly Service, 1967.

Curry, George. *James F. Byrnes*. New York: Cooper Square

Publishers, 1965.

Dahl, Robert A. *Congress and Foreign Policy*. New York: Harcourt, Brace, 1950.

Dallin, David J. *Soviet Russia in the Far East*. New Haven, Conn.: Yale University Press, 1948.

Davies, John Paton, Jr. *Foreign and Other Affairs*. New York: W. W. Norton, 1964.

Divine, Robert A., ed. *Causes and Consequences of World War II*. Chicago: Quadrangle Books, 1969.

―――. *Second Chance: The Triumph of Internationalism in America during World War II*. New York: Atheneum, 1967.

Druks, Herbert. *Harry S. Truman and the Russians, 1945-1953*. New York: R. Speller, 1967.

Dulles, Foster Rhea. *China and America: The Story of Their Relations since 1784*. Princeton, N.J.: Princeton University Press, 1946.

Dulles, John Foster. *War or Peace*. New York: Macmillan, 1950.

Fairbank, John K. *China Perceived: Images and Policies in Chinese-American Relations*. New York: Alfred A. Knopf, 1974.

―――. *China: The People's Middle Kingdom and the U.S.A.* Cambridge, Mass.: Belknap Press, 1967.

Farnsworth, David N. *The Senate Committee on Foreign Relations*. Urbana, Ill.: University of Illinois Press, 1961.

Feis, Herbert. *The Atomic Bomb and the End of World War II*. Princeton, N.J.: Princeton University Press, 1966. 2nd ed. rev., 1970.

―――. *The China Tangle: The American Effort in China from Pearl Harbor to the Marshall Mission*. Princeton, N.J.: Princeton University Press, 1953.

―――. *Churchill—Roosevelt—Stalin: The War They Waged and the Peace They Sought*. Princeton, N.J.: Princeton University Press, 1957.

————. *From Trust to Terror: The Onset of the Cold War, 1945-1950.* New York: W. W. Norton, 1970.

Ferrell, Robert H. *George C. Marshall.* New York: Cooper Square Publishers, 1967.

Fishel, Wesley R. *The End of Extraterritoriality in China.* Berkeley, Calif.: University of California Press, 1952.

Fleming, Denna Frank. *The Cold War and Its Origins, 1917-1960.* 2 vols. Garden City, N.Y.: Doubleday, 1961.

Freeland, Richard M. *The Truman Doctrine and the Origins of McCarthyism: Foreign Policy, Domestic Politics, and Internal Security, 1946-1948.* New York: Alfred A. Knopf, 1972.

Gaddis, John Lewis. *The United States and the Origins of the Cold War, 1941-1947.* New York: Columbia University Press, 1972.

Gardner, Lloyd C. *Architects of Illusion: Men and Ideas in American Foreign Policy, 1941-1949.* Chicago: Quadrangle Books, 1970.

Gardner, Lloyd C., Schlesinger, Arthur, Jr., and Morgenthau, Hans J. *The Origins of the Cold War.* Waltham, Mass.: Ginn, 1970.

Gittings, John. *The World and China, 1922-1972.* London: Eyre Methuen, 1974.

Goldman, Eric F. *The Crucial Decade—And After: America, 1945-1960.* New York: Vintage Books, 1960.

Graebner, Norman A. *Cold War Diplomacy: American Foreign Policy, 1945-1960.* Princeton, N.J.: D. Van Nostrand, 1961.

————. *The New Isolationism: A Study in Politics and Foreign Policy since 1950.* New York: Ronald Press, 1956.

————, ed. *An Uncertain Tradition: American Secretaries of State in the Twentieth Century.* New York: McGraw-Hill, 1961.

Guhin, Michael A. *John Foster Dulles: A Statesman and*

His Times. New York: Columbia University Press, 1972.

Halberstam, David. *The Best and the Brightest.* New York: Random House, 1972.

Halle, Louis J. *The Cold War as History.* New York: Harper Colophon Books, 1967.

Harper, Alan D. *The Politics of Loyalty: The White House and the Communist Issue, 1946-1952.* Westport, Conn.: Greenwood Publishing Corp., 1969.

Hartmann, Susan M. *Truman and the 80th Congress.* Columbia, Mo.: University of Missouri Press, 1971.

Herz, Martin F. *Beginnings of the Cold War.* Bloomington, Ind.: Indiana University Press, 1966.

Iriye, Akira. *Across the Pacific: An Inner History of American-East Asian Relations.* New York: Harcourt, Brace & World, 1967.

―――. *The Cold War in Asia: A Historical Introduction.* Englewood Cliffs, N.J.: Prentice-Hall, 1974.

Isaacs, Harold R. *Scratches on Our Minds: American Images of China and India.* New York: John Day, 1958.

Kahn, E. J., Jr. *The China Hands: America's Foreign Service Officers and What Befell Them.* New York: Viking Press, 1975.

Keeley, Joseph. *The China Lobby Man: The Story of Alfred Kohlberg.* New Rochelle, N.Y.: Arlington House, 1969.

Kennan, George F. *American Diplomacy, 1900-1950.* Chicago: University of Chicago Press, 1951.

Kirkendall, Richard, ed. *The Truman Period as a Research Field.* Columbia, Mo.: University of Missouri Press, 1967.

Koen, Ross Y. *The China Lobby in American Politics.* New York: Harper & Row, 1974.

Kolko, Gabriel. *The Politics of War: The World and United States Foreign Policy, 1943-1945.* New York: Random

House, 1968.

Kolko, Joyce, and Kolko, Gabriel. *The Limits of Power: The World and United States Foreign Policy, 1945-1954.* New York: Harper & Row, 1972.

Kubek, Anthony. *How the Far East Was Lost.* Chicago: Henry Regnery, 1963.

LaFeber, Walter. *America, Russia, and the Cold War, 1945-1975.* 3rd ed. rev. New York: John Wiley & Sons, 1976.

Lasswell, Harold D., and Lerner, Daniel, eds. *World Revolutionary Elites: Studies in Coercive Ideological Movements.* Cambridge, Mass.: M.I.T. Press, 1965.

Liang, Chin-tung. *General Stilwell in China, 1942-1944: The Full Story.* New York: St. John's University Press, 1972.

Lohbeck, Don. *Patrick J. Hurley.* Chicago: Henry Regnery, 1956.

Lukacs, John. *A New History of the Cold War.* 3rd ed. rev. Garden City, N.Y.: Anchor Books, 1966.

McLane, Charles B. *Soviet Policy and the Chinese Communists, 1931-1946.* New York: Columbia University Press, 1958.

McNeill, William Hardy. *America, Britain, and Russia: Their Co-operation and Conflict, 1941-1946.* Royal Institute of International Affairs. *Survey of International Affairs, 1939-1946.* Edited by Arnold Toynbee. London: Oxford University Press, 1953.

Manchester, William. *American Caesar: Douglas MacArthur, 1880-1964.* London: Hutchinson & Co., 1979.

Matthews, Donald R. *U.S. Senators and Their World.* Chapel Hill, N.C.: University of North Carolina Press, 1960.

May, Ernest R., and Thomson, James C., Jr., eds. *American-East Asian Relations: A Survey.* Harvard Studies in American-East Asian Relations, No. 1. Cambridge, Mass.: Harvard University Press, 1972.

Bibliography

Moorad, George. *Lost Peace in China.* New York: E. P. Dutton, 1949.

Morgenthau, Hans J. *In Defense of the National Interest: A Critical Examination of American Foreign Policy.* New York: Alfred A. Knopf, 1951.

Oksenberg, Michel, and Oxnam, Robert B. *China and America: Past and Future.* New York: Foreign Policy Association, 1977.

——, eds. *Dragon and Eagle. United States-China Relations: Past and Future.* New York: Basic Books, 1978.

Paterson, Thomas G., ed. *The Cold War Critics: Alternatives to American Foreign Policy in the Truman Years.* Chicago: Quadrangle Books, 1971.

Phillips, Cabell. *The Truman Presidency: The History of a Triumphant Succession.* New York: Macmillan, 1966.

Purifoy, Lewis McCarroll. *Harry Truman's China Policy: McCarthyism and the Diplomacy of Hysteria, 1947-1951.* New York and London: New Viewpoints, 1976.

Riggs, Fred W. *Pressures on Congress: A Study of the Repeal of Chinese Exclusion.* New York: King's Crown Press, 1950.

Robinson, James A. *Congress and Foreign Policy-Making: A Study in Legislative Influence and Initiative.* Homewood, Ill.: Dorsey Press, 1962.

Romanus, Charles F., and Sunderland, Riley. *China-Burma-India Theater.* Vol. 1: *Stilwell's Mission to China.* Vol. 2: *Stilwell's Command Problems.* Vol. 3: *Time Runs Out in CBI.* In *United States Army in World War II.* Edited by Kent Roberts Greenfield, Office of the Chief of Military History, U.S. Department of the Army. Washington, D.C.: U.S. Government Printing Office, 1953-59.

Rothman, David J. *Politics and Power: The United States Senate, 1869-1901.* Cambridge, Mass.: Harvard University Press, 1966.

Salisbury, Harrison E. *War between Russia and China.* New York: W. W. Norton, 1969.

Schaller, Michael. *The U.S. Crusade in China, 1938-1945.* New York: Columbia University Press, 1979.

Seton-Watson, Hugh. *Neither War nor Peace: The Struggle for Power in the Postwar World.* New York: Frederick A. Praeger, 1960.

Shewmaker, Kenneth E. *Americans and Chinese Communists, 1927-1945: A Persuading Encounter.* Ithaca, N.Y.: Cornell University Press, 1971.

Snell, John L. *Illusion and Necessity: The Diplomacy of Global War, 1939-1945.* Boston: Houghton Mifflin, 1963.

――――, ed. *The Meaning of Yalta: Big Three Diplomacy and the New Balance of Power.* Baton Rouge, La.: Louisiana State University Press, 1956.

Spanier, John W. *American Foreign Policy since World War II.* 4th ed. rev. New York: Frederick A. Praeger, 1971.

Steele, A. T. *The American People and China.* New York: McGraw-Hill, 1966.

Stromer, Marvin E. *The Making of a Political Leader: Kenneth S. Wherry and the United States Senate.* Lincoln, Neb.: University of Nebraska Press, 1969.

Sutter, Robert G. *China-Watch: Toward Sino-American Reconciliation.* Baltimore: The Johns Hopkins University Press, 1978.

Theoharis, Athan. *Seeds of Repression: Harry S. Truman and the Origins of McCarthyism.* Chicago: Quadrangle Books, 1971.

――――. *The Yalta Myths: An Issue in U.S. Politics, 1945-1955.* Columbia, Mo.: University of Missouri Press, 1970.

Thomas, Elbert D. *Chinese Political Thought: A Study Based upon the Theories of the Principal Thinkers of the Chou Period.* New York: Prentice-Hall, 1927.

Bibliography

———. *The Four Fears*. Chicago: Ziff-Davis, 1944.

———. *Thomas Jefferson, World Citizen*. New York: Modern Age Books, 1942.

Thomson, James C., Jr. *While China Faced West: American Reformers in Nationalist China, 1928-1937*. Cambridge, Mass.: Harvard University Press, 1969.

Tompkins, C. David. *Senator Arthur H. Vandenberg: The Evolution of a Modern Republican, 1884-1945*. East Lansing, Mich.: Michigan State University Press, 1970.

Treadgold, Donald W., ed. *Soviet and Chinese Communism: Similarities and Differences*. Seattle, Wash.: University of Washington Press, 1967.

Tsou, Tang. *America's Failure in China, 1941-50*. 2 vols. Chicago: University of Chicago Press, 1963.

Tuchman, Barbara W. *Stilwell and the American Experience in China, 1911-45*. New York: Macmillan, 1970.

Ulam, Adam B. *Expansion and Coexistence: The History of Soviet Foreign Policy, 1917-67*. New York: Frederick A. Praeger, 1968.

———. *The Rivals: America and Russia since World War II*. New York: Viking Press, 1971.

Utley, Freda. *The China Story*. Chicago: Henry Regnery, 1951.

Varg, Paul A. *The Closing of the Door: Sino-American Relations, 1936-1946*. East Lansing, Mich.: Michigan State University Press, 1973.

———. *Missionaries, Chinese, and Diplomats: The American Protestant Missionary Movement in China, 1890-1952*. Princeton, N.J.: Princeton University Press, 1958.

Vincent, John Carter. *The Extraterritoriality System in China: Final Phase*. Cambridge, Mass.: East Asian Research Center, distributed by Harvard University Press, 1970.

Westerfield, H. Bradford. *Foreign Policy and Party Politics:*

Pearl Harbor to Korea. New Haven, Conn.: Yale University Press, 1955.

White, Theodore H., and Jacoby, Annalee. *Thunder out of China*. New York: William Sloane Associates, 1946.

Williams, William Appleman. *The Tragedy of American Diplomacy*. New York: World Publishing Company, 1959.

Young, Roland. *Congressional Politics in the Second World War*. New York: Columbia University Press, 1956.

Zagoria, Donald S. *The Sino-Soviet Conflict, 1956-1961*. Princeton, N.J.: Princeton University Press, 1962.

Articles

Brogan, Denis W. "The Myth of American Omnipotence." *Harper's* 205 (December, 1952): 21-28.

Edinger, Lewis J., and Searing, Donald D. "Social Background in Elite Analysis: A Methodological Inquiry." *American Political Science Review* 61 (June, 1967): 428-45.

Fairbank, John K. "Assignment for the '70's." *American Historical Review* 74 (February, 1969): 861-79.

———. "Our Chances in China." *Atlantic* 178 (September, 1946): 37-42.

LaFeber, Walter. "New Perspectives on American-East Asian Relations." *Journal of Asian Studies* 32 (August, 1973): 679-82.

May, Gary. "The 'New China Hands' and the Rape of the China Service." *Reviews in American History* 4 (March, 1976): 120-27.

Schlesinger, Arthur M., Jr. "The New Isolationism." *Atlantic* 189 (May, 1952): 34-48.

Stone, Lawrence. "Prosopography." *Daedalus* 100 (Winter, 1971): 46-79.

Tsou, Tang. "The American Political Tradition and the American Image of Chinese Communism." *Political Science Quarterly* 77 (December, 1962): 570-600.

Bibliography

———. Review of *Americans and Chinese Communists, 1927-1945: A Persuading Encounter*, by Kenneth E. Shewmaker. *Journal of Asian Studies* 31 (August, 1972): 937-39.

Tuchman, Barbara W. "If Mao Had Come to Washington: An Essay in Alternatives." *Foreign Affairs* 51 (October, 1972): 44-64.

Wertenbaker, Charles. "The China Lobby." *The Reporter* 6 (April 15, 1952): 4-24.

———. "The World of Alfred Kohlberg." *The Reporter* 6 (April 29, 1952): 19-22.

Unpublished Papers and Dissertations

Fetzer, James Alan. "Congress and China, 1941-1950." Ph.D. dissertation, Michigan State University, 1969.

———. "Congress and China, 1947: The Congressional Effort to Aid Chiang Kai-shek." Paper read before symposium on "The United States and China," n.d.

Fishel, Wesley R. "The Abolition of Extraterritoriality in China." Ph.D. dissertation, The University of Chicago, 1948.

Leary, William M., Jr. "Smith of New Jersey." Ph.D. dissertation, Princeton University, 1966.

Index

267

Index

Chicago, 60

Chicago Sun, 90

China: American perceptions of, 41, 126, 140, 143–44, 174, 188, 202–3, 207–9, 214–16, 218, 220–21, 225–26; Americans crave explanation concerning, 144, 174, 188; as focus of Soviet-American mistrust, 87, 145–46; Japanese forces in, 119, 124; political situation in, 67, 86, 113, 118, 207, 214; recedes as political issue, 189, 203, 205–6; signatory to Declaration of the United Nations, 41; sits on Security Council, 46; Truman Administration develops policy in, 117–30, 189–96; United States policy problems in, 126–27, 149–50, 173–74, 186, 199 + 00, 204–5, 208, 218–21; wartime United States policy toward, 40–42. *See also* Chiang Kai-shek; Chiang Kai-shek, Madame; Chinese Communist Party; Chinese Nationalist Government; Chou En-lai; Kuomintang Party; Manchuria; Mao Tse-tung; North China; Yalta Conference

China Aid Act, 220

China-Burma-India theater (CBI), 41–42

China correspondents, 112, 182–83, 200. *See also* Jacoby, Annalee; White, Theodore H.

China hands, 76; attacks on, 114, 220–22 (*see also* Bridges, Styles; Dondero, George; Hurley, Patrick J.; Kohlberg, Alfred; Loeb, William R.; Vandenberg, Arthur H.); China policy recommended by, 80–85, 87, 104, 211, 235, n. 18; critique of policy recommended by, 84–85; and Hurley, 76, 81–83, 85, 211; views of, ignored, 124, 208,

210–12, 216; views of, on Chiang, 104, 126–27, 200, 219. *See also* Atcheson, George; Atcheson message; Davies, John Paton, Jr.; Service, John S.; Vincent, John Carter

China Lobby, 91, 219–20

China policy scenario, 125–26

China White Paper, 220–21, 223

Chinese Communist Party (CCP), 40, 44, 76–78, 86, 220; ideology of, 78–80; and Kuomintang, 42, 119; and Soviet Union, 78–79, 221; support for, in China, 43; and United States, 79–80, 82–83, 145–47, 205, 214–15, 225–26. *See also* Chu Teh; Mao Tse-tung

Chinese Exclusion Act, 40–41, 57

Chinese Nationalist Government, 40, 43, 86, 119, 224–25. *See also* Kuomintang Party

Chinese Nationalist Party Constitutional Conference, 55

Chou En-lai, 82–83

Chungking, 47

Churchill, Winston S., 19–20, 67–68

Chu Teh, 201

Cleveland Council on World Affairs, 48, 50

Clubb, O. Edmund, 146

Coffee, John M., 241, n. 29

Collective security, 31, 215

Committee for a Democratic Far Eastern Policy. *See* Committee for a Democratic Policy Toward China

Committee for a Democratic Policy Toward China (Committee for a Democratic Far Eastern Policy), 133–36, 189

Concord (New Hampshire) Cham-Chamber of Commerce, 105

Congress, U.S. *See* U.S. Congress

Connally Resolution, 28

Connally, Tom, 27, 91, 153; and

269

Index

Index

Index

Vandenberg, Arthur H., 218, 244, n. 9; attacks State Department, 111–12, 114, 154–55, 184, 222; and bipartisanship, 26, 50, 165, 206, 222–23; chairman of Senate Foreign Relations Committee, 222; criticized by Thomas, 152–56; and Dulles, 16, 26, 50, 52, 206; as isolationist, 15–16, 23, 50; and Moscow Conference of Foreign Ministers, 109, 114; at San Francisco Conference, 24, 26, 52–53; tries to clarify issues in China, 112–13, 156, 200; and United Nations, 17, 22–26, 53, 66; views of, on China, 50–54, 65, 110, 112–13, 156, 209, 222–23; views of, on peacetime alliances, 15–17, 25, 51, 109–10; views of, on Soviet Union, 22–26, 52–54, 109–11, 114–15, 156, 206; and wartime ideals, 24–25, 51; wartime views of, on Far East, 50–52; and Yalta Far Eastern agreement, 108–9, 111, 114–15, 155, 222. *See also* Conservatives

Versailles Conference, 217

Versailles, Treaty of, 29, 58, 217

Vietnam War, 226

Vincent, John Carter: attacks on, 92–93, 139, 221–22; director of State Department Office of Far Eastern Affairs, 92, 119; and Mansfield, 132–33; recommendations of, for Marshall mission, 190–91; speech of, to Foreign Policy Association, 128–30, 148, 174–76, 194–95; and State Department defense, 175; views of, on American military intervention in China, 119–20, 127. *See also* China hands

Vladivostok, 146

War, Department of. *See* U.S.

Department of War

Washington, George, 217

Washington Post, 99, 177

Wedemeyer, Albert C.: and China hands, 81–82, 85, 184, 221, 238, n. 56; commands United States forces in China, 82, 118–19, 122–24, 127, 137, 146–47, 175, 195; criticism of, by noninterventionists, 134–35, 138, 168

Wheeler, Burton K., 16, 237, n. 41

Wherry, Kenneth S, 91, 98–100, 165–66, 169. *See also* Conservatives

White, Theodore H., 112, 182–85, 188, 247, n. 59

White, Wallace, 244, n. 9

Wiley, Alexander, 17, 113–14

William, Maurice, 60

Wilson, Woodrow, 15, 27–31, 34, 36, 217–18

World War II: America debates how to stay out of, 217; and China-Burma-India theater, 39–46

Yalta conference (Crimea Conference), 15, 17–19, 23–24, 29, 38; and Far East, 45–46, 53–54, 56–57, 62, 66, 69–70, 114. *See also* Bridges, Styles, collaborates with Hurley; Roosevelt, Franklin D., and Hurley; Vandenberg, Arthur H., and Yalta Far Eastern agreement

Yenan, 76–78, 134

Zaibatsu, 61